The New Guide To

WRITING A PERFECT RESUME

The Complete Guide to Writing Resumes, Cover Letters, and Other Job Search Documents

by

Greg Faherty

Certified Professional Résumé Writer

Owner, www.A-Perfect-Resume.com

TABLE OF CONTENTS

INTRODUCTION   3

CHAPTER 1: What is a Résumé & Why Do I Need One?   5

    The Résumé   5

    The Cover Letter   6

    Why A Professional Résumé?   6

    Why Does a Professional Résumé Work Better?   7

CHAPTER 2: The Anatomy of a Résumé   10

    Basic Résumé Format   10

    The Sections of a Résumé   12

    Contact Information Heading   12

    The Head Line   13

    The Summary   14

    Professional Experience   16

    Other Information   17

    The Cover Letter   18

    Basic Resume Types   19

        Reverse Chronological   20

        Functional   21

        Semi-Functional   22

        Curriculum Vitae   23

        Federal Résumé   26

CHAPTER 3: Writing Your Résumé   29

    Extroverts & Introverts   29

    Keywords   29

    Action Verbs & Adverbs   34

    Résumé Pitfalls   26

    Résumé Template   40

Résumé Companies   42

Before & After Samples   46

CHAPTER 4: Different Résumés & Their Purposes   **62**

American Résumés   62

Reverse Chronological   62

Functional   69

Semi-Functional   72

Curriculum Vitae   76

Federal Résumé   80

International Résumés   85

Special Situations   88

CHAPTER 5: The Cover Letter   **96**

Writing A Cover Letter   96

The Parts of the Cover Letter   101

Cover Letter Samples   101

Advertised Jobs vs. Cold Calling   105

Final Cover Letter Tips   105

CHAPTER 6: Other Documents   **107**

Thank You Letters   107

Biographies   109

Personal Profiles   111

Personal Statements   111

Business Card Résumés   113

Reference Pages   114

CHAPTER 7: Succeeding in the Electronic Age   **115**

No PDFs!   115

ATS-Formatted Résumés   116

HTML & XML Résumés   118

Plain Text / Ascii File Résumés   118

CHAPTER 8: Building a Great Résumé   **123**
    Creating Exceptional Bullets   123
    Gathering Your Skills   124
    The Correct Order for Your Information   126
    How Far Back Should I Go?   127
    How Much is Too Much?   128
    Summing it all Up   135

CHAPTER 9: I Have My Résumé. Now What?   **136**
    Using the Résumé   136

CHAPTER 10: Interviewing   **139**
    Do Your Homework   139
    The Pre-Interview   139
    Appearance is Everything   140
    Getting Through the Interview   142
    Keeping Quiet   143
    After the Interview is Over   143
    Getting What You're Worth   144

CHAPTER 11: Final Thoughts   **145**

APPENDIX 1: Sample Résumés, A-Z   **146**
    Academic Officer   147
    Administrative Assistant 1   149
    Athlete   150
    Attorney   152
    Business Student   153
    Business Owner   154
    Chef   155

Chief Financial Officer	156
Chief Technology Officer	158
Controller	160
Construction Executive	161
Dentist	163
Editor	164
Electrician	165
Executive (Information Technology)	166
Graduate Student	167
Graphic Design Manager	168
Home Care Provider	170
Human Resources Manager	171
Intelligence Officer	173
Interior Designer	175
International Curriculum Vitae	177
International Résumé	179
IT Project Manager	181
IT Support Technician	183
Janitorial (Senior Custodian)	184
Media Buyer	185
Nurse	187
Oil/Gas Driller	189
Operations Manager	191
Paralegal	193
Physician	194
Sales Representative	195
Teacher	197
Veterinarian	198
Web Developer	200
X-Ray Technician	201
Zookeeper	202

APPENDIX 2: Suggested Resources   **204**

APPENDIX 3: Proofreading Your Résumé   **206**

APPENDIX 4: Printing Your Documents   **207**

APPENDIX 5: Action Verbs and Adverbs   **208**

SPECIAL BONUS COUPONS   **213**

ABOUT THE AUTHOR   **214**

ISBN-13: 978-1523288724

ISBN-10: 1523288728

This publication is designed to provide accurate information regarding the subject matter covered. It is intended for general informational purposes only. It is sold with the understanding that the publisher is not rendering legal, accounting, or other professional advice.

Greg Faherty, CPRW, individually or corporately, does not accept any responsibility for any liabilities resulting from the actions of any parties publishing, purchasing, or using the materials contained within this book, and cannot accept responsibility for the individual results of people using the information contained within this publication.

All business and personal names used in the samples contained within this book are fictional or have been changed to protect the privacy of any individuals.

GREG FAHERTY, CPRW

Certified Professional Resume Writer

Owner, www.a-perfect-resume.com

Featured in "Designing a Cover Letter to 'WOW' Hiring Personnel, 2nd Ed"

Featured in "Cracking the Code to Pharmaceutical Sales"

Featured in "Professional Cover Letter Examples for Managers & Executives"

Regular contributor to Forbes.com, BusinessInsider.com, Lohud.com and the

Westchester/Rockland Journal News

Examiner.com's New York Resume Examiner

Contact Information & Social Media:

www.twitter.com/gfahertycprw

www.linkedin.com/in/gregfaherty

www.facebook.com/APerfectResume

INTRODUCTION

A Perfect Résumé...and More

That's the tag line for my business. I write résumés and cover letters and all sorts of job search documents for a living. If you're reading this book, you're probably aware there are a lot of résumé books out on the market. Some are simply compilations of 'award-winning résumés,' or 'résumés that have gotten people jobs.' Others are instructional guides that imply that by using their methods, you're *guaranteed* to get a new, wonderful job.

If that's what you're interested in, you're probably reading the wrong book. Try something in the fairy tales section of the bookstore or library instead.

But if you're reading this because **you want to know how to get more interviews,** or **take your career to the next level,** then you've come to the right place.

The purpose of this guide isn't just to show you what a good résumé looks like, although I will do that. And it isn't to teach you how to write your own résumé, although you'll learn that as well. The purpose of this book is to show you *how* and *why* a good résumé works, so you can determine what areas yours needs help in, improve it, and, most importantly, use your résumé to get more interviews.

The biggest myth relating to the professional résumé is that résumé writers guarantee their résumés will get you jobs. Any résumé writer who promises this is pulling your leg. The function of the résumé is to help people obtain *interviews*; the résumé (and, by association, the cover letter) is simply a tool used to get hiring managers and recruiters interested in the applicant, interested enough to contact the person for an interview. That's why I'll be providing advice on interviewing as well. More on that later, though.

Your résumé and cover letter are marketing or advertising tools. When you see an appealing ad on TV, there's a good chance you'll go to the store or check out the product online. The better the ad, the more people will think about buying the product or service. But if the product turns out to be a dud, do you buy it just because the ad was interesting? Of course not. The same goes for résumés; they're a tool to get your foot in the door. The difference between the well-written, professional résumé and the poorly written résumé is the professional résumé gets a lot more interviews for the applicant. *50% to 100% more, on average.* And following the law of percentages, the more interviews you get, the better the odds of landing the job you want.

TIP: If a writer 'guarantees' you'll get a job, make sure it's a 100% money-back guarantee!

So now we know what the résumé is for. What else will this book tell you? After reading **Perfect Resumes & Cover Letters**, you'll know the different formats (types) of résumés, and when to use each one. You'll learn what the purpose of the cover letter is. You'll see lots of examples of résumés that worked and résumés that didn't, with explanations of why. You'll discover the most dangerous pitfalls of résumé writing and usage, such as not using the correct punctuation or grammar.

In addition to the information about résumés, you'll also find helpful hints on searching for jobs in the electronic age, using the multitude of networking services available on the internet, and the importance of other documents, such as thank you letters.

Most importantly, you'll see why the résumé is one of the most important documents in your life, and understand why it's so critical that your résumé meets the professional standards that human resource representatives, recruiters, and hiring managers look for.

TIP: A good résumé could mean the difference in thousands of dollars a year for you.

CHAPTER 1: WHAT IS A RÉSUMÉ, AND WHY DO YOU NEED ONE?

Any book about résumés should start at the beginning, with an explanation of what a résumé is. According to Funk & Wagnall's New International Dictionary of the English Language, a résumé is defined as: "A summary, as of one's employment record."

Note the key word in that definition: "summary." A résumé should be exactly that, a summary of your employment and educational history, along with any other information that might be important to a potential employer, such as computer skills, language skills, and other points of interest. The résumé is not a detailed, lengthy biography, nor is it simply an outline. Placing too much or too little information in a résumé will result in a fast ride to the trash bin, either electronic or physical.

The Résumé

A résumé must immediately grab the interest of the reader in order to be effective. The amount of time the average hiring manager, human resources representative, or recruiter spends on the first reading of a résumé is anywhere from 30 seconds to two minutes. Whatever the specific time might be, the fact of the matter is this: your résumé only has a very short chance to capture the reader's interest. The job of the professional résumé writer is to create a document that grabs the reader's attention right away and details the applicant's most important facts without overloading the reader, while at the same time making sure to not leave anything out. This is one of the most difficult parts of résumé writing, and it's the reason why professional résumés perform so much better than home-prepared résumés. Think about it. If you owned a company that sold a product, would you hire your mother to write the marketing materials, or your best friend's sister to create your advertisements? Probably not! Yet when it comes to job hunting, that's exactly what too many people do. They don't market the product—themselves—effectively.

So, what is a résumé? A résumé is a document that succinctly and effectively summarizes your employment and academic background, demonstrates how you can benefit an employer, and interests an employer in speaking with you personally. And that brings us to the second half of your marketing tool: the cover letter.

The Cover Letter

The cover letter is the companion to the résumé. It's an introduction, both to you and your résumé. It's the first thing the reader sees. In a way, it's the first impression before the résumé even has a chance to make an impression, which is why the cover letter is so important.

What else does the cover letter do? It announces the type of job or career the applicant is searching for, and it provides some space to include extra information that might not fit in the résumé, or information the applicant wishes to emphasize. Examples of this might be sales numbers, awards, or special skills.

It is a generally accepted rule that an effective résumé package includes a professional résumé and a professional cover letter. Having a great résumé and pairing it with a poorly written cover letter is like giving someone your business card and omitting your telephone number. You've only given them half the information they need.

*TIP: Remember, the résumé and cover letter package is your **only** chance to impress someone who has never met you or spoken to you. Be sure to make the best impression possible.*

Why a professional résumé?

OK, now you know what the résumé and cover letter are for. But why worry so much about writing one? After all, there are plenty of books out there containing hundreds of sample resumes for you to copy, and on top of that there are software packages where you can pick a résumé format, plug in your information, and behold! A complete résumé, ready to use. In fact, most standard word processing software comes with résumé templates already loaded in. So why spend all that money on a book that teaches you the secrets of professional résumé writing, and then makes you do all that hard work?

The reason is simple: *professional résumés get people more interviews. A lot more.*

Surveys have shown (and my own work as a résumé writer, both with my own company and others, backs this up) that, on average, job seekers who write their own résumés with no training receive approximately a 3% return on the résumés they send out. That means if you write your own résumé without help, you'll average about three interviews for every 100 résumés you send out. *Three out 100.* Would you bet money on those odds? I know I wouldn't. Yet people constantly bet their entire careers on bad résumés.

Let's take it a little further. People who make a real effort to prepare a good-looking résumé by studying résumé books have a higher rate of success, maybe 10 to 15 interviews out of 100 résumés. That's about the same as people who go to a non-certified writer or who use a cheap, fly-by-night online résumé service. Better odds than before, but still not that great, considering it's your future you're betting on. You've basically doubled your chances, which is a decent return on your investment at best.

However, nothing compares to a résumé written by an experienced, professionally trained and certified résumé writer. Those return, on average, *25 to 35 interviews for every 100 résumés sent out.* That's **more than five times** the number of interviews than if you write it yourself, with no help, and **three times** the number of interviews you'll receive if you use a $10 guidebook or a hire $69.95 résumé company. Will the professional resume cost more? Yes, of course. But think about that return on investment. Does it seem like a good one? It should, considering the potential difference in salary those extra interviews could mean.

My goal is to get you as close to that 25% mark as I can, by showing you how a professional résumé writer prepares a résumé.

Why does a professional résumé work so much better?

Maybe you think you're a great writer, or you've read hundreds of résumés yourself, so you know what to do and not to do. I hear it all the time. "I work in Human Resources." "I got an 'A' in English in college." "I do all the hiring at my job." "Writing is easy."

Wrong.

This is like me saying, "I pumped gas in high school. I used to change the spark plugs in my 1979 Mustang. I bought a new car two years ago. So let me fix the engine of your race car."

Would you want me to do it? I don't think so. You'd want a professional, right?

Or maybe you think the résumé doesn't matter, because your qualifications are so fantastic. If you believe any of these things, you couldn't be more wrong.

The fact is, you need a professional résumé writer for the same reason someone else needs someone with *your* particular skills.

Think about these things:

What job do you do?

How many other people do that job?

How many of those people will be applying for the same jobs as you?

What makes you **stand out** from all those other people?

While I can't answer the first two questions, I can answer the second two. On average, for every job opening today, there are anywhere from 50 to 500 people applying for it. *50 to 500*. It doesn't matter if you're a computer programmer, an electrician, a teacher, a corporate officer, an IT manager, or a nurse. You're facing tough competition, because a lot of those people who are applying for that job have the same—or better—qualifications as you.

In order to stand out, you need is a résumé that makes you sound like the most qualified candidate, without resorting to exaggeration or outright lies.

*(Important Note - for most companies today, lying on a résumé is considered an acceptable reason for **immediate employment termination**. In other words, if anything on your résumé isn't true, your employer can fire you for it.)*

Another reason professional résumés are more effective has to do with the impression you're conveying to the reader. A prospective employer obviously wants an employee who's willing to work hard, go the extra mile, and do whatever it takes to succeed. The professional résumé conveys this attitude. It shows that the applicant is aware of how a well-written résumé is important to the job search process, and has put in the time, effort, and, yes, money, to produce the highest quality product possible.

Never forget how important this aspect of the job search process is. You wouldn't wear a dirty shirt or a torn suit jacket to an interview, would you? So why would you send in a résumé with typographical errors, poor grammar, or an out-of-date format? All you're doing is telling the employer you put no effort into the résumé, which translates as "I don't care."

That's not the type of attitude hiring managers are looking for.

TIP: You only have one chance to make a first impression. The more professional your résumé appears, the better a first impression you make.

Above all, you want your résumé to shine like a diamond in a pile of rocks. Unless you're handing in a résumé as a formality for a position where there are no other applicants, there are going to be many, *many* other people applying for the same job. That number could be dozens; it could be *hundreds*.

How will you stand out in that kind of crowd? How can you get your résumé noticed?

There's only one way: make your résumé sound better than everyone else's!

This book won't turn you into a professional résumé writer - no book can, no matter what it says on the cover. But I can get you a lot closer to the perfect résumé than you'd get if you used a template, or only read books containing sample résumés. By providing you with the benefit of my years of experience as a résumé writer and industry expert, I can give you all the tools you'll need to craft a résumé that's much better than the one you've been using.

I'm giving you the hammer, the nails, the wood, and the blueprints.

The rest is up to you.

CHAPTER 2: The Anatomy of a Résumé

Basic Résumé Format

As previously noted, a résumé is a summary of a person's career, laid out in a specific style, or **format**. That format can vary slightly depending on a person's career level and job type, but every résumé has the same basic parts:

Headline

Summary

Employment

Education

Training

Computer Skills

Additional Information

On the next page, you'll see an example of a very simple resume, which illustrates all the basic parts listed above.

NAME
Address • City, State, Zip Code • (555) 555-5555 • email address

A highly talented and accomplished Customer Service professional with skills and experience in Customer Relations, Sales, Sales Support, and Telemarketing

SUMMARY OF QUALIFICATIONS

- More than 11 years of customer service and sales support experience.
- Proven ability to meet or exceed all sales and customer service goals.
- Able to develop, maintain, and strengthen business relationships with clients.
- Recognized for exceptional problem-solving and analysis abilities.
- Pleasant personality, hard working, and dedicated to customer satisfaction.
- Outstanding verbal and written communication skills.

PROFESSIONAL EXPERIENCE

COMPANY ONE, Old City, NY   2000 – Present
Customer Service Specialist
Respond to pricing inquiries, providing accurate and timely information and quotes. Perform calculation of credit adjustments and forward adjustments accordingly. Carry out order processing activities, utilizing AS400 system. Coordinate invoicing and shipping functions.
- Improved shipping accuracy 15% in first year.
- Supported more than $1M in new sales activity.
- Developed and implemented new reporting procedures.

COMPANY TWO, Old City, NY   1992 – 2000
Customer Relations Representative (1996 – 2000)
Assisted customers with inquiries and resolved potential customer service issues. Member of select inter-divisional cross-training program, designed to increase efficiency through sharing of knowledge of operations.
- Saved company $500,000 by bringing training programs in-house
- Recognized by sales department for outstanding customer service.

Sales / Marketing Coordinator, Photo Division (1992 – 1996)
Tracked sales data and maintained customer purchase histories for Regional Sales Manager.
- Brought in $40,000 in new sales by marketing services to existing customers.
- Earned Marketing Coordinator of the Year award (1993).

EDUCATION

Associate's Degree in Business, Dellwood Community College (1992)

TRAINING

Sales Management, Strategic Sales, Solution Selling, 7 Habits of Highly Successful People

COMPUTER SKILLS

Windows 95/98/2000, Word, Excel, proprietary database and business systems

The Basic Sections of a Résumé

A résumé contains different sections, each containing a specific type of information. Using the example on the previous page, let's examine each of the main, basic sections of a résumé.

1. The Contact Information Heading

Every résumé must have a contact heading at the top of the first page; this is the person's name and contact information.

Name

Address • City, State, Zip Code • (555) 555-5555 • email address

---

Contact information should always include the following: Name, full street address, city/state/zip code, at least one telephone number, and an email address. Don't leave any piece of contact information out. The résumé isn't the place to worry about privacy. If a company can't contact you easily, they won't contact you at all. Companies will email you or call you, so be sure to use an email address and phone number that you check frequently, and don't share with other people.

TIP: Use an email address that's easy for someone to read and remember.

Don't use 'cute' emails. A recruiter isn't going to be impressed when they see hotdogluvr27 or wildthing1965. The best bet is to use an email address with some combination of your name. If you don't have one, set one up for free at Yahoo or Gmail and use it only for your job search.

People often insert pictures or graphics into the contact heading. *Don't do this!* I can't emphasize that enough. *G*raphics can cause major format issues when someone opens up the résumé on their computer, or stores it in a database and then tries to retrieve it later. If you want to place a line across the top of the page, as is shown in the example, go to Format, and then Borders and Shading in your word processor's tool bar line, and choose one of the selections there. Never use a Drawing Tool or Insert Graphics function. That's when problems start.

Another thing to remember is not to confuse the contact heading with the header/footer function.

TIP: NEVER use a header or footer in a résumé!

The reason for this is simple: If you cut and paste your résumé into an email or a company's web form, or if you need to save the résumé as a plain text (ascii) file, *the header and footer will be lost!* These sections don't transfer, which means the person at the other end will receive a résumé with no contact information or name on it! As you might imagine, these résumés, of which there are many, end up in the trash. They're useless. And before you say, "But Greg, I sent my résumé as a Word attachment, so the header should have still been there when the company opened the file," remember this: a) the person at the other end might not have the same word processing system, or version, you do; b) many companies automatically download the files they receive directly into a database, where again the headers and footers can be lost; and c) often people open attachments directly from the email, to avoid viruses. Again, the header could be lost. Better to play it safe. *Always avoid headers and footers.*

Sometimes you might see a résumé where the top heading only contains a name, while the contact information appears at the bottom of the page. This is a style that used to be quite popular, but has become outdated in recent years. Stay away from this type of format.

2. The Headline

Over the past few years the headline, sometimes called a **tag line**, has taken the place of the old, familiar Objective, which is no longer used in résumés. The reason the Objective has fallen out of favor is that it tells the employer what the applicant is looking for, and pins the applicant down to that one type of position. Today, employers prefer to see how the applicant best fits in the company's needs. To put it bluntly, employers care more about what *they want* than what the applicant is interested in.

Omitting the Objective also helps the applicant because it eliminates the potential for meaningless statements such as "seeks position that will allow extensive career growth," or "seeks profitable position with good opportunities to make a difference." These types of statements are useless because they offer no practical information about the applicant. You might as well just say, "I want a job, any old job."

A good Headline sums up the applicant's professional expertise in one short sentence:

A highly talented and accomplished Customer Service professional with skills and experience in Customer Relations, Sales, Sales Support, and Telemarketing

An alternative to the Headline is to insert a keywords list at the top of the page, which serves the same purpose:

Customer Service ~ Customer Relations ~ Sales ~ Sales Support ~ Telemarketing

Regardless of the style, the headline not only helps the reader determine what type of position the person is applying for / qualified for, but it grabs the reader's attention so he or she will read the rest of the résumé.

3. The Summary

The Summary section highlights the applicant's main skills and /or achievements. The three basic formats are the vertical bullet point list, the horizontal bullet point list, and the paragraph. Here are examples of each, with tips for when to use them.

Vertical Bullet List – used most commonly on mid-level and entry-level résumés, and résumés where there's an above-average amount of space available.

SUMMARY OF QUALIFICATIONS

- More than 11 years of customer service and sales support experience.
- Proven ability to meet or exceed all sales and customer service goals.
- Able to develop, maintain, and strengthen business relationships with clients.
- Recognized for exceptional problem-solving and analysis abilities.
- Pleasant personality, hard working, and dedicated to customer satisfaction.
- Outstanding verbal and written communication skills.

Horizontal Bullet List – used primarily when space is at a premium.

SUMMARY

• More than 11 years of sales support experience.	• Proven ability to meet all sales goals.
• Able to develop and maintain business relationships.	• Highly adept at account management.
• Recognized for exceptional analysis abilities.	• Aggressive but pleasant style of sales.
• Familiar with in-house and cold-call sales.	• Excellent communication skills.

Paragraph Style – best for senior management, executive, and corporate officer résumés.

SUMMARY OF QUALIFICATIONS

Highly talented and accomplished Sales Management executive with more than 11 years of experience directing sales and marketing operations. Proven ability to hire, train, and manage successful sales teams. Able to develop and maintain effective business relationships. Recognized for consistent record of increasing sales revenues and profitability. Adept at all aspects of departmental management, including P&L, forecasting, accounting, and goal setting. Proficient at formulating and implementing effective sales strategies, business policies, and operational procedures. Outstanding negotiation, presentation, and communication skills.

Certain résumés, such as sales-oriented résumés, often include a bulleted list of accomplishments as part of the summary, or as a separate sub-section:

SUMMARY OF QUALIFICATIONS

Highly talented and accomplished Sales Management executive with more than 11 years of experience directing sales and marketing operations. Proven ability to hire, train, and manage successful sales teams. Able to develop and maintain effective business relationships. Recognized for consistent record of increasing sales revenues and profitability. Adept at all aspects of departmental management, including P&L, forecasting, accounting, and goal setting. Proficient at formulating and implementing effective sales strategies, business policies, and operational procedures. Outstanding negotiation, presentation, and communication skills.

Selected Accomplishments

- Increased annual revenue $4 million (25%) in first year at current position.
- Earned Regional Director of the Year for Sales Performance six consecutive years.
- Built Northeast Region into company's Number One sales region.

A good Summary provides a brief but accurate overview of the applicant's qualifications without presenting any extraneous information. This is not the place to discuss specific projects, details of job descriptions, or personal qualities. In fact, personal qualities (good listener, independent thinker, pleasant attitude) should never be included anywhere on a résumé. In this day and age, it's expected that you listen well, show enthusiasm, and can work independently. Placing this information in a résumé simply wastes space.

Just as importantly, the Summary sets the professional tone of the résumé. Never give in to the temptation to use a conversational or casual tone just to make the résumé stand out. That style worked well in the 1980s and early '90s, but today all it gets you is a quick trip to the garbage can. Here's an example of a line from a Summary on a résumé I once had to critique, written by the CEO of a Fortune 500 company:

> "I am a true captain of the industry, and I guarantee that I'll triple your company's revenue in one year."

There are two things wrong with this statement: One, the first half of the statement is too casual, conveying a tone that's distinctly non-professional. Two, no one can guarantee they'll make a company money. There are too many variables involved. That's why it's better to list what you've done before, and let those facts serve as an indication of what you can do in the future. Here's how I re-worked that sentence on the new résumé:

> Highly experienced at leading corporate functions. Proven ability to dramatically increase revenue, year after year.

Using the original résumé, the client received zero interviews in three months. Using the revised résumé, the client obtained a new position five weeks later as a corporate officer.

4. Professional Experience

This section is the highlight of the résumé; this is where the meat is. In a standard Reverse Chronological résumé, the Professional Experience section will resemble this:

PROFESSIONAL EXPERIENCE

COMPANY ONE, Old City, NY   2000 – present
Customer Service Specialist
Respond to pricing inquiries, providing accurate and timely information and quotes. Perform calculation of credit adjustments and forward adjustments accordingly. Carry out order processing activities, utilizing AS400 system. Coordinate invoicing and shipping functions.
- Improved shipping accuracy 15% in first year.
- Supported more than $1M in new sales activity.
- Developed and implemented new reporting procedures.

Now, there are several variations to this format; some styles work better than others, depending on a person's employment background. However, there are certain basic guidelines you should follow in order to get the best performance out of your résumé. They are:

☞ Use a short paragraph to describe the basic job functions. Don't waste a lot of space describing the company; instead, keep the information centered on your job duties and regular activities.

☞ Use a bullet point style for the accomplishments listed under each job. Bullet points make the accomplishments stand out from the job description, help the reader find information rapidly, and give the résumé a much neater appearance. Bullet points should never be more than three lines long; in most cases one or two lines is best. The most important or relevant bullets should come first.

☞ White space. Placing twenty or thirty bullet points under one position makes the résumé hard to read. There's no reason to have that much information under one job. The résumé is an *overview* of your experience, not a detailed biography. Remember the KISS rule: Keep It Short and Simple. If for some reason it's really necessary to have a lot of bullets under one position, separate them into categories, or group them by topic area, with each category separated by a sub-heading (See Chief Financial Officer example in Appendix I).

☞ Avoid placing dates along the left margin. This goes back to the fact that many résumé recipients scan résumés into databases for storage. Having the dates on the left side, and all of the employment information indented, results in a jumbled, confused résumé after database storage. And if a person can't read the résumé...well, by now you know where those documents end up.

An exception to this general format is the functional résumé. In a functional résumé, the Experience section has the information grouped by category, but with no job/company data, followed by a separate section for Employment History where jobs are listed by title, company name, and years of service. At the end of this chapter you'll see an example of this style.

5. Other Information
Depending on the applicant's qualifications and background, other sections found in

the résumé could include Education, Licenses and Certifications, Computer or Technical Skills, Language Skills, Professional Organizations, Community Organizations, Professional Development and Training, Awards and Recognition, Publications, and anything else that might be important.

Tip: A résumé used in the United States should NEVER include any personal information such as hobbies, interests, marital status, or children. Foreign résumés are different, and we'll cover those later.

Sometimes there will be exceptions to the general format. For instance, a recent college graduate should place their Education section after the Summary and before the Experience. A hands-on technology professional often needs to place the Technical Skills section right after the Summary. Sales professionals, as we've seen before, might include a special list of top accomplishments before the Experience section.

The Cover Letter

No, it's not part of the résumé, but we use it with the résumé, right? So here's an example of how. The information in a cover letter can be adjusted to match the type of position being applied for. I tell my clients they should always customize their letters, based on the job they're applying for. When doing this, though, remember to always paraphrase, or re-write, what's in the ad, rather than quoting directly.

Compare this job description to the two cover letter samples below it:

Job description

Requirements: More than 7 years of experience in sales of pharmaceuticals or other medical / healthcare products. Strong familiarity with cardiology profession. Ability to communicate with, and sell to, doctors, hospital personnel, and surgeons. Willing to travel.

Sample paragraph from cover letter 1

In addition to the skills and achievements listed above, I have more than 10 years of experience in pharmaceutical sales, and have a proven record of success selling to doctors, hospital personnel, and surgeons. I'm very familiar with the cardiology profession; in fact, I was responsible for all cardiac care product sales for the Southeast region. I am willing to travel.

Sample paragraph from cover letter 2

In addition to the skills and achievements listed above, I have an extensive background in pharmaceutical sales. I've been effective at selling and promoting products to healthcare professionals at all levels. I have particular expertise with cardiac care products, such as the ones manufactured by your company. I am willing to travel.

In the first letter, the applicant quoted the advertisement almost word for word; that's a red flag to a prospective employer, who might think the applicant is either lying or simply too lazy to write their own information in their own words. By rephrasing the ad, the applicant provides all the right information, in a manner that seems original but still touches on the correct keywords and phrases.

Basic Résumé Types

'Résumé' is a general term applied to any document summarizing a person's employment record, but there are distinct types of résumés, each of which has its own purpose. These will be discussed in depth in Chapter 4, but for now let's familiarize ourselves with the basic formats we'll be discussing throughout the book.

1. The Résumé

I use this term, except where noted otherwise, to describe the U.S. or American résumé. The U.S. résumé is normally one to two pages in length, and uses a bullet point format to display accomplishments. There are three basic formats for the U.S. résumé: **Reverse Chronological** (the jobs are listed from most recent to earliest), **Functional** (the information from the various jobs is broken down into categories, and then followed by a brief employment history), and the **Semi-Functional** or **Combined Chronological – Functional** (positions are separated into sections based on industry, and then listed in reverse chronological order under each section). Of these, the Reverse Chronological is the most common, followed by the Functional.

Take a look at the samples of each basic type on the next 3 pages and get to know their differences, and what they have in common.

REVERSE CHRONOLOGICAL
Mockingbird Lane • Tulsa, OK 12121 • (555) 555-2222 • name@email.com

SUMMARY
Award-winning Accounting professional with 10 years of management experience in accounting and accounts payable. Proven ability to supervise effective teams, oversee daily operations, and improve workflow, efficiency, and accuracy. Talented project manager, familiar with technology implementations, program management, and vendor relations. Expertise in financial reporting, reconciliations, data review, payroll processing, closings, general ledger, and budget preparation. Able to liaison to, and establish relationships with, vendors and service providers.

PROFESSIONAL EXPERIENCE
Company Name, Tulsa, OK   2003 – Present
Accounts Payable Vendor Project Specialist (contract position)
Research payments dating back to fall of 2002 that were processed incorrectly by PeopleSoft system, due to data entry errors. Contact customers, verify payment amounts, and enter updated information into system to ensure refund checks printed and distributed. Research and update vendor maintenance file, deleting and/or activating individual files.
- Identified and eliminated $100,000 of erroneous billings.
- Streamlined data processing and management procedures.
- Brought company up to date in terms of vendor payments.

Company Name, Tulsa, OK   1996 - 2003
Accounts Payable Supervisor
Oversaw daily activities of Accounts Payable department. Supervised staff of five A/P specialists and one data entry clerk. Managed invoice and payment processing for $1.5 million in weekly check runs. Improved efficiency and accuracy by introducing 100% reconciling of invoices versus checks, reducing errors and producing dramatic savings.
- Recognized for improving workflow and accuracy of data entry process.
- Earned an Outstanding Performance award for completing a critical refund check project.

Company Name, Tulsa, OK   1992 – 1996
Accounts Payable Supervisor (1994 – 1996)
Supervised operations of accounting department, managing team of six A/P professionals. Prepared financial statements and reports, reconciled accounts to general ledger, and approved journal entries. Reviewed and processed 1099 forms for IRS filings.
- Processed, reviewed and approved check requests; coordinated daily check runs averaging $75,000.

EDUCATION
Course work in Accounting and Finance, Strayer College Washington, DC

COMPUTER SKILLS
MS Office, Access, Associate Masterpiece, PeopleSoft (Financials, HR, GL, Payroll), QuickBooks

FUNCTIONAL
P.O. Box 222 • 115 Whitehorse Rd. • Anytown, CT 00022 • (555) 555-2222 • name@aol.com

Recent graduate with strong academic background in Communications and desire to work in field of Broadcast and Broadcast Journalism. Previous project management experience.

SUMMARY OF QUALIFICATIONS
- Academic background in Communications, Mass Media, and Public Relations.
- Expertise in analysis, research, planning, and presentation for projects.
- Previous professional experience in project and business management.
- Hard working, detail oriented, and able to multi-task effectively.
- Excellent communication skills. Able to work independently or as part of a team.

EDUCATION
BA in Communications, University of Connecticut, Storrs, CT (2015)
Emphasis in Interpersonal Communications
- *Course work:* The Process of Communication, Principles of Public Speaking, Interpersonal Communication, Small Group Communication, Research Methods in Communication, Nonverbal Communication, Cross-Cultural Communication, Effects of Mass Media

BACKGROUND & ACCOMPLISHMENTS
Academic Projects
- Prepared and delivered presentation on nonverbal communication., focusing on Kinesics.
- Researched and discussed five areas of body movement: gesture, touching behavior, posture, facial expression, and eye behavior.
- Part of team involved in semester-long project to create and launch public relations campaign for Hartford's minor league hockey team.
- Evaluated strategy, strengths, weaknesses, and overall effectiveness of campaign that introduced new marketing and advertising strategies and increased attendance 20%.
- Conducted research of communications processes within actual organizations. Carried out semester-long analysis of Amazon.com and Ebay.
- Compiled historical data for both organizations, identified value chains, discussed differences between each company and its main competitors.

Project and Business Management
- Foreman, Sales Representative, and Customer Relations Associate for construction company.
- Planned and managed multiple projects simultaneously, ranging from $2,000 to $78,000. Negotiated agreements, prepared estimates.
- Communicated with clients to determine specifications. Monitored progress of projects to ensure all requirements met and schedules adhered to.

EMPLOYMENT HISTORY
Supervisor / Equipment Operator, Harry's Construction, Anytown, CT (2010 – Present)

COMPUTER SKILLS
Windows, Word, Excel, PowerPoint, Outlook, WordPerfect

SEMI-FUNCTIONAL
125 Northwest Park Ave. • Okra, FL 22339 • (555) 555-2222 • name@media.com

SENIOR BUSINESS & COMMUNICATIONS PROFESSIONAL

SUMMARY

Senior Executive with more than 15 years of experience in Business Operations and Academics. Proven ability to oversee daily operations of multiple business locations and to produce dramatic increases in revenue and sales. Consistent record of reducing costs and improving profitability. Able to develop and implement effective business policies and procedures. Adept at creating classroom curricula and instructing university-level classes in Business and Finance. Expertise in International Economics. Outstanding presentation, leadership, and communication skills.

BUSINESS & MANAGEMENT EXPERIENCE

MEDIA COMMUNICATIONS, Salem, FL   2006 – Present
Senior Director, International Business Operations
Supervised team of 150 sales and administrative personnel at five locations across North and South America. Responsible for P&L, recruiting, and overall sales and business management.

- Expanded company's presence in South America, opening two new offices in 2000.
- Increased sales revenues from $4 million in 1996 to $32 million in 2002.
- Negotiated key accounts with government of Brazil, increasing revenue by 22%.
- Reduced operating costs 18% by lowering headcount for sales teams.

CARLSBAD COLOR, Panama City, FL   2004 – 2006
Sales Director (1993 – 1996)
Managed all sales for international manufacturing and distribution company.

- Opened seven new offices, including company's first in Panama and Puerto Rico.
- Achieved $22 million growth in revenue (200%) in only three years.
- Supervised international team of eight sales managers in the US and overseas.

Senior Sales Representative (1989 – 1993)
Conducted sales of full array of company's product line, in North and South America.

- Ranked Number One in Sales four consecutive years.
- Earned Salesman of the Year each year, for exceeding goals by 15% or more.

ACADEMIC EXPERIENCE

College of Business, City, FL   2003 – Present
Assistant Professor
Instruct undergraduate classes in Economics, Business, Finance, and Management.

- Developed new courses in International Economics and International Business.
- Awarded Teacher of the Year in 1995 and 2001.
- Introduced internship program for seniors, placing students with international businesses.

EDUCATION
MA in International Finance, Minescongo University, New York, NY
BA in Business Administration, minor in Spanish, Minescongo University, New York, NY

COMPUTER SKILLS
Windows, MS Office, Project, Visio, QuickBooks, SAP, Oracle Financials, Internet

LANGUAGES
Fluent in Spanish and Italian

2. The Curriculum Vitae

In general, the curriculum vitae (or CV) is a much longer document than the American résumé, with no set page length. It's most commonly used for academic positions, medical or scientific research positions, graduate school admission, and in the fine arts. The CV is also a very common type of employment history document outside of the U.S., where it's used in several European countries as well as some Latin American countries. Today many foreign countries, such as Australia, are switching over to a format similar to the American résumé, while others, such as Japan, have their own distinct required formats.

The CV uses a paragraph or combined paragraph and bullet point style for job histories, tends to include more details than a résumé, and also includes personal information, which American résumés typically do not.

CVs often include lengthy sections detailing publications, awards, research projects, grants, and speaking engagements, while in the US these are usually listed in separate documents rather than on the résumé, in order to keep the résumé short.

On the next two pages you'll see an example of a short curriculum vitae. Compare it to the résumés you previously looked at and you'll get an idea of how different and specialized these documents are.

CURRICULUM VITAE

19 Cunningham Circle		Phone: (555) 555-1212
City, MA 02368	name@attbi.com	Work: (555) 555-1212

SENIOR ACADEMICIAN SPECIALIZING IN SOCIAL BEHAVIOR

SUMMARY

Award-winning and accomplished Professor with extensive background in Social Work, Human Behavior, and International Social Policies. Licensed Diplomate in Clinical Social Work with previous academic and clinical experience. Highly adept at developing, enhancing, and instructing courses and field seminars in Social Work and Human Diversity. Skilled at curriculum development, student advising, research, and public/college service. Comprehensive training in field, with numerous fellowships and foreign language / cultural expertise. More than 30 publications and presentations in field. Outstanding project and program management experience. Excellent communication skills.

EDUCATION

Ph.D. in Social Policy, Planning, Community Organizing, and Administration
College Graduate School of Social Work, Hill, MA

M.S.W. in Social Work
School of Social Work, Boston, MA

BA, School of Public and Community Services
University of Massachusetts, Boston, MA

PROFESSIONAL BACKGROUND

State College, City, MA   2003 – Present
Associate Professor, Graduate School of Social Work (2005 – Present)
Instructed courses in Social Work Practice I/II/IV, Human Diversity and Social Work, and Human Behavior I/II, as well as conducting field and directed study courses in Health Policy and Supervision, and International Social Work (Barbados).

Prepared classroom materials and updated curricula. Personally developed International Social Work field study class for Barbados. Acted as Visiting Lecturer at Boston College, instructing Introductory Research and Community Advocacy.

Served as student advisor for 25 graduate students per semester, and field liaison. Lead Faculty member for Social Work Practice II and Human Diversity courses. Active member of several campus committees, including serving as Committee Chair for M.S.W. Admissions, Student Services, and Health / Mental Health Concentration.

Earned tenure in 1999, recognized by graduate organization for Outstanding Performance. Conducted research from 1998 to 2002 in association with Adoption Crossroad, on persons working with adopted children or adoptive parents. Evaluated program's training component.

Project Director, Special Program (2003 – 2005)
Performed program planning, fiscal management, federal grant reporting, and staff supervision. Administered grant. Completed annual / mid-year evaluations. Supervised program coordinator. Served as Lecturer from 1994 to 2000, on Research Methods and Community Organizing and Social Change. Organized seminars on Managing Graduate Studies.

NAME, MSW, Ph.D. • Page 2

(State College, continued)

Coordinator, M.S.W. Admissions (2003 – 2004)
Oversaw enrollment and admissions functions for School of Social Work. Managed recruitment of culturally diverse students.

Graduate School of Social Work, City, MA   1995 – 2003
Adjunct Professor (2001 – 2003)
Co-instructed course in Comparative Social Policy, supervised student field activities in Cuba.

Field Supervisor, Scholars Program (1996 – 2001)
Oversaw graduate-level social work students in field studies in Boston Public School System. Worked with educational coordinator, provided summary evaluation reports on student progress.

Consultant, Special Conference (1995 – 1996)
Conducted research on Boston's Caribbean community for conference design purposes. Prepared and delivered demographic data on research results.

Major Hospital, Boston, MA   1991 – 1995
Field Staff Director, Special Program (1991 – 1995)
Hired and managed multi-cultural staff of nursing professionals and human services workers responsible for conducting field studies with local families, interviewing participants and drawing blood samples for analysis regarding levels of lead according to geographic location in city.

Project Coordinator, Office of Treatment Improvement (1991)
Managed oversight and administered $800,000 budget for program that involved providing services for individuals with substance abuse problems. Hired and supervised professional staff.

ADDITIONAL EXPERIENCE

Clinical Field Work Instructor, Hospital, City, MA (1990)
Clinical Social Worker, Hospital, City, MA (1989)

LICENSES AND CERTIFICATIONS

Massachusetts Licensed Clinical Social Worker
Board Certified Diplomate in Clinical Social Work

COMPUTER & LANGUAGE SKILLS

MS Office, SPSS, WordPerfect
Fluent in Spanish and Haitian Creole

PROFESSIONAL DEVELOPMENT

Certificate in Latin American Studies, Andres Bello Cultural Institute, Trinidad, West Indies
Certificate in Addictions, Moorehouse College, Atlanta, GA

COMMUNITY & PROFESSIONAL INVOLVEMENT

Member, The Council on Social Work Education
Chair, Caribbean American Educational Coalition

3. The Federal Résumé

Federal résumés have a very distinct style, one that's different from the standard résumé formats or the curriculum vitae. In fact, there is more than one type of federal résumé, as different formats are needed depending on the agency you're applying to, and the level of the position you're applying for. However, the majority of federal agencies use what we call the standard federal résumé format, which is what we'll discuss in this book.

Like the CV, the federal résumé includes personal information below the heading. It also typically includes the names of supervisors and their contact information, salary history, and complete addresses of the places of employment (as opposed to simply city and state in a standard résumé).

Usually federal résumés are accompanied by documents known as KSAs (Knowledge, Skills, and Abilities), which include responses to specific questions asked in a federal job posting. KSA responses can run anywhere from one to two pages each.

On the next pages you'll find an example of a typical federal résumé.

For more information on the different résumé formats and the uses of each, please refer to Chapter 4. Also, Appendix 1 contains a list of sample résumés from a wide variety of industries, job sectors, and professions.

If you still feel you need more information, feel free to contact me at **sales@a-perfect-resume.com**, or visit my website, **www.a-perfect-resume.com**.

FEDERAL RÉSUMÉ

NAME
Address
City, State, Zip
email
Social Security Number: 123-456-7890

Vacancy No: ABC-1234
Job Title/Grade: Level 4
US Citizen: Yes
Veteran's Preference: No

SUMMARY

Highly talented and accomplished Investigator with special expertise in business and financial fraud. Previous experience with City of New York and US Secret Service. Superior skills in document preparation, research, and communications. Contributed to arrest and apprehension of several wanted individuals. Excellent record of prosecution for investigated cases. Strong knowledge of federal, state, city, and local laws and requirements.

Investigations • Case Review • Witness Interviews • Documentation • Research
Data Analysis & Verification • Currency Assessment • Fraud Investigation
Evidence Management • Surveillance • Team Leadership • Case Management

WORK EXPERIENCE

Job Title: Investigator / Senior Investigator
Employer: Bureau of Fraud Investigation, NY City Human Resource Administration
Address: New York, NY
Dates of Employment: 10/2008 – Present
Hours Per Week: 40+
Pay/Grade Level: $65,000/yr
Supervisor: Bob Hoskins, 555-555-5555 (okay to contact)
Carry out investigations of fraud for city's Dept. of Social Service & Human Resource Administration. Maintain average case load of 40 to 60 investigations per week. Review case records and complaints against applicants and program participants suspected of fraud. Schedule and conduct interviews of witnesses, complainants, and suspects. Communicate with local, state, and federal agencies. Prepare summary reports and recommendations. Verify recipients' identities and application data. Determine eligibility of welfare recipients to receive social services.

Saved close to $200,000 by identifying 20 cases of fraud. Promoted to Senior Fraud Investigator after only 2 years. Developed effective contacts within law enforcement agencies and city agencies. Eliminated backlog of outstanding cases. Played key role in arrest and apprehension of individuals wanted by law enforcement, including NY City Warrant Squad and US Marshals. Recognized for having 6 cases prosecuted out of 20 filed.

Name
SSN: 123-456-7890
Page 2

INTERNSHIPS

Job Title: Intern
Employer: NY City Dept. of Housing Preservation & Development
Address: New York, NY
Dates of Employment: 06/2007 – 08/2007
Hours Per Week: 40+
Pay/Grade Level: $10,000/yr
Supervisor: Bob Hoskins, 555-555-5555 (okay to contact)
Assisted with investigations of contractors and businesses doing business with City of New York, specifically work involving city-owned houses and buildings. Carried out investigations in response to complaints of poor quality work or financial fraud. Interviewed witnesses and suspects. Maintained evidence. Performed surveillance duties.

Job Title: Intern
Employer: United States Secret Service
Address: New York, NY
Dates of Employment: 10/2006 – 12/2007
Hours Per Week: 40+
Pay/Grade Level: N/A
Supervisor: Tim Leary, 555-555-5555 (okay to contact)
Provided investigatory assistance for agents In Counterfeit, Bank Card Fraud, Credit Card Fraud, Wire Transfer Fraud, Check Fraud, and Identity Theft divisions. Sorted and identified counterfeit currency sent to Secret Service from Federal Reserve. Prepared and organized case filed, evidence, and other data.

EDUCATION

BS in Behavioral Science, with Major in Criminal Justice and Minor in Paralegal Studies, Marist College, Poughkeepsie, NY (2007)

Diploma (with Honors), Xavier High School, New York, NY (2003)

TECHNICAL SKILLS

MS Office, Outlook, Lexis-Nexis, Internet research. Type 50 wpm.

CHAPTER 3 - Writing Your Résumé

Most people find it difficult to write about themselves. People generally fall into two categories when it comes to writing their own résumés: the **extrovert** and the **introvert**.

The **extrovert** is the person who has no trouble putting down all their job functions and accomplishments. They leave out no details, no matter how small. A résumé written by this type of person can extend to six or seven pages, especially if the person works in a technical field or has held several jobs during their career. The extrovert describes every job and project to excess, frequently including the name and model of every piece of equipment used, who they reported to, loads of data about the company they worked for, and an employment history going back to the very beginning of their career, even if it was forty years ago. The extrovert also will frequently include all of the details of their academic background, even going so far as to list classes taken in college back in 1968.

No matter how well written this type of résumé is, it will not be effective in getting the applicant interviews. Remember, your résumé only has one minute at best to pique the interest of the reader. A recruiter or human resource agent who picks up a six-page résumé is more likely to toss it aside than read it.

TIP: The résumé is a summary, not a biography. Keep it short; 2 pages is best.

The **introvert** has the opposite problem. A typical introvert might be a person who has a fifteen-year career filled with accomplishments and achievements, and yet puts together a one-page résumé with hardly any details in it. Each position has the job title and company followed by two or three lines of description. This type of résumé doesn't convey any important information to the reader, and so it also ends up being tossed aside.

TIP: Too much information is a no-no, but the résumé must give an accurate overview of the person's qualifications and achievements. Too little information is as bad as too much.

Keywords

A keyword is any word that draws attention to your résumé, by matching your résumé to the job description the employer is trying to fill. Most people think of keywords as a list of words in a résumé designed to attract the attention of search engines, and that is the main reason for including them in your résumé. But keywords have been around longer than computers—we just didn't call them keywords!

There are two basic types: general and job- or industry-specific.

General keywords are those that apply to a wide variety of jobs, such as leadership, budget control, organizational skills, analytical skills, or strategic planning.

Specific keywords are those that apply to a particular job or industry. It's important you know the right ones for your industry, and the jobs you're interested in, so you can make sure you include them on your résumé.

Back when companies first started using databases and search engines to store and find résumés, people often created separate keyword sections on the résumé to aid the computers in their searches. Today, thanks to the dramatic improvements in computer technology, we don't need to do that. We simply incorporate keywords and phrases into the résumé itself. The most common place to do this is in the Summary.

Before you can incorporate your keywords, however, you have to know them. The best way to do this is to pick out a few jobs you're interested in, and read the ads carefully to find the important or common words and phrases. Look at the sample ad below, for a Human Resources Manager:

Responsibilities:
• Responsible for the overall function of the HR Department
• Administration of personnel functions and payroll
• Ensure new employee orientation is delivered to foster positive attitude toward company goals.
• Coordinates management training in interviewing, hiring, terminations, promotions, performance review, safety, and sexual harassment and advises management in appropriate resolution of these issues
• Advise managers and employees consistent with company policies, procedures, and programs and facilitate resolution of employee relations issues.
• Recommends and implements changes to meet the changing needs of the business
• Design and implement salary administration and performance review program to ensure effectiveness, compliance, and equity within organization and conduct wage surveys within

labor market to determine competitive wages.

• Recruitment to ensure the Company is adequately and suitably staffed on a timely basis to meet the Company's requirements

• Administration of the Company's benefit plans and management of compensation packages, including proactive recommendations for changes in accordance with prevailing or foreseen employment requirements.

Requirements Qualifications:
• A highly motivated individual with strong sense of integrity
• The ability to handle a wide variety of confidential information on a regular basis
• Positive approach and pro-active working style
• Strong knowledge of employment law and relevant regulations
• Good organizational and analytical skills
• Spanish preferred but not required
• Excellent interpersonal and communication skills with staff at all levels
• Strong ability to work independently
• Knowledge of payroll and benefits plan systems a plus
• At least 3 years experience in similar management capacity

• Bachelor's degree in Human Resources Management or related discipline.

Sounds like a standard ad, right? Can you pick out the keywords a résumé writer would include in the résumé? Go back and circle your choices, and then look below to see how well your picks match up to those a professional résumé writer would make.

Responsibilities:
• Responsible for the **overall function of the HR Department**
• **Administration of personnel functions and payroll**
• Ensure **new employee orientation** is delivered to foster positive attitude toward company goals.
• Coordinates **management training** in **interviewing, hiring, terminations, promotions, performance review, safety,** and **sexual harassment** and advises management in appropriate **resolution of these issues**
• Advise managers and employees consistent with **company policies, procedures, and programs** and facilitate **resolution of employee relations issues.**
• **Recommends and implements changes** to meet the changing needs of the business

• **Design and implement salary administration and performance review program** to ensure effectiveness, **compliance**, and equity within organization and **conduct wage surveys** within labor market to determine competitive wages.

• **Recruitment** to ensure the Company is adequately and suitably staffed on a timely basis to meet the Company's requirements

• **Administration of the Company's benefit plans and management of compensation packages**, including proactive recommendations for changes in accordance with prevailing or foreseen employment requirements.

Requirements Qualifications:
• A highly motivated individual with strong sense of integrity
• The ability to handle a wide variety of **confidential information** on a regular basis
• Positive approach and pro-active working style
• Strong knowledge of **employment law and relevant regulations**
• Good **organizational** and **analytical skills**
• **Spanish preferred** but not required
• Excellent interpersonal and communication skills with staff at all levels
• Strong ability to work independently
• Knowledge of **payroll and benefits plan systems** a plus
• At least **3 years experience** in similar management capacity
• **Bachelor's degree in Human Resources Management** or related discipline.

What I've done is place in bold everything that is actually important for the job. The next step is to incorporate these skills into the Summary section of the résumé, in such a way that they're all included, but the Summary doesn't sound like a repeat of the job description.

SUMMARY

Talented Human Resources Management Professional with 10+ years of experience overseeing all HR department functions, including benefits, compensation, recruiting, and performance reviews. Special expertise in developing and implementing new employee orientation, compliance, and salary administration programs. Background includes conducting wage surveys and creating new procedures to keep pace with corporate growth and change. Familiar with managing confidential information and serving as department subject matter expert in employment law. Excellent organizational and analytical skills. Multi-lingual in French and Spanish. Hold SPHR designation.

That's how the Summary would look on the résumé. Now look at it again to see where I've worked in the keywords:

SUMMARY

Talented Human Resources Management Professional with **10+ years of experience** overseeing all **HR department functions**, including **benefits, compensation, recruiting, and performance reviews**. Special expertise in **developing and implementing new employee orientation, compliance**, and **salary administration programs**. Background includes conducting **wage surveys** and creating new procedures to keep pace with corporate growth and **change**. Familiar with managing **confidential information** and serving as department subject matter expert in **employment law**. Excellent **organizational** and **analytical skills**. Multi-lingual in French and **Spanish**. Hold SPHR designation.

I hit all the key points of the ad while making sure the Summary didn't sound like a plagiarized or copied statement. I did this by rewording the information and including other facts about the applicant's career not asked for in the ad, such as the SPHR designation.

Just as important as what I included was what I left out: the non-essential skills. Can you find those in the ad? Go back and look. Then check out the list below:

Positive attitude
Advise managers
Proactive recommendations
Integrity
Interpersonal skills
Communication skills
Work independently

Why weren't these attributes, skills, and phrases included? Go back once more and read the list carefully. Notice the one main difference between those words and the keywords we selected? All the words in the above list are *personal qualities*, not professional skills. You'll see these personal qualities, and others similar to them, in every job posting you read, in almost every field. But professional writers don't include them on the résumé or cover letter. Why? *Because the employer* **expects** *you to have them*. Do you think they're going to hire someone who isn't trustworthy? Or who can't work independently? Or who has a negative attitude? Of course not. So don't waste space on your résumé with information that's not necessary. If you don't have the basic personal qualities most jobs call for, you've got bigger problems than your resume!

TIP: Never include personal qualities in your résumé. Stick to professional skills.

Before you create the Summary to your own résumé, go through several ads and find the common keywords. Then make sure to include them in your Summary (assuming, of course, you have those skills. Never put a skill on your résumé if you don't have it).

Action Verbs and Adverbs

Because the idea of the résumé is to grab the reader's attention, it's important that every sentence and every bullet point convey a sense of action and/or accomplishment. There are two basic types of sentences, **active** and **passive**. Active sentences convey *action*, naturally, while passive sentences do not. Both sentences have their uses in traditional writing, but in résumés it's important to use as many active sentences as you can, in order to keep the reader's interest.

Look at the examples below and see if you can pick out the passive and active sentences.

1. Reviewed files to ensure accuracy.
2. Completed over 36 projects in one year.
3. Responsible for all staffing assignments.
4. Familiar with all aspects of office operations.
5. Friendly and courteous to clients entering building.
6. Achieved major increases in sales each year.

Ready for the answers?

Sentences 1, 2, and 6 are active sentences; 3, 4, and 5 are passive.

TIP: Active sentences indicate the person is doing, or did, something.

If you were reading a résumé, which of these bullets would catch your eye first?

• Managed and improved office operations.

• Familiar with all aspects of office operations.

The first one, right? It tells us the applicant not only knows what he or she is doing, but was good at it, and accomplished something. The second sentence only says the applicant had knowledge, not that he or she actually did anything or achieved anything. In the first sentence, the action verbs–'Managed,' 'improved'–grab the reader's attention. The second sentence is 'blah,' and just sits there, begging to be overlooked. That's not what you want.

TIP: Action verbs grab a reader's attention and make them want to keep reading.

Sometimes even an action verb isn't enough to make a bullet stand out. That's where **adverbs** come in. Adverbs are words that describe verbs and make them sound better.

Look at the following examples.

Increased sales every year.
Dramatically increased sales every year.

Produced changes in operational procedures.
Effectively produced changes in operational procedures.

Calculated large volumes of information.
Accurately calculated large volumes of information.

See how the use of the adverbs (the 'ly' words) at the beginning of each sentence makes the sentence even stronger? Professional résumé writers use adverbs when the action being described doesn't stand out very well on its own.

Below you'll see a sample job description from a résumé, before and after the use of adverbs and action verbs. Notice how we don't use adverbs for every bullet, just the ones that need it.

Before

$8.7 million dollar territory at large manufacturer of medical supplies. Started as Sales Representative, then Sr. Sales Rep. Managed a staff of three clinical specialists. Carry out sales of products by developing relationships with healthcare professionals. Grew territory 39% in 2006-2007, meeting 130% of goal. Awards included Pacing Rep of the Region in 2002, CRDM National Rep of the Quarter in 2007, District Representative of the Year in 2004 and 2006, and President's Club in 2007. Grew market share 34% in 2007. Increased revenues each year.

After

Manage $8.7M territory for manufacturer of medical and related products. Promoted twice, from Sales Representative to Senior Sales Rep to current role. Supervise 3 clinical specialists. Develop relationships with healthcare professionals.
- Delivered 39% territory growth from 2006 to 2007 (130% of goal).
- Earned Pacing Rep of the Region in 2002 and CRDM National Rep of the Quarter in 2007.
- Recognized as District Representative of the Year 2x (2004, 2006).
- Received President's Club Award in 2007 while growing market share 34%.
- Dramatically increased sales revenue every year.

Here is the **After** description again, this time with the action verbs in bold, and the adverbs in italics:

Manage $8.7M territory for manufacturer of medical and related products. **Promoted** twice, from Sales Representative to Senior Sales Rep to current role. **Supervise** 3 clinical specialists. **Develop** relationships with healthcare professionals.
- **Delivered** 39% territory growth from 2006 to 2007 (130% of goal).
- **Earned** Pacing Rep of the Region in 2002 and CRDM National Rep of the Quarter in 2007.
- **Recognized as** District Representative of the Year 2x (2004, 2006).
- **Received** President's Club Award in 2007 while **growing** market share 34%.
- *Dramatically* **increased** sales revenue every year.

When writing your own job descriptions, remember to always use action verbs and adverbs. You can find a good list of these in Appendix 5 of this book.

Résumé Pitfalls – What to Watch Out For

Whether you're writing your own résumé or having one done for you, there are certain things to watch out for. Knowing these potential pitfalls can save you a lot of time, money, and aggravation in the long run.

1. Writing your own résumé

We've already covered this somewhat, but I want to go over it again. *People who write their own résumés don't get as many interviews as do those who have their résumés professionally written.* And that goes for having your best friend, co-worker, parent, sibling, or in-law write the résumé for you. Unless one of these people is a professional résumé writer, they're probably not going to do a much better job than you would yourself.

The biggest danger of writing your own résumé is that you'll make a mistake, resulting in the résumé getting tossed into the trash. Part of my job as a résumé writer is reviewing and critiquing people's résumés, and it's simply astounding to see the documents people use for their job searches. Now, one typo or misspelling on a résumé or cover letter isn't going earn it a trip to the garbage bin, but anything more than that probably will. Spell check is a basic component of all word processing systems, and I recommend every person use it, for every document they write. What I *don't* recommend is depending only on spell check. How many times have you seen words such as *to, two,* and *too; for, fore,* and *four; form* and *from,* and so on slip through spell check? You can't blame the software. The words are spelled correctly, after all. And that's all your computer is checking for. Some people use grammar check, which can catch some problems, but not everything. There have even been occasions where I've seen the letter 'f' omitted from the word 'shift,' resulting in a truly embarrassing typo that made its way into a cover letter distributed to hundreds of potential employers. How many positive responses do you think *that* applicant received?

But typos, spelling or grammatical, are only one level of the problems encountered in résumés. More sinister is language usage. This is a trap even semi-professional writers fall into. There's a reason the study of reading and writing is called the Language Arts. Writing is an art, just like painting, sculpting, or composing. It doesn't matter if you're writing poetry, novels, technical papers, newspaper articles, or résumés. A good writer needs to have a way with words, and needs to be able to meet the demands and guidelines of the subject matter. The world's greatest novelist might not be able to write a decent article for a medical journal, because the two styles of writing are completely different. A person might write exceptional technical reports, but not be able to put together an effective résumé.

Because the résumé must convey, in a short format, not only the key facts of a person's work history, but *why* that person would be a benefit to a prospective employer, it requires specific types of word usage and sentence structure.

A résumé is centered on actions and results. Look at these sentences from actual résumés written by applicants, and then compare them to the same facts, rewritten by a professional résumé writer:

Old: Sold car batteries, engine parts, and accessories to general public. I made $375K in my first year, better than any of the other sales people.

New: Achieved $375,000 in sales of automotive parts in first year, ranking Number One for the office.

Old: I started my company in 1989. By 1992 it was making $995,000 per year, and employed 311 people.

New: Established a new company and grew annual revenue from zero to almost $1M in only 3 years. Increased staff from 1 to more than 300.

Old: I was the only person in my team that was able to repair and troubleshoot technical problems the other technicians couldn't figure out.

New: Served as the final escalation point and team lead for all technical issues.

Were you able to see the difference? Each of the new sentences started with an action verb to grab the reader's attention and indicate something was accomplished. Also, in every case the new sentences moved the most important piece of data to the beginning of the sentence, where it's more likely to be read if someone is just skimming the résumé. This is just one example of how a professional résumé writer crafts words and phrases into effective statements.

Another example of résumé grammatical standards is the omission of certain words and types of phrases. Résumés, unlike cover letters, *are never written in the personal or first-person format.* The words 'I,' 'we,' 'me,' 'my,' 'our,' 'mine,' 'he,' and 'she' are never used in a résumé. In addition, resumes also frequently use incomplete phrases to denote accomplishments and job functions, especially in the bullet points. Look at these examples:

- Achieved $29 million in sales over two years.
- Founded and directed a successful video production company.
- Oversaw production operations for five international factories.
- Managed a team of seven project managers across the state of New York.
- Owned and operated the largest plumbing supply store in San Francisco.

All of the above sentences are technically incomplete, according to standard grammatical rules, because they lack a subject (I, me, etc.) but they are perfectly acceptable, in fact *preferable*, for the résumé format. The incomplete sentence makes its point quickly and saves valuable space on a document.

Let's look at a couple of examples of how a professional résumé writer uses language and format to create top-performing content, using the extrovert and introvert we spoke about earlier.

The Extrovert

Original Document

Project: eBusiness Strategy, major west coast power company

Title: eBusiness Technology Strategist

This project was to develop a strategy for eBusiness group to define the applications architecture roadmap to support SCE Intranet strategy and programs. Application areas include: Portal Platform Services, Web Content Management, Business Application Integration, Workgroup Collaboration Services, etc. As a Technical Analyst, I was involved in analysis of Technology trends, Industry Best practices for B2C, B2E and B2B areas of Utility industry. As part of four-person project team I was responsible for developing major sections of ebusiness Strategy document and B2E portal roadmap presentation.

Accomplishment: A quality product was produced and submitted to client's CIO in a very challenging time frame, which was well received by client's upper management.

New Document

Project: eBusiness Strategy, major west coast power company

Title: eBusiness Technology Strategist

Served as Technical Analyst on four-person project team. Developed major sections of eBusiness strategy document and key B2E portal roadmap presentation. Facilitated success for project involving development of application architecture definition strategies. Successfully completed project on time, delivering well-received presentation to client CIO.

The Introvert

Original Document

2001-2003 Car Dealership, Dallas, TX

General Manager

Increased vehicle sales 170%. Managed Inventory. Increased service hours. Supervised staff. Recruited to next job.

New Document (after interview with client to gather additional information)

Car Dealership, Dallas, TX   2001 – 2003

General Manager

Supervised car dealership with staff of 120. Oversaw sales, P&L, inventory, parts, repairs, and customer service.

- Increased vehicle sales 170%, from 80 per month to 310 per month.
- Improved gross sales from $2M to $8M, while tripling gross profit levels.
- Took market share from 6% to 12% and ranked in the Top 50 for the nation.
- Grew revenues by adding additional service hours.

For the extrovert, we had to condense the information to the essential facts. For the introvert, we needed to add more information than what the client previously had on the resume. In both cases, the content needed to be adjusted as well (this is called *wordsmithing*) in order to create a resume that would meet the standards HR offices look for.

These are just some of the pitfalls associated with writing your own résumé, or having it written by someone who isn't qualified to write résumés.

"But Greg," you might be asking, "why not use one of the many professional templates available today on the internet?" Good question. Let's take a look.

Résumé Templates and Software Packages

Thanks to the computer age, templates and cookie-cutter résumé software packages are everywhere. But just because they're common doesn't mean they're going to produce a résumé that works.

Résumé templates and software packages give you a choice of many different formats to choose from, and they often include all sorts of fancy fonts, headings, and graphics. These things look great to *your* eye, but they're annoying to human resources personnel and hiring managers. Odd fonts and unusual formats make the résumé harder to read, especially for someone who has to read dozens, maybe hundreds, of résumés each day. And if the resume is hard to read, chances are it won't get read at all.

TIP: Résumés should be written in a professional-looking font that's easy on the eyes. Studies have shown the following fonts are best for this: Times New Roman, Arial, Century, Verdana, Calibri, and Lucida. Stick with one of these, and you'll be safe.

Graphics are another résumé writing sin. Vertical lines, pictures, and unusual bullet point styles all appear on peoples' résumés to this day, even when hiring professionals and résumé writers are doing their best to teach people this only hurts their chances of getting an interview. Today's résumés need to be fax, email, database, and scanner-friendly, and graphics play havoc with all of these. At best they cause smudges or don't transfer at all; at worst they interfere with format, even going so far as to jumble up the order of words and sentences. When that happens... well, you can imagine how effective a résumé is when a person can't even read it.

Pretty smiley-face bullets and their kin serve only one purpose: they demonstrate the applicant has no idea of what a professional document looks like. Would you use a smiley face, or a heart, or a Microsoft Windows symbol as a bullet point on a business letter or technical report? Of course not. So why would you put one on a résumé? Your best bet is a round, black dot. Nice and simple. In some cases, especially for entry level résumés or certain industries, such as the sales or entertainment fields, an arrow is acceptable, but only rarely.

While we're at it, let's take a moment and discuss another pitfall, one that strikes novice and professional alike: Always make sure to select a bullet that transfers well when you format your résumé into an *ascii*, or *plain text*, file, as you'll often have to do when applying for jobs. Many bullet point symbols with turn from this:

- I look like a normal bullet point.

to this:

$$X&!!'''" I look like a normal bullet point.

Wow. That simple bullet morphed into something guaranteed to ruin any chance you have of getting a positive response to your résumé.

The reason for this problem is that not all bullet symbols, or even symbols in general, are created equal; that is, they're not supported in the plain text format used for pasting your résumé into a form on a website, or into the body of an email. This includes copyright and trademark symbols, foreign words that have accents over certain letters, and even quotation marks and hard carriage returns, depending on how old your software is.

TIP: Always go back and double-check your document after you've cut and pasted it into an email or a web submission form. Be prepared to correct any changes.

Another pitfall of the template goes back to the idea of how well you write. A template supplies all your headings for you, but you still need to pick the information that's going to go under each one, and then write it in clear, correct, professional-sounding English. This is the big stumbling block for most people. Even if the book or software shows you how to format the résumé, *you still have to write it!* How will you choose which verb leads off each sentence? Will your sentences make sense? Will the facts be in the proper order? Will your punctuation be correct?

As most résumé writers, human resource personnel, and recruiters know, the answer to many of those questions will be 'No!'

There's no shame in admitting you can't write a good, effective résumé; 98% of our population can't. Everyone has their own niche, their own areas where they have skills. I've found mine as a professional writer. I'm not a mechanic, or a plumber, or a doctor. This is what résumé templates and software can't to do for people—give them the ability to write the *content* of the résumé. Hopefully, after reading this book and studying the samples and instructions, you'll be able to craft something that stands out from the crowd. However, it's good to know that if the résumé you write doesn't work as well as you want it to, you can always use the **discount coupons** at the back of this book to get a professionally-written résumé.

2. Résumé Companies

Let's say you've decided that a professional résumé is the way to go. How do you decide what company to use? Open a phone book, or do an internet search, and you're likely to be overwhelmed by the number of résumé companies and 'professionals' out there. The fact is, just like in any profession, there's a chance you could pick the wrong company and end up paying hundreds of dollars for a résumé that doesn't work any better than the one your nephew wrote for you a month ago. Many of these companies are of the 'fly by night' variety, and many don't use professionals writers at all.

So how can you choose?

The first thing you want to do is make sure the person writing your résumé is a Certified Résumé Writer. There are three national organizations that certify résumé writers: the Professional Association of Résumé Writers and Career Coaches (PARWCC), the National Résumé Writers Association (NRWA), and the Professional Résumé Writing and Research Association (PRWRA). A certification from any of these organizations means the writer has passed an intensive examination and has demonstrated the ability to prepare an effective résumé, as judged by a panel of highly experienced and certified résumé writers. While certification doesn't automatically confer expertise (just like doctors, writers can graduate at the top or bottom of the class, or anywhere in between), it does greatly improve the odds your résumé will be well written.

The second thing to find out is how many years of experience your writer has, and if they're familiar with your field. Contrary to popular belief, the best writer is not necessarily someone who's worked in your field. Often the best writer is the one who's written résumés in a wide variety of fields, for people in all walks of life. However, the writer should have a basic understanding of your job, recognize the important skills, and be able to take your information and shape it into an effective document.

Important Résumé Fact: When you apply for a job, the first person who reads your résumé won't be an expert in your field; he or she will most likely be a recruiter or human resources representative. If they feel your résumé matches the description of the available job, they'll forward it to the appropriate hiring manager or supervisor. That means your résumé must be written in such a way that it can be understood by a layman, and yet contain all the information needed to impress the person you would be working for. This is a fine line, one that résumé writers walk every day.

Third, but by no means last in importance, is to look at sample résumés posted on the company's website. You want to make sure your résumé is going to be customized to best display your skills. Many companies out there, local and national alike, use a template and cookie-cutter approach to résumé writing. That means every client gets a résumé that looks exactly the same. While the format these companies use may be effective in many cases, the fact is, the same résumé format isn't going to work for everyone. A writer, or company, must be adaptable to meet the needs of *all* its clients. An information technology professional, physician, international student, and police officer all have different needs, as does the person re-entering the work force, moving to Australia, or changing careers. If every résumé on a website looks identical, or if they have the same extraneous graphics and bullets you've seen in software package templates, those are signs you might want to proceed with extreme caution.

Finally, compare prices. A résumé package today can run anywhere from $69 to $800, depending on the company, your level of experience, and where you live. But beware of the two extremes. A company offering a $69 résumé for everyone is probably either using the cookie-cutter method of writing, using non-certified writers, or cutting corners somewhere. That's not to say you might not get a good résumé from them, but to me it's kind of like seeing a brand new car for sale that's ten thousand dollars cheaper than what any of the other dealerships are selling it for. When I see that, I hear the alarms inside my head saying, 'buyer beware.'

The same goes for the other end of the spectrum, the company that's selling you a résumé for $600 or $700. Unless you happen to be the CEO of a Fortune 50 company, odds are that's too much to pay. This is a firm that's either catering strictly to high-end executives or is trying to make itself seem more prestigious by raising the prices of its products.

Somewhere in between these two extremes is where most résumé companies lie, and this is the zone you probably want to focus on, at least initially. Sure, two or three hundred dollars seems like a lot to pay for a couple of sheets of paper, but when you consider it could mean a difference of many thousands of dollars in your paycheck, or even getting a paycheck at all, it's money well spent.

Other things to look for in a reputable résumé company? Some type of guarantee. Whether it's a free rewrite after 30 or 60 days, or a money-back guarantee, it doesn't matter. As long as you have a commitment on the company's part that they'll stand by their product.

Today most companies offer some variation on a 60 day rewrite guarantee, which means if you haven't received an increased number of interviews within 60 days, they'll rewrite the résumé for free. There are two things to notice about this: One, it's not a money-back guarantee. Most résumé companies don't offer those any more. And two, it's not guaranteeing you a job. Why? Because although a professional résumé is going to be much more effective than your old one in getting you interviews, having one doesn't mean you're going to get the job you want. People don't like to hear this, but it's a cold, hard fact. The résumé is only one part of the job search process. A good one increases the number of interviews you get, which increases your odds of getting a job. But "sure things" don't exist. And there are several reasons why.

Please pay attention: in order for your résumé to work, *you must send it out.* I don't mean five or six résumés and then give up; I mean sending out 20 or 40 a week. Flood the market, send it in for every job you qualify for, and some you think are a little beyond your skill level.

Even the best professional résumé averages only 30 interviews for every 100 résumés sent out. That's 3x - 5x better than a résumé prepared by your sister's boyfriend's uncle, but it still means you have to send out a lot to get a good return.

30% of 100 is a pretty good number. 30% of five is less than two interviews, which isn't so great. Especially when there's a lot of competition in the marketplace. No résumé company is going to back their guarantee if you're not holding up your end of the deal. I once had a client who said she'd only gotten one interview in 60 days using my résumé and she wanted her money back. When I asked her how many positions she'd applied for, she told me "two." She was surprised when I told her that meant I'd written her an exceptional résumé.

Another reason companies don't like to give money back is that even if the new résumé gets a person a lot of interviews, the writer can't control what happens during the interview. If an applicant dresses wrong, isn't prepared, or just doesn't have the qualifications some of the other applicants have, no job offer is going to be made. This will happen—you aren't going to be the best candidate for every job you interview for. Accept it and move on to the next interview; sooner or later you'll hit the jackpot.

Another thing writers can't control is what people do with their résumés after they receive them. People think it's okay to make changes to the documents, which is a lot like trying to fix the engine of your new car yourself, instead of bringing it to the shop. You're not only going to create problems, you'll also void the warranty.

As a job seeker, it pays to be aware of the job market in your area. At the time this book is being written, the national average for getting a job is 45-60 days. That means it takes a minimum of 45 days for your résumé to be received, read, read again, have an interview (or two) scheduled with the company, and then have the company make the decision to hire you.

Now compare that to the 60 day guarantee most companies give. Sure, we're proud of our work, but we have to be realistic as well. 60 days might not be enough time for companies to reach the interviewing stage in the process. If you're working, and can afford to be patient, do yourself a favor and don't request the rewrite until after at least 60 days have passed. Having two different versions of your résumé out there at the same time can lead to other problems, like having both versions end up on the same person's desk. Talk about confusing!

I once had a client who requested a rewrite because he hadn't heard anything after 45 days. Since he was still working at the time, I counseled him to wait another two weeks, just in case. He did, and one week after our conversation he received three interviews and ended up accepting one of the offers. Had he sent in a different version of his résumé for the same position, it could have raised red flags at the company and cost him a job.

Before and After Samples

Now that we've learned about proper résumé format, bullet points, keywords, and action verbs, let's take a look at some before and after samples and see how those rules get put into effect when writing a résumé. Each of the before and after samples you'll see are actual résumés I received and then re-wrote. Examine them carefully, and try to see where I've put into use the lessons we've gone over in the previous chapters.

BEFORE 1

Address • city, state, zip • phone number • email address

Management professional with recent MBA in change management and business strategy
Summary of qualifications
10 years of increasingly responsible management positions.
Expertise in consumer services, warehousing, workflow, and change management.
Proven ability to establish and lead effective teams and successful businesses.
Consistent record of increasing productivity, sales, and profitability.
Able to identify areas for improvement and implement policies and procedures.
Excellent problem solving, reporting, financial, and communication skills.

Professional Experience
Company 1, City, CO   2005 - Present
Warehouse Coordinator
Oversee operations of 3rd-party warehouses in Denver and Phoenix. Manage and coordinate
receipt and delivery of products and services. Supervise staff of 5 and carry out training.
Work closely with account executives to meet customer needs. Manage customer billing, and
product/services billing. Maintain inventory. Monitor and report on productivity. Research
inventory discrepancies and determine causes.

Identify areas for improving productivity and deliver recommendations to Operations
Manager.
As member of Safety and Ergonomics teams, contributed to cost control by achieving zero
lost-time accidents since 2005.
Developed and implemented several safety improvements for warehouse.
Provide effective inventory control for 55 clients in Denver region and 50 clients in Phoenix;
maintain total of more than 2,900 inventory items between 2 facilities.
Played major role in Denver facility earning Most Valuable Business Service Center Award in
2006.
Company 2, City, CO   1998 - 2002
Manager / Outside Sales Representative
Managed $1.5 million dollar retail store, largest of 5 locations in company. Supervised staff of 5
outside and inside sales representatives. Carried out sales and customer service training.
Monitored sales. Resolved customer service issues.

Built store to 33% higher revenue than next-largest location.

Enhanced efficiency by developing monthly reports and new spreadsheets.

Communicated frequently with vendors to ensure customer needs met.

Increased sales average of 12% per year, by diversifying business offerings.

- Promoted from Inside Sales Representative to Manager.

- Ranked as Number One Outside Sales Representative.

Education

- MBA in Change Management/Business Strategy, University of Colorado (2007)

Course Work: Designing Effective Organizations, Organizational Development, Strategic Management, Marketing Strategy, Performance Management, Customer Relationship Management, Marketing Management, Managing Individuals and Teams

BA in Economics, University of Colorado (2004)

- Minor in Business Administration

- Dean's List student

Included Course Work: Micro & Macro Economics, Money & Banking Systems, Corporate Accounting, Financial Accounting: Reporting & Analyses, Corporate Finance, International Finance, Labor Economics, Industrial Economics, Business Ethics and Society

Computer Skills
MS Office, Access, Oracle, Acrobat

****In this example, the spacing isn't consistent, the headings don't match, the bullet format is not uniform, nothing stands out, and the use of action verbs is poor. Also, it goes onto a second page with no name heading.***

AFTER 1

ADDRESS • CITY, STATE, ZIP • PHONE NUMBER • EMAIL ADDRESS

Management professional with MBA in Change Management and Business Strategy

SUMMARY OF QUALIFICATIONS

➤ 10 years of increasingly responsible management positions.

➤ Expertise in change management and leadership

➤ Proven ability to establish and lead effective teams and successful businesses.

➤ Able to identify areas for improvement and implement policies and procedures.

➤ Consistent record of increasing productivity, sales, and profitability.

➤ Excellent problem solving, reporting, financial, and communication skills.

PROFESSIONAL EXPERIENCE

COMPANY 1, City, CO   2005 - Present

WAREHOUSE COORDINATOR

Oversee operations of warehouse in Denver and 3rd-party warehouse in Phoenix. Manage and coordinate receipt and delivery of products and services. Supervise staff of 5 and carry out training. Work closely with account executives to meet customer needs. Manage customer billing and product/services billing. Maintain inventory. Monitor and report on productivity. Research inventory discrepancies and determine causes.

• Identify areas for improving productivity and deliver recommendations to Operations Manager.

• As member of Safety and Ergonomics teams, enhanced profitability by achieving zero lost-time accidents since 2005. Developed and implemented several safety improvements for warehouse.

• Provide effective inventory control for 55 clients in Denver region and 50 clients in Phoenix; maintain total of more than 2,900 inventory items between 2 facilities.

• Played major role in Denver facility earning Most Valuable Business Service Center Award in 2006.

COMPANY 2, City, CO   1998 - 2002

MANAGER / OUTSIDE SALES REPRESENTATIVE

Managed $1.5 million dollar retail store, largest of 5 locations in company. Supervised staff of 5 outside and inside sales representatives. Carried out sales and customer service training. Monitored sales.

- Built store to 33% higher revenue than next-largest location.
- Enhanced efficiency by developing monthly reports and new spreadsheets.
- Communicated frequently with vendors to ensure customer needs met.
- Increased sales average of 12% per year, by diversifying business offerings.
- Promoted from Inside Sales Representative to Manager.
- Ranked as Number One Outside Sales Representative.

EDUCATION

MBA in Change Management/Business Strategy, University of Colorado

- Course Work: Designing Effective Organizations, Organizational Development, Strategic Management, Marketing Strategy, Performance Management, Customer Relationship Management, Marketing Management, Managing Individuals and Teams

BA in Economics, minor in Business Administration, University of Colorado

- Dean's List student
- Course Work: Micro/Macro Economics, Money & Banking, Corporate Accounting, Financial Accounting: Reporting & Analyses, Corporate Finance, International Finance, Labor Economics, Industrial Economics

BEFORE 2

Street address • City, state, zip

Phone number

Enthusiastic high achiever with excellent communication skills

Comfortable working in a team or with minimum supervision

Highly proficient in creation, management and casting of project from creation of concept to production

Years of experience as principle singer with considerable dance training and performance

Ability to direct and "fine tune" productions of all types

Familiar with light and sound design and all aspects of show production

Very organized and detail oriented

Excellent trouble shooting abilities

Musical Director: Taught music to singers and non singers for numerous large production shows for Norwegian Cruise Line. Responsible for every aspect of singer's performance from solo work to achieving natural body movement in all genres' of music represented in show.

Production Manager: Responsible for teaching, performing in and managing all aspects of traveling character shows for Paramount Productions, ranging from mall shows to circuses.

Casting: Responsible for planning and executing national audition tours for cruise ship casting for Paramount Productions, Charlotte, NC. Auditioned singers and taught hip hop, ballet and jazz dance combinations. Also reviewed video submissions for casting.

Performance: Principle performer with 25 years experience with Walt Disney World, Tokyo Disneyland, Sea World, Special Event and Convention Companies: Norwegian Cruise Line, Royal Caribbean Cruise Line, Dinner Theatre, Studio Recording

Coaching: Very experienced in many styles of vocal coaching. Have taught audition workshops for singers and dancers. Have extensive training in classical, musical theatre and pop styles of singing therefore able to help vocalists achieve results in any style of music. Also able to work with performers in areas including body movements, interpretation and presentation.

Special Event Planner: Promotions Chairperson for local chapter of nationally recognized program, Sanford Main Street, Inc. Responsible for planning and execution of St. Patrick's Day Festival, Oktoberfest, monthly car cruises, assisted in Fourth of July Celebration with estimated 85,000 in attendance, Entertainment Chairperson for Annual Tour of Homes in Sanford, Florida with Sanford Historic Trust

In this sample, no bullets are used, the actual employment history isn't given, there's no focus to the résumé to let the reader know what the applicant is looking for, and the tone is too conversational.

AFTER 2

Street Address • City, State, Zip • Phone Number • email address

Entertainment Management ~ Production Manager ~ Special Event Planner

Talented entertainment management professional with strong background coordinating and leading productions, special events, and performances. International experience in theater, stage, and music. Proven ability to train, lead, and direct successful teams and projects. Adept at negotiating with vendors and suppliers, meeting deadlines/schedules, and resolving problems. Excellent communication skills.

Show Production • Event Management • Musical Direction • Staff Coordination
Project Management • Theater / Stage Production • Training & Coaching
Scheduling • Negotiations • Budget Control • Creation & Casting • Problem Solving

PROFESSIONAL BACKGROUND & ACCOMPLISHMENTS

Show Production

- Extensive international experience in all aspects of show production, including development, casting/auditions, training, lighting, sound, and live production.
- Worked closely with stage directors to ensure casts show-ready. Facilitated stage productions, musicals, dinner theater, and other performances for traveling and single-site productions.
- Served as Production Manager for Las Vegas / Broadway-style review shows and dinner theater for major cruise lines, including Norwegian Cruise Lines and Paramount Productions.
- Supervised musical training and show production for 'character-themed' shows. Arranged auditions, instructed cast in music, and taught hip-hop, ballet, and jazz dance.
- Selected and coordinated casts ranging from 5 to 15 persons for shows in US and Latin America.
- Assisted with management of more than 20 major productions from 2002 to 2005.

Name • Page 2

(Background & Accomplishments, continued)

Special Event Management

- Served as Promotions Chairperson for local chapter of Mainstreet USA. Planned and organized several major events each year, including festivals and monthly events.
- Obtained and negotiated agreements with vendors, auditioned and hired talent, obtained necessary permits, and coordinated stage set up. Administered project budgets.
- Oversaw St. Patrick's Day Festival, Oktoberfest, 4th of July Celebration, and monthly car cruises.
- Supervised volunteers for events ranging as large as 85,000 attendees.

Coaching & Training

- Trained performers in dance and vocals for theater and stage productions.
- Instructed audition workshops for singers and dancers.
- Provided training in classical, theater, and pop styles of singing.
- Worked with dancers and performers on body movement, interpretation, and presentation.

EMPLOYMENT HISTORY

Barbara Bauman, Private Entertainer / Production Manager, Sanford, FL (2005-Present)

Contract Roles with Disney World, Tokyo Disneyland, Sea World, and others (2002-2005)

EDUCATION & TRAINING

Course work in Musical Theater & Dance, Jacksonville University, Jacksonville, FL

ADDITIONAL INFORMATION

Computers: MS Office, Internet

BEFORE 3

Address

City, State, Zip

Phone Number

Email address

EXECUTIVE CHEF   Specializing in Authentic Italian and American and Kosher Cuisine.

EXECUTIVE DUTIES

- Supervision of entire kitchen staff and their daily duties.
- Appointing daily work details to include times and job descriptions.
- Reviewing on a weekly basis function sheets to include all ordering of meats, fish, groceries, And all kitchen supplies.
- Keeping food costs within percentage limits. Currently working at a 14% average.
- Reviewing and overseeing weekly menus for our customer satisfaction.
- Artistic skills includes garde manger detail, ice sculptures
-

2007-present   EXECUTIVE CHEF

RESTAURANT 1, CITY. NY.

- Specializing in authentic Italian and American cuisine
- Preparation and supervision of all aspects of operation
- Supervision of kitchen staff and all job details.
- Supervision of all catering banquets and planning of all menus pertaining to restaurant and catering hall.
- Ordering of all items to include back and front of house.

1999-2007   EXECUTIVE CHEF

RESTAURANT 2, CITY, NY

- Specializing in authentic Italian and American and kosher cuisine
- Preparation and supervision of all appetizers, sauces, gravies, soups, salads, entrees, and desserts.

- Supervision of all kitchen staff and job details.
- Working with a 13% to 15% food cost.

1996-1999   EXECUTIVE CHEF

RESTAURANT 3, CITY, NY

- Specializing in Italian and regional Italian and American cuisine
- Supervision of all kitchen staff and their job details, 15 kitchen employees under my supervision.
- Worked with a 15%to 17% food cost.
- Ice sculptures and garde manger detail.

1988-1995   EXECUTIVE CHEF

RESTAURANT 4

- Specializing in American and Italian cuisine.
- Supervision of 8 kitchen staff and their daily duties.
- Reviewing and creating new weekly menus for ala carte dining.
- Ice sculptures

1975-1988   CO-EXECUTIVE CHEF

RESTAURANT 5, BX, NY.

- Specializing in Italian and American cuisine.
- Supervision of 30 employees and assistant chefs and cooks.
- Keeping food cost at a great percentage with the amount of parties on a weekly basis.

In this résumé, the spacing and format are inconsistent, there are hardly any action verbs, there are numerous grammatical errors, and the résumé goes back too far in time. There is also information missing from some of the jobs, and the résumé goes onto a second page with no name heading.

AFTER 3
Street Address • City, State, Zip • phone number • email address

---

SENIOR CULINARY PROFESSIONAL
Executive Chef – Chef de Partie

~ SUMMARY OF QUALIFICATIONS ~

- Specialize in Glatt Kosher, Italian, American cuisine, and *garde manger* work for established catering houses and restaurants.
- Expertise in ala carte service up to >6,000 covers per month, catering multiple events for parties of all sizes, and overseeing kitchen activities.
- Regionally recognized as **Ice Sculptor** specialist by multiple NY State newspapers.
- Consistent record of reducing costs through competitive bidding, implementing vendor discounts, streamlining portioning of proteins and fish, and effectively utilizing labor.

~ PROFESSIONAL EXPERIENCE ~

RESTAURANT 1, City, NY   2014 – 2015
Executive Chef
Responsible for 60-seat Italian-American restaurant and 150-seat catering facility. Supervise kitchen staff of 6. Responsible for purchasing all kitchen supplies. Oversee kitchen, catering, and delivery operations. Led complete kitchen layout redesign.
- Improved profitability by re-engineering menu and setting new prices for restaurant and catering operation

RESTAURANT 2, City, NY   1999 – 2014
Executive Chef
Directed catering operations for high-volume facility with 3 banquet rooms, capable of handling >500 guests per event. Managed off-premise catering and kosher catering for special events, including 150 weddings per year. Supervised kitchen staff. Prepared appetizers, sauces, gravies, soups, and entrees from scratch.
- Successfully carried out more than 150 off-premise kosher weddings and events per year
- Produced more than $4M in annual revenue and 50,000 covers through upscale menu preparation and design. Grew covers per year from 30,000 to 50,000.
- Built high volume of repeat business for upscale seder dinners
- Prepared more than 30 new homemade hors d'oeuvre recipes for catering menu
- Increased catering profit levels by maintaining a 14% food costs
- Reduced costs by performing ice sculpting in house instead of purchasing

RESTAURANT 3, City, NY   1996 – 1999
Executive Chef
Supervised staff of 12 and oversaw all kitchen operations for high-volume catering facility with - 3- banquet rooms and 900 guest capability. Specialized in authentic regional Italian cuisine.
- Grew revenue from $6M to $9M+ and increased covers per year from 40,000 to 75,000.
- Directed food preparations for more than 250 weddings per year
- Implemented both sauté and cook-to-order pasta stations for all weddings. Introduced hors d'oeuvres, desserts, and entrees to increase menu choices.
- Maintained food costs at less than assigned goal of 17%

RESTAURANT 4, City, NY   1988 – 1995
Executive Chef
- Managed ala carte and catering operations for multi-room facility with capacity of over 400.
- Supervised staff of 8 and coordinated all kitchen activities, food preparation, and service.
- Prepared weekly menus for ala carte dining and introduced custom Italian specialties.
- Oversaw regionally popular Sunday brunch service.
- Brought ice sculpting in house to reduce kitchen costs.

CAREER NOTES: Previously held position of **Co-Executive Chef** at RESTAURANT 5, supervising kitchen staff and operations, managing catering functions, and producing over $15M per year in revenue. Details available on request.

~ EDUCATION & TRAINING ~
Course work in Business Management
All appropriate food services, safety, and health training

~ LANGUAGES ~
Conversational in Spanish

~ COMPUTER SKILLS ~
MS Office, Internet

BEFORE 4

Street Address

CITY, MI 12345

Phone Number

Email

OBJECTIVE:

To obtain a position that will enable me to utilize and develop my knowledge and skills, as well as provide a beneficial source of experience.

SKILLS:

Knowledgeable in Microsoft Word, Excel, PowerPoint, Access, Lotus Notes and Lean Manufacturing.

EDUCATION:

Lawrence Technological University; Southfield, Michigan

MBA (Career Integrated MBA = CIMBA)

Wilberforce University; Wilberforce, Ohio.

BS Psychology (1997)   G.P.A   3.93 / 4.00

WORK EXPERIENCE:

Manufacturing Supervisor   Company 1, city, MI   07/01 - Present

Responsibilities encompass training and managing of 30 United Auto Workers in the manufacturing of wheel spindle bearings.

- Involved in training programs with employees in order to provide a safe work environment and insure the production of quality parts by performing daily audits.
- Evaluate team member performance and conduct reviews on an annual basis.
- Assist with the implementation of methods and procedures that maximized the utilization of equipment and manpower.
- Schedule manpower requirements and order the raw materials needed to meet the daily and weekly schedules.
- Work with maintenance to eliminate downtime and improve part quality.

Training Coordinator   company 2, City, MI   07/00 – 07/01

- Provided training on Microsoft Office Software (Word, Excel, Access, PowerPoint, and Lotus Notes) to all employees within the company.
- Prepared and maintained all documentation related to enrollment and confirmation of class schedules.

Training Coordinator   -company 3, City, MI   06/98 – 07/00

- Performed audits for ISO 9000 certification and also maintained the Corrective Action Logs.
- Responsible for providing training on Microsoft Office Software (Word, Excel, PowerPoint and Access). Prepared and maintained all documentation related to enrollment and class schedules.
- Organized the Brand Segmentation database for all GM PEP vehicles and assisted in maintaining the database for GM – Onstar. Also assisted in pulling and releasing part numbers in the company's GPDS system.
- Created a monthly newsletter with current information of events taking place within the organization.

Mathematics Tutor   University 1; City, OH.   01/95 - 04/97

- Assisted students in learning how to solve difficult mathematics equations to prepare them for classes and examinations.
- Responsible for filing documents and typing.
-

AWARDES RECEIVED:

Awarded 4 year Academic Scholarship Wilberforce University.

Presidential Award 1994/ 1995 / 1996 for Good Academic Performance.

Dean's List 1993 – 1996 and National Dean's List 1993 – 1996.

This résumé presented a host of technical issues. The font and spacing were not consistent, in many instances it was difficult to tell where one position ended and the next one began, the sections were not in the correct order, the résumé went to a second page with no name heading, and it contained a multitude of spelling and punctuation errors.

AFTER 4
Street ▪ City, MI 12345 ▪ phone number ▪ Email

Training ● Learning & Development ● Training Manager ● Manufacturing Manager

Talented and accomplished Management professional and corporate trainer with more than 8 years of experience. Expertise in quality assurance, safety, LEAN manufacturing, and performance improvement training. Consistent record of contributing to higher production and customer service levels. Adept at preparing training materials and programs.

~ PROFESSIONAL EXPERIENCE ~

COMPANY 1, City, MI   2001 - Present
Manufacturing Supervisor
Trained and supervised staff of 30 United Auto Workers in manufacturing setting. Monitored staff performance and provided annual evaluations. Prepared schedules. Ordered raw materials. Conducted regular safety and quality audits. Directed training program.
- Increased quality 10% by reducing equipment downtime and improving parts inspections.
- Enhanced productivity by maximizing equipment and resource utilization.
- Improved efficiency through better preventive maintenance programs.
- Reduced costs by resolving scrap issues and minimizing raw material usage.
- Worked closely with maintenance team to eliminate downtime and increase part quality.
- Ensured all team members completed required safety and equipment training.

COMPANY 2, City, MI   2000 – 2001
Training Coordinator
Carried out training in Lotus Notes and MS Office, including Access and PowerPoint, for all employees. Prepared and maintained training documentation.
- Conducted classes of 10 or more and created department-specific training manuals.
- Prepared specialized training sheets for employees to use after completing classes.

COMPANY 3, City, MI   1998 – 2000
Training Coordinator
Oversaw MS Office training. Actively involved in quality initiatives and database management.
- Conducted audits for ISO 9000 certification and maintained corrective action logs.
- Prepared and managed all training-related documentation and schedules.
- Organized brand segmentation database for key vehicle program and assisted with management of other databases.
- Created department-specific training manuals and ancillary documentation.
- Facilitated quality improvement by developing quality surveys distributed to customers.

~ EDUCATION ~

Career-Integrated MBA (CIMBA), Lawrence Technological University, Southfield, MI
BS in Psychology, Wilberforce University, Wilberforce, OH

~ ADDITIONAL INFORMATION ~

Computers: MS Office, Access, Lotus Notes, proprietary databases and systems
Recognition: Dean's List student and Presidential Academic Award winner (Wilberforce Univ.)

CHAPTER 4: Different Résumés and Their Purposes

Earlier in this book I gave an overview of the basic types of résumés (American, Curriculum Vitae, Federal, International). Now it's time to take a closer look at each one, and provide an explanation as to when and why they should be used.

The American, or Standard, Résumé

As stated previously, the three basic types of American résumés are the Reverse Chronological, the Functional, and the Combined Chronological – Functional.

Let's start with the **Reverse Chronological**. This is the résumé most people are familiar with, what we call the 'standard résumé.' It's most useful in the following situations:

☞ Someone with one to 20 years of experience in the same, or a similar, field of work, who has held increasingly responsible positions. An example of this would be a person who's in sales, started out with retail sales, moved to equipment sales, and gradually worked his or her way up the ladder to a sales management or territory management position.

☞ Someone who has held similar positions in one field throughout their career, such as a teacher who has taught at four different schools, or a salesperson who has been an account executive with several different companies.

The Reverse Chronological résumé can be used for any industry, and any level of employment. From entry-level associate to chief executive officer, in sales, construction, management, operations, international marketing, science, education, and janitorial services. From accountant to zookeeper, the Reverse Chronological résumé is appropriate and effective.

Approximately 70% of all U.S. résumés written fall into this category. On the following pages you'll see three examples of 'typical' reverse chronological résumés.

Chronological 1

CIVIL ENGINEER

Local Address
PO Box 4578
Jubail, KSA 22558

(M) +696 45 881 9926
name@ymail.com

Permanent Address
689 Hidden Circle Drive
Columbia, NY 02356 USA

Highly accomplished Civil Engineer & Construction Manager with Middle East experience

Proven ability to manage and improve construction initiatives in Middle East and America. More than 17 years of construction industry experience, including 8 years in road and drainage work. Special expertise in overseeing multiple projects simultaneously, ensuring compliance, monitoring costs, and coordinating multi-cultural teams. Excel at directing sewerage, drainage, infrastructure, and roadway projects. Consistent history of completing projects on-time/ahead of time and within/below budget. Consistent history of increasing safety and quality, and building long-term relationships with clients, stakeholders, and government officials. Highly familiar with adapting Western processes and best practices into Middle Eastern work culture. Skilled at overseeing all project phases from planning to turn over. on PM, EPC, and EPCM contracts.

Core Competencies:
Project/Program Management ~ Construction Planning ~ Site Supervision ~ Budgeting
Inventory Control ~ Procurement ~ Relationship Management ~ Curb & Gutter Installation
Cost Control ~ Process Optimization ~ Roadway Construction ~ Storm Water Management

PROFESSIONAL EXPERIENCE

BUFFSTER CORPORATION, Jubail Industrial City, KSA ~ 2010 – Present
Lead Field Civil Engineer- (Construction Manager)

Oversee construction of roads, culverts, storm drainage channel, sea water cooling, industrial and sanitary waste water collection networks, 34.5kV distribution network, road lighting, telecommunication network, earthworks, and more for $91.75M, 30 sq. km. site development project. Also manage earthworks, instrumentation, procurement, logistics, site safety, inventory control, and compliance. Supervise 30 employees, including project and construction managers, mechanical/civil/electrical/telecom/roads supervisors, QC manager, and safety manager. Coordinate 245 trades workers from various countries. Review and approve $3.1M in monthly invoices. Communicate with local municipalities, investors, stake holders, and EPC firms.

Accomplishments:

- Directed completion of 26,000 meters of drainage channel, 760 meters of sand asphalt-lined open channel, 18 culverts, 94 over-sized drains, 400 meters of twin pipe culverts, 2320 meters of road-to-toe ditches, and 917 meter cast-in-place inlet drop structure.
- Oversaw installation of 20km of heavy and light duty paving in center of active industrial area.
- Improved safety and quality more than 25% by implementing project's first quality and safety programs, with bonuses and awards for achieving performance goals.
- Achieved 40 million safe man hours without a work lost accident on Jubail 2 and more than 2.5 million safe working hours on current site.
- Reduced rework-related costs 3% by conducting productivity studies and identifying issues.
- Increased productivity 5% by developing and implementing checklists and work programs.

Civil Engineer ~ Page 2

MALPHEES CONSTRUCTION, Cascade, MI, USA ~ 2004 – 2010
Senior Project Manager

Planned and managed large commercial and residential construction projects for $200M construction company. Directed horizontal and infrastructure projects as large as $59M, including road networks, storm water drainage systems, sanitary waste systems, pump stations, bridges, culverts, runways, and railroads. Frequently served as Lead Manager on complex initiatives. Served as liaison to consultants, developers, engineers, and government officials.

Accomplishments:
- Installed double-lane medium duty road as part of Day River Tech project. Led construction of integrated storm water drainage system with reinforced concrete pipe, precast manholes, outfall structure, and curb and gutter system.
- Oversaw construction of privately funded highway access road with heavy, medium, and light duty pavement sections. Developed traffic management plan. Completed portions of project at night due to heavy highway traffic. Project included drainage system and 2 small bridges.
- Lead Manager for $59M golf course and luxury commodities project. Coordinated roadwork, drainage systems, culverts, and sanitary systems with state and local authorities.
- Recognized for completing projects within budget and meeting accelerated timelines.

THE WHITNEY HOOCH CONTRACTING COMPANY, Mayfield, PA, USA ~ 1995 – 2004
Project Engineer / Assistant Project Manager

Managed turnkey medical, research, and educational facilities construction projects for private and public sectors. Oversaw construction document reviews, budgeting, equipment, materials sourcing, subcontractor evaluations, and quantity take-off/verification. Defined scopes of work for subcontractors. Supervised project teams. Served as College Recruiter for project and field engineers. Also served as Quality Control Engineer.

Accomplishments:
- Lead Project Manager for $7M medical facility at Georgia Institute of Technology.
- Played key role in negotiations, pre-construction, and project close-out for $175M in projects.
- Quality Control Engineer for $90M laboratory project at Centers for Disease Control.

EDUCATION

BS in Civil Engineering, w/specialization in Construction Management, Clemson University, Clemson, SC

CERTIFICATIONS & TRAINING

Six Sigma, Safety, Quality, Leadership, Management, HR, Practical Construction Documentation

ADDITIONAL INFORMATION

Affiliations: American Business Association, Construction Managers Association of America
Computers: MS Office, Timberline, Prolog, Salesforce.com, AutoCAD, Eversuite, Infoworks

Chronological 2

HEALTHCARE EXEC, M.D.,FACP

6451 Well Way • Shantyville, IL 55889 • 748-898-8837 • brocal@kmail.com

Talented Hospitalist specializing in Internal Medicine

— PROFILE —

Experienced Hospitalist specializing in Internal Medicine, with proven ability to reduce patient length of stay and improve overall quality and efficiency of healthcare in hospital environments. Played major role in establishing two start-up hospitalist programs. Previous experience as Academic Attending. Fellow, American College of Physicians. Board Certified in Internal Medicine. ACLS/BLS certified. Illinois licensed. Well-developed leadership and business skills.

— PROFESSIONAL EXPERIENCE —

BELLA HOSPITAL, Shantyville, IL   2007 - Present
Hospitalist

Senior member of team of 8 that manages all aspects of inpatient care, from admission and diagnosis to discharge, for 35% of hospital's patients. Communicate extensively with primary care physicians, specialists, families, consultants, nurses, and discharge planners. Monitor patients throughout stay and coordinate movement of critically-ill patients through ICU and other departments. Assist with team scheduling. Co-manage surgical patients, including orthopedic cases and stroke cases. Code Blue Team Lead and Rapid Response Team Member.

- Actively involved in improving patient care by developing general admission protocol that resulted in fewer calls to doctors from nurses and more accurate DVT prophylaxis.
- Assisted in creation of effective medical reconciliation form for discharging patients.

AMERICAN HOSPITAL, Shantyville, IL   2002 - 2007
Hospitalist

Member of team that established and managed hospital's first Hospitalist program. Assisted with all administrative functions, including physician scheduling. Served on multiple committees. Prepared and conducted in-service classes. Designed and developed new healthcare programs. Provided coverage for internal medicine outpatient programs. Participated in quality improvement and education program development. Gave well-received Grand Rounds on VTE. Member of Rapid Response Team and served as Code Blue Team Leader.

- Member of ER Committee and QA/QI Committee.
- Designed highly successful VTE protocol and VTE in-service program for nurses.
- Played key role in increasing levels of care as Member of Program and Education Committee, and by developing and participating in Quality Improvement.
- Recognized as member of team that lowered average patient length of stay by half-day.
- Maintained 100% compliance with JCAHO core measures for myocardial infarction and CHF.
- Contributed to 150% increase in business by improving relations with local physicians.
- Aided team in growing from 4 to 10+ physicians by actively recruiting new hospitalists.
- Recognized for achieving reductions in patient length of stay through implementation of new protocols, 24-hour care, and better communication with nurses and discharge coordinators.
- Prepared and conducted lectures on Updates in Internal Medicine.

Healthcare Exec, M.D., FACP • Page 2

COLLEGE OF ILLINOIS MEDICAL SCHOOL, Shantyville, IL   2004 - 2007
Associate Clinical Professor
Academic Attending at teaching hospital. Performed teaching rounds and delivered lectures to groups of residents. Supervised residents on daily bedside rounds. Evaluated patient care plans. Instructed students during physical examinations and reviewed differential diagnoses. Assisted residents in preparing for morning reports.

- Contributed to improved patient care and resident education as member of team that created hospitalist elective rotation for family practice residents.
- Earned reputation for one of most popular rotations. Consistently increased residents' knowledge of acute inpatient care and management of diabetes, hypertension, cholesterol, and other issues.

— ADDITIONAL EXPERIENCE —

HEALTHY LASER SPAS, Shantyville, IL   2005 - 2009
CEO / Medical Director / Founder
Established and directed company specializing in laser hair removal, laser skin rejuvenations, microdermabrasion, chemical peels, acne treatment, botox injections, and other procedures. Hired and supervised administrative personnel, laser technician, and esthetician. Managed marketing, advertising, and website. Performed all medical procedures. Developed policies and procedures.

- Grew business from startup to 600 clients and gross profits $150K per year.
- Improved efficiency through online calendaring, online billing, and patient-facing website.
- Sold business for profit in 2009.

— EDUCATION —
Doctor of Medicine, University of Illinois at Chicago, Chicago, IL
BS in Biology, University of Illinois, Urbana, IL

— LICENSURE & CERTIFICATIONS —
Board Certified in Internal Medicine
ACLS/BLS Certified
Illinois Licensed
Fellow, American College of Physicians (ACP)

— PROFESSIONAL DEVELOPMENT —
Completed course in Hospitalist Procedures
Certified to operate Aesthetic Lasers
Certified in Microdermabrasion
Certified in Laser Safety
Certified in Botox & Fillers

— PROFESSIONAL ORGANIZATIONS —
American College of Physicians
American Medical Association

CHRONOLOGICAL 3

IT PROJECT MANAGER, PMP

6727 Washington Irving South • Plainfield, MN 44110 • (234) 658-8712 • mw223@nsn.com

IT PROJECT MANAGEMENT PROFESSIONAL / CERTIFIED PMP

Talented and accomplished Certified Project Management Professional with extensive background planning and leading wide variety of successful IT projects. Adept at leading full project life cycles, from inception to closure. Highly familiar with coordinating multi-disciplinary teams for infrastructure build-outs, system migrations, technology implementations, data conversions, process design, and custom development projects, among others. Excellent leadership and problem-solving skills.

Key Skill Sets:
Project Management • Program Management • Budget Control • Infrastructure Design
Technical Consulting • Enterprise Security • System Migration • Technology Implementation
Data Center Migration/Build Out • Analysis & Reporting • Technology Selection

PROFESSIONAL EXPERIENCE

HIGHWAVE CORP., Plainfield, MN   2010 – 2015
Project Manager
Played major role in establishing project management position for IT consulting firm. Developed all policies and procedures. Led project teams of 3 to 8 individuals. Administered project budgets up to $2 million. Oversaw complete project life cycles based on Statement of Work (SOW). Provided technical assistance to sales teams as needed. Supported customers in banking, manufacturing, academic/university, city government, and retail sectors.

- Managed Enterprise Security projects for clients to implement RSA token authentication and IPass security products. Coordinated internal, client, and subcontractor teams.
- Led internal Vulnerability Assessment Services project. Reduced errors and improved accuracy. Built repeatable delivery framework for all vulnerability assessment opportunities with standardized SOW documentation. Defined processes.
- Planned and led major system migration for large financial organization. Project included improvements to legacy system and migration to new version of UNIX environment.
- Oversaw several IP Telephony projects. Directed implementation of systems as large as 500 users. Replaced and configured Call Manager servers.

EUGENIX, Plainfield, MN   2006 – 2010
Project Manager, Enterprise Technology
Supervise teams of 3 to 10. Administered project budgets as large as $2 million. Directed internal projects at multiple facilities for large healthcare analytics company.

- Carried out integration of acquired company. Migrated and consolidated servers, PCs, email, and related services. Standardized operations to reduce cost of having remote office.
- Carried out migration of data center to centralized facility. Led virtual project team. Set up hardware space, arranged transportation, and testing systems.
- Directed 6,000 sq. ft. data center build-out. Coordinated vendors and internal teams.
- Member of team that created PMO from scratch. Developed processes and documentation.

Project Manager, PMP

Page 2

(Eugenix, continued)

- Successfully completed 1ˢᵗ phase of development project to create interface to HEAT support system. Improved efficiency by integrating 2 distinct applications into 1.
- Selected to take over failing infrastructure design project, part of larger development project. Resolved on-going issues and brought project on-track.
- Migrated customer environment from leased facility to internal data center, with HP SuperDome technology. Led migration of development, test, and production devices. Introduced new data management and storage technology to increase productivity.
- Oversaw installation of HP OpenView at main data center. Deployed database SPIs for several customers. Assisted with construction of command center to monitor systems.

HEALTHCARE INFORMATION SYSTEMS, Plainfield, MN   2004 – 2006
Technical Consulting Services Project Manager (2005-2006)
Implementation Project Manager (2005)
Planned and led wide variety of projects for large healthcare technology firm.

- Managed major automated data conversion project for 4 legacy products. Oversaw client conversions nationwide. Developed conversion programs and initial processes.
- Implemented integrated client-server product for new clients.
- Formulated policies and procedures for newly-formed implementation team.

Account Manager (2004)

CAREER NOTES: Previously held positions of **Assistant Project Manager**, DOOGIE TECH SYSTEMS and **IT Support Tech**, GOOD SAMARITAN CENTER. Details available upon request.

EDUCATION

Masters Certificate in Project Management, George Washington University, Arlington, VA
BS in Business Administration, University of Minnesota, Minneapolis, MN

CERTIFICATIONS & PROFESSIONAL DEVELOPMENT

PMI Project Management Professional (PMP)
ITIL-Foundation Level Certification

ADDITIONAL INFORMATION

Computers: MS Office, Project, Visio, proprietary systems and databases
Affiliations: Project Management Institute (national and Minnesota chapters)

You may have noticed that all three reverse chronological résumés had different styles. There is no one style for résumés, although certain fonts and formats do work better. But within each résumé type, a writer has several options, style-wise, all of which will work equally well.

The **Functional** résumé is the second most common résumé in the U.S., with over 20% of the résumés in use today being of this variety. The Functional résumé is dramatically different from the Reverse Chronological, in that the information normally placed under each job is instead placed under a specific subject heading, and the employment history receives its own section on the résumé.

The Functional résumé is most often used for the following reasons:

☞ A person has worked in more than one field, and would like to showcase them equally.

☞ A person is looking to make a dramatic career change.

☞ A person has a lot of skills, but they're either scattered throughout the résumé, too far back in their career to list in the usual manner, or the result of non-professional experience. This is often the case with recent graduates.

The Functional résumé has an advantage in these cases, because it allows the writer to place the most important skill sets first in the résumé, regardless of how long ago employment was in that particular area. It places the emphasis on the skill, rather than on where and when a person worked, or what position title was held.

Look at these two examples of Functional résumés:

NAME
3901 Drive, Apt. 1234 • Dallas, NY 12345 ▪ (555) 555-1212 • name@email.com

Risk Analysis • Mitigation • Program Administration • Lending • Underwriting • Business Analysis

SUMMARY OF QUALIFICATIONS

➢ Strong financial background includes underwriting, credit analysis, risk analysis, and reporting.
➢ Adept at performing collateral assessments, debt ratio analyses, and loss mitigation to lower risk.
➢ Skilled in program administration, monitoring of markets, and preparation of documentation.
➢ Able to apply knowledge of applicable laws and regulations to facilitate regulatory compliance.
➢ Recognized for "program knowledge, organization, teamwork, and quality of work" (2011).

PROFESSIONAL BACKGROUND & EXPERIENCE

Risk Management & Compliance
• Carried out risk management relating to property values and loan conditions.
• Reviewed credit packages to ensure compliance with federal, state, and bank regulations.
• Provided business development managers with information on changing guidelines.
• Met bank guidelines and quality requirements, enabling sale of loans in secondary market.

Underwriting
• Evaluated applications to ensure accuracy and validity of employment and credit data.
• Reviewed customer loan applications, including credit histories, income documents, disposable income, debt ratios, property types, appraisals, titles, regulations, and customer disclosures.
• Ranked #1 in pre-screen volume and led team of 6 with 80 approvals in 1 month (Wells Fargo).
• Key member of team that increased monthly loans 30%, despite 50% reduction in staff.

Management
• Reviewed files and countersign loans completed by junior underwriters.
• Supervised and trained a junior underwriter who ranked #1 in number of approvals.
• Improved efficiency by changing processes to streamline workflow.
• Supervised a staff of 15 in a high-volume food service environment.

EMPLOYMENT HISTORY

FANCY RESTAURANT, Dallas, NY **Assistant Manager**	2012 - 2015
BANK, Dallas, NY **Senior Underwriter III**	2004 - 2011
BANK FINANCIAL, Dallas, NY **Mortgage Underwriter**	2000 - 2004

EDUCATION

BS, Finance with Management concentration, College, Bristol, TN

COMPUTER SKILLS

Word, Excel, PowerPoint, Access, proprietary databases, Experion, TransUnion, Equifax, LexisNexis.

Functional - IT
126 New Street • City, State 12121 • (555) 555-1212 • name@att.net

Network and Systems Administration ~ Help Desk Services ~ IT Support

TECHNICAL SKILLS

Operating Systems:	Windows 98/NT/2000/XP/2003
Networking:	LAN/WAN, TCP/IP, Ethernet, IIS, IPX/SPX, FTP, NetBEUI, NetBIOS, DHCP, DNS, fiber optics, network security, network access configuration
Applications:	MS Office, Outlook, Acrobat, PageMaker, Norton Firewall, Norton Ghost, Photoshop, FrontPage, antivirus software, MS Internet Security, Acceleration Server 2000, Norton Utilities, HTML, Arachnophilia
Hardware:	PC/server assembly and repair, routers, switches, hubs, cabling, peripherals

PROFESSIONAL BACKGROUND & ACCOMPLISHMENTS

Information Technology
- Multiple certifications, including A+, MCP, and Network +. Familiar with system and network administration, technical support, and maintenance.
- Determined system requirements, designed, configured, installed, and supported small networks. Performed subnetting. Set up and configured security protocols.
- Configured network access and implemented system enhancements.
- Carried out PC troubleshooting, including hardware, software, and operating systems.
- Installed and upgraded operating systems for desktops and networks. Upgraded hardware.
- Conducted end user training in general PC and software usage.

Technology and Electronics
- Constructed and assembled electrical test fixtures for military and commercial contracts.
- Ensured accuracy of wire lists against schematics, identified discrepancies, and recommended changes. Assisted with quality control.
- Built electrical control panels for precision roll feeders. Performed troubleshooting and testing at customer sites to evaluate accuracy of electro-mechanical assemblies.
- Supervised scheduling of production and testing of feed assemblies.

Business Operations
- Reviewed design package part lists from customers and sourced primary and secondary vendors.
- Carried out inventory control, stock maintenance, and requisitions.
- Assisted managers with scheduling and with forecasting of material needs and labor.

EMPLOYMENT HISTORY

Wiring Technician/Purchaser, TECHNOLOGIES, INC., Fall River, MA (2008 – 2015)
Precision Roll Feeder Technician, ELECTRONICS, INC., Cranston, RI (2006 – 2008)
Customer Service Representative, OTHER COMPANY, Warwick, RI (2003 – 2006)

EDUCATION & CERTIFICATIONS

Microsoft Certified Systems Administrator (MCSA), Roger Williams University, Providence, RI
A+ / Network + / MCP, Roger Williams University, Providence, RI
AS in Electronics Technology, New England Institute of Technology, Warwick, RI

In the first résumé, the client is looking to leverage their underwriting, management, and risk management skills in order to look for jobs outside of the underwriting industry. In the second résumé, a person who's been working in electronics for their entire career is now seeking a position in information technology, and wants to showcase the skills and academic experience in that area over previous work experience. In both cases, the Functional résumé is the best format for presenting the skills and abilities that will interest a prospective employer.

Even though the Functional résumé has been used effectively for many years now, it's still regarded negatively by some résumé writers and recruiters. This is because people sometimes use the functional format to hide large gaps in their employment record. While it's true some people use the Functional résumé for this purpose, I don't see anything negative about it. The gaps are not hidden so much as de-emphasized; anyone familiar with reading résumés knows to read the employment history that follows the functional section, and to check the dates. If there is a gap, the reviewer will ask the applicant about it during an interview, and the applicant must be prepared to explain it. The functional format is simply a way to emphasize the applicant's skills *before* the gap is noticed; all too often someone who's qualified for a job and using a standard Reverse Chronological résumé is eliminated from the interview process simply because his or her résumé doesn't showcase the applicant's skills sets soon enough.

*TIP: Remember, the purpose of the résumé is to get the reader interested enough in you to schedule an interview. **Never lie or falsify information on a résumé;** this is a sure way to be fired later, when your credentials are checked. However, there's nothing wrong with rearranging the order of the data on a résumé so your most important skills get showcased first.*

As you might expect, the **Combined Chronological / Functional Résumé,** or **Semi-Functional Résumé,** incorporates aspects of both the Reverse Chronological and Functional formats. It's not as common as either of those two, but there are certain times when it can be a very effective tool, such as for a person who has perhaps been working at two positions simultaneously, in different fields, or for someone who has held a full time job in one area, and done an extensive amount of volunteer or military work at the same time. The Combined

Chronological / Functional résumé offers this type of client the opportunity to separate his or her background into distinct areas, while still utilizing the chronological format.

In the following example, you can see how the client's career included two entirely distinct areas (hands-on technical work and management), either of which might have gotten lost or obscured in a traditional Reverse Chronological Résumé. At the same time, the Functional résumé would not have been appropriate for this person, due to his senior-level management experience. The Combined résumé allowed the client to apply for positions in either of his areas of expertise, by listing the key achievements and also showcasing leadership skills and a timeline of promotion.

NAME
14352 Lane • City, CA 12345 • 555-555-5555 • name@email.com

Highly Experienced Mechanical Design Engineer with expertise in CNC Programming and Design for Manufacture and strong Management skills

QUALIFICATIONS

- Extensive background in Mechanical Design Engineering, Team and Project Leadership, Manufacturing Process Selection, Root Cause Analysis, Material Selection, and Process Mapping.
- Experienced in Finite Element Analysis, Process Automation, Fixture/Tool Design, Quality Systems, Robust Manufacturing, and Component System and Assembly Part Design.
- Proven ability to improve cycle times, certify vendors, develop new processes, streamline workflow, reduce costs, and perform both design and manufacturing.
- Excellent problem solving, leadership, Six Sigma, communication, and purchasing skills.

SELECTED PROJECTS & ACCOMPLISHMENTS

- Achieved >100% reduction in cycle time and tooling costs by transitioning creep feed grinding of airfoils to 5 Axis machining. Authored complex simultaneous 5 Axis CNC programs.
- Reduced cost on multiple components through value engineering and re-design techniques.
- Slashed costs 45% for manufacturing processes and 175 components, through effective management of Centaura Lid Lift Mechanism.
- Grew first time yield builds from 73% to 98% for EC Actuators and Motion Control devices.
- Developed highly profitable robust manufacturing processes and equipment for new products.
- Improved productivity through automation of production processes for employers/clients.
- Increased efficiency by introducing Lean Six Sigma processes.
- Created and implemented successful QA and continuous improvement programs.
- Contributed to profit growth by benchmarking CAD/CAM systems and implementing Unigraphics.

Name • Page 2

PROFESSIONAL EXPERIENCE

COMPANY, city, CA • 2000 - Present
Mechanical Manufacturing Design Engineering Consultant

- Designed prismatic cell, airfoil, patent-pending canvas stretching machine, button cell program, capital equipment components, fixtures for production processes, and more for clients and employers.

COMPANY, city, CA • 1998 - 1999
Manufacturing Engineering Manager

- Developed process for manufacturing compressor wheel matrix, described by CAM system vendors as "the most complex project we have ever seen."
- Produced major programming time savings by eliminating need for Command File Structure.

COMPANY, City, CA • 1997 - 1998
Manufacturing Engineering Manager

- Developed and improved production process for manufacture of UHV vacuum chambers and complex precision mechanical components and assemblies.
- Actively involved in new product development and manufacturing. Set up machine tools, performed grinding of HSS tools, and debugged CNC programs.

COMPANY, City, CA • 1989 - 1997
President / Owner

- Formulated successful, complex CNC programs for Roders HSC, 5 Axis, HAAS, NIGATA, Fadal machining centers and Fagor control lathes.
- Prepared complex assembly drawings and instruction sheets for operators.
- Produced production drawings from multiple file formats, including SAT-IGES-DXF-STEP and others, utilizing multiple CAD systems.

EDUCATION

INSTITUTE OF TECHNOLOGY, city, state
BS in Mechanical Engineering
Advanced Technological Certification in Mechanical Engineering

- Completed Irish State Apprenticeship in Machine Tool Technology. (City and Guilds Certificates)

COLLEGE, city, state
AA in Mechanical Technology

- Completed Advanced CNC Programming utilizing Mastercam V9.0

The Curriculum Vitae

Commonly referred to as the **CV**. The CV is often confused with the International résumé, because both are frequently used outside of the United States. But there are distinct differences. International résumés usually follow America's one or two-page rule, even though they might have different format requirements from the American résumé. However, the CV does not follow American or International résumé format restrictions; it has its own format requirements. On top of that, there are different requirements for international CVs and American CVs. The confusion gets even worse when you consider that many foreign countries have switched to a résumé format, but continue to use the term CV. I'll discuss that more later in this chapter.

Let's start with the **international CV**. In many countries, including the UK, France, Spain, Italy, Germany, and Russia, the CV is still frequently used instead of a résumé. Here are some basic CV format facts:

➤ There is no page restriction. Although they generally run from three to five pages, CVs are as long as they need to be to accurately provide all the required information.

➤ Personal information is not only acceptable, it's usually required, and often placed near the top of the first page. This could include sex, marital status, age, birth date, nationality, and even hobbies. This type of information is never found on U.S. résumés, except in the case of certain federal résumés.

➤ After the personal information there may or may not be a summary section; it's not mandatory, but is often used anyway.

➤ Academic information comes before employment history, and usually includes high school as well as college and graduate work.

➤ All CVs are written in reverse chronological order; the functional format is never used.

➤ The information provided under each job is either in a paragraph format, or a combined paragraph and bullet point format. In either case, information is not summarized to the same degree as in American résumés, and a job description can run anywhere from a paragraph to a full page. The type of information provided (job functions and achievements) is the same, but the language is more formal in style, with fewer incomplete sentences.

➤ Following the employment section, all the other information is presented in the same style as an American résumé; that is, computer skills, languages, publications, and any other pertinent information.

> Unlike a résumé, CVs often contain long lists of publication, presentations, and research credits.

In the United States, the CV is used primarily for high-level academic, research, medical, and legal positions. The more upscale graduate school programs may also require one as part of their entrance documentation requirements, and occasionally people involved in the fine arts will need one. Healthcare CVs are used by medical researchers, some physicians and surgeons, and any healthcare professional applying for certain non-profit, government, or international agency positions.

The main difference between the U.S. CV and the international CV is that, like the American résumé, U.S. CVs normally don't include personal information..

On the following pages is an example of a typical U.S. curriculum vitae.

ACADEMIC CURRICULUM VITAE

ACADEMIC CV

190 Bedford Ave. #118 ▪ City, NY 12345 ▪ 123-456-7890 ▪ email@email.com

DIGITAL MEDIA ARTS INSTRUCTION
Adjunct Professor – Instructor - Teacher

Digital Media Arts professional with more than 9 years of academic instruction experience. Adept at developing lessons and curricula, delivering presentations and demonstrations, and coordinating projects. Strong technical background includes interactive technologies, computer animation, digital photography and video, sound design and recording, and digital editing. Experienced at assisting students in the creation of film packages for festivals and broadcasting. Skilled at implementing new tools to facilitate learning and meet changing industry needs.

Core Competencies:
Interactive Design –Lesson Planning – Performance Technologies – Cinematography
Sensor-Based Technology –Broadcasting – Workflow Management – Document Control
Process Improvement – Interior Design – Sculpture – Mold Making – Woodworking

EDUCATION

MA in, Interactive Communications, New York University, New York, NY
- *Studies focused on Digital Photography, Animation, and 3D Modeling.*

BFA in Art & Technology Studies, Art Institute of Chicago, Chicago, IL
- *Studies focused on Sound, Film, Video, and Computer Programming.*

PROFESSIONAL EXPERIENCE

HOFSTRA UNIVERSITY, NY   2014-present
Adjunct Professor

Instruct classes in computer animation. Prepare lessons and class materials, configure computer-based activities. Provide one-on-one and group assistance as needed. Oversee hands-on technical training utilizing Photoshop, Flash, Illustrator, After Effects, and Cinema 4D.
- Led sessions in traditional and digital animation, scanning of materials, colorizing of frames, and conversion of drawings into movies. Instructed storyboarding and movie development.

NEW YORK UNIVERSITY, New York, NY   2005 – Present
Media Coordinator, Tisch School of the Arts

Lead video editing seminars for undergraduate film students. Provide one-on-one film production instruction and technical support, from conceptualization through to creation of film packages for festivals, advanced classes, and broadcast projects. Update and maintain a digital media archive.
- Actively involved in developing and producing media materials, website content, brochures, and other collateral for the university.
- Improved communications between media coordinators and technical support department by recommending the use of new technologies.

Name ▪ Curriculum Vitae ▪ Page 2

UNIVERSITY OF CHICAGO, Chicago, IL   2000 – 2005
Manager, Film & Media Operations
Oversaw all multimedia functions for the department's main theater and directed all film archiving and preservation activities. Inspected, repaired, shipped, and received films. Trained projectionists and ensured all technical and media needs were met for classes. Evaluated and purchased hardware and software. Supervised up to 15 student employees per semester.

- Set up and managed the department's off-site film library. Maintained and cataloged more than 1,000 donated, rare, obscure, and/or mainstream films.
- Managed the Preservation of the Cinema Media Studies' rare and valuable film collection.
- Aided the student-run Fire Escape Films in acquiring movies for screenings. Also provided creative programming input and resolved technical issues.
- Reduced costs through effective price comparisons for purchases.
- Introduced state-of-the-art procedures, including scanning film and slides into digital format, software-based video editing, and more, to support staff presentations, research, and projects.

INDEPENDENT PROGRAMMING ASSOCIATES, Chicago, IL   1997 – 2000
Video Editor/Machine Room Operator
Carried out editing of television programs, independent documentaries, and commercials. Created and formatted motion graphics. Performed digital soundboard operation for editing sessions. Prepared and shipped videos to television stations for broadcast. Utilized digital routing system for graphics, video editing, and compositing activities.

CAREER NOTES: Additional experience includes **Art & Music Curator** at TRANS PECOS (Brooklyn, NY) and D'AMELIO GALLERY (New York, NY) and **Art Instructor** for the CITY OF PITTSBURGH (Pittsburgh, PA). Also own and operate sustainable clothing company, LIFTED MYTH (Brooklyn, NY) and serve as Designer.

TECHNICAL SKILLS

MS Office, Arduino, Avid, Final Cut, Photoshop, After Effects, Premier, Illustrator, film archiving, prototyping, digital photography/videography, wearable technologies, computer animation

AFFILIATIONS

Issue Project Room

AWARDS & RECOGNITION

Issue Project Room and The String Orchestra of Brooklyn Composer Commission (2012)
Community Arts Assistance Program, Department of Cultural Affairs, Chicago, IL (2003)

PERFORMANCES & EXHIBITIONS

Complete list of more than 40 available on request
Portfolio and Media Samples available at www.myportfolio.fun

Federal Résumés

Although a federal résumé serves the same purpose as a standard résumé—presenting a person's qualifications and experience—it looks very different than a résumé or curriculum vitae. That's because the federal government has its own set of formatting rules that must be followed. To make things even more confusing, certain agencies within the government often have further guidelines and formatting conventions. The standard federal résumé, though, follows these format conventions:

1. Limited formatting. The résumé is written without the use of special fonts (Times Roman or Arial are preferred), bold is limited to section headings only, and there is little to no underlining, bold, italics, graphics, tabs, or section breaks.

2. Personal information. Unlike a standard résumé, on a federal résumé you include your social security number, citizenship, data of birth, and any other special information the application calls for.

3. Employment history. For each job, you must provide the months/years employed, salary, grade level (if a government position), hours worked per week, supervisor's name and contact information, and if it is okay to contact the supervisor for a recommendation.

4. Format. Depending on the agency's requirements, federal résumés either list all the job responsibilities and accomplishments in a long paragraph (Block Format) or in a combination of paragraphs and bullet points (Bullet Format). When in doubt, go with the block format, as it's the more classic and common style.

5. Education. Some agencies prefer it to come before the employment, and some after. Unlike a standard résumé, you're supposed to include your high school information as well as your college and graduate school degrees.

6. Other information. Training, technical skills, presentations, languages, and any other information come after the employment history, and complete lists should be provided, as in a curriculum vitae.

7. Length. The federal résumé can be any length, but most agencies prefer a document that's between three and five pages. The higher the level of the position being applied for, the longer the résumé can be.

8. Keywords. Federal agencies use special software to read and sort résumés, separating out the ones that best match the advertised job opening. They do this by scanning for keywords, so it's vital to include as many of those in your résumé as you can.

FEDERAL RESUME

FEDERAL OPTION 3
Address
Phone
Email
SSN: 123-45-6789

VACANCY IDENTIFICATION NUMBER: AL-2245
JOB TITLE AND GRADE: Storekeeper, G11

U.S. Citizen: Yes
Federal Employee: Yes
Highest Grade Level and Dates: G10, 2015

"Mr. Cherenfant has worked extremely hard to learn the basics required to successfully serve as a 2nd Radio Electronics Technician. He has proven the ability to identify the various communications paths used on the Kaiser-class T-AO Ship, including Demand Assigned Multiple Access (DAMA) subsystems, External Modem Interface for High Data Rate (HDR AN/WSC-3) Line of Sight (LOS), High Frequency (HF) Voice and Fleet SIPRNet Messaging (AN/URT-23). He also demonstrated the ability to provide block diagrams of the above circuits to include all switchboards and patch panels. In addition, he has completed the Navy Local Element (LE) Electronic Keying Material Systems (EKMS), User Computer Based Training (CBT). He has also become proficient in the use of the Common Message Processor for the preparation of outgoing messages." —David A. Van Sant, Ship's Communication Officer, USNS Kanawha (T-AO 196), Military Sealift Fleet Support Command (MSFSC), Letter of Recommendation, 2009

PROFESSIONAL SUMMARY

Affect overall organizational communications and IT strategy by volunteering time exceeding the 8-month minimum training requirement; over four-year period to train as 2nd Radio Electronics Technician (2nd RET) in conjunction with performing as Supply Utilityman and executing inventory, logistics, and Storekeeper duties and responsibilities. Excel academically, as evidenced by 94% overall rating while attending Penn Foster Career School for IT and Network Computer Training. Received Letters of Recognition and Recommendation to advance to 2nd RET qualified status three years consecutively. Received accolades including the Secretary of Defense Medal for the Global War on Terrorism, two *On-the-Spot* bonus awards for superior service, performance, and Most Outstanding Team Member relating to managing preparation for various successful inspections. Expedited training requirements by accelerated certification and completion of Secure Terminal Equipment (STE) and Career Management Systems (CMS).

WORK EXPERIENCE

2nd Radio Electronics Technician (RET) Training, WM-9985-09 (848)   05/2007 to Present
Storekeeper Assistant in Training, WM-9994-15/9994-16 (852)   Hours/week: 50+
Military Sealift Command (MSC)   Salary: $23,688+ per year
Norfolk, VA   Supervisor (Current): Mr. Smith
                                                                       Telephone: (123) 456-7890
                                                                       OK to Contact: Yes

Shipboard Operations and Support: Perform tracking and monitoring of processed messages, using/maintaining equipment involved in transmissions relating to 2nd RET during hands-on training. Assist Communications Department and train and receive instruction on essentials of cache of communication paths for use on *Kaiser*-class T-AO United States Navy Ships (USNS), including satellite, LOS, HF voice, messaging, and IT installation and management. Illustrate block diagrams of circuits, to include switchboards and patch panels. Accomplish and complete ongoing Navy computer-based training. Use Common Message Processor for preparation of outgoing messages. Continue ongoing preparation, study, and practical application of other material for 2nd RET position, including *Basic Communications Course* and *Windows Server 2003 LAN Manager Course*. Execute general supply operations and provision for basic life essentials, to include perishable procurement, food handling and preparation, serving meals, busing tables, and collecting and processing laundry. Maintain staterooms, latrines, passageways, and common areas. Direct performance evaluations and assessments for onboard performance relating to the supply department. Use Supply Management-5 (SM5) to order supplies and the Haystack for tracking and monitoring availability of supplies from the Fleet & Industrial Supply Centers (FISCs).

Apply security directives, procedures and equipment to ensure system security and protection for confidential information. Maintain security of messages, records, logs, and files. Apply procedures for destroying messages to prevent the use of obsolete documents and for security purposes. Operate radio cryptographic equipment, sending messages via the AN/-WSC-3 transceiver, and use the Communications Status Board to review data, classifying it as routine, priority, immediate, or operational. Send messages through the Common-User Digital Information Exchange System (CUDIXS) and through the alternative, two-way Fleet SIPRNET Messaging (FSM) system, sending them online.

Communications Systems Maintenance and Support: Apply knowledge of shipboard exterior communication systems to perform drafting of messages and procedures to set up Demand Assigned Multiple Access (DAMA) and to construct audio and data circuitry, antennas, and coupling. Maintain radio transmitting and receiving equipment, evaluate system integration, and assess interoperability between systems and programs. Perform software and hardware installation, applying instructions on design and implementation, and conduct systems analysis, design, development, implementation, and acceptance testing. Implement Internet Protocol (IP), Local Area Network (LAN), and Wide Area Network (WAN) information assurance plans. Participate in training in performance of Command, Control, and Communications (C3) Computer and Intelligence Systems and Communications Security (COMSEC) protocols. Implement Internet Protocol (IP), Local Area Network (LAN), and Wide Area Network (WAN) information assurance plans, and complete required maintenance data forms. Provide technical and supervisory liaison between work centers.

Troubleshooting, Diagnostics, and Quality Control: Use test equipment and specialized tools to perform tests and repairs of electrical/electronic components, cables, and connectors. Troubleshoot, assess, and evaluate systems to localize and isolate malfunctions and initiate repairs or replacement of faulty parts or subassemblies. Identify root causes of malfunctions to systems, subsystems, circuits, parts, inventories, and installed equipment. Complete maintenance reports and logs. Provide intense diagnostics to isolate problems and identify maintenance on more than 260 individual pieces of electronic equipment. Participate in Quality Control (QC) activities and in developing the master schedule of weekly preventive maintenance requirements. Read and interpret schematics and block diagrams, use test equipment and hand tools to troubleshoot and repair electronic equipment, and repair electrical/electronic cables and connectors. Manage inventory and complete maintenance data forms. Conduct test operations relating to systems and subsystems. Direct and supervise repairs.

Communications Procedures and Processes: Apply extensive on-the-job (OJT) training on communications procedures and fundamentals to ensure reliable, secure, and speedy communications. Work with low and high frequency spectra applicable to maritime operations, including low-range voice and Very High Frequency (VHF) systems aeronautical radio navigation and communications, Ultra High frequency (UHF) system line-of-sight or short-range communications, and Super High Frequency (SHF) communications. Operate the AN/WSC-3 transceiver, the US Navy's standard UHF satellite terminal and Line-Of-Sight (LOS) transceiver. Utilize the Demand Assigned Multiple Access (DAMA) system, designed to allow control of multiple circuits. Clean, repair, and maintain antennae and participate in routine maintenance of the hard-drives.

COMSEC Procedures and Cryptographic Equipment: Apply security directives and maintain strict confidentiality of information, following standard procedures for the transmission of messages, record-keeping, maintenance of logs and files of printed and transmitted messages, and storing of digital copies in the appropriate electronic format ("classified" or "unclassified"). Apply procedures for destroying messages to prevent the use of obsolete documents and to free up memory. Operate radio cryptographic equipment, sending messages via the AN/-WSC-3 transceiver and use the Communications Status Board to review data, classifying it as routine, priority, immediate, or operational. Send messages through the Common-User Digital Information Exchange System (CUDIXS) and through the alternative two-way Fleet SIPRNET Messaging system (FSM), sending them online. Eligible to attain Secret Clearance upon 2nd Radio Electronics Technician Certification.

Communications Security and Cryptographic Equipment: Apply security knowledge gained during the Secure Terminal Equipment (STE) Operator Training Course and the Local Element CMS Training Interactive Course, including the Electronic Key Management System (EKMS) for establishing an electronic security system to limit access to confidential information. Participate in the Department of Defense's Information Assurance Awareness class to stay abreast of security information and the latest computer technology.

Successfully completed the Secure Terminal Equipment (STE) Operator Training Course via a CD-ROM disk and the Local Element CMS Training Interactive Course online, gaining knowledge of the Electronic Key Management System (EKMS) for establishing an electronic security system for direct access to confidential information to ensure access only to authorized individuals. Acquired knowledge of devices used in cryptography, incorporating the electronic key system, office phone-like Secure Terminal Equipment (STE), the small laptop-like Data Transfer Device (DTD), and Simple Key Loaders (SKLs).

IBM-based Computer Systems (Windows and Internet Environment): Prior to employment with Military Sealift Command, participated in evening computer courses at the Stanley Isaacs Center, receiving initial training in computer, LAN-based systems. Furthered knowledge while with Pitney-Bowes and working on computers in the offices of Deutsche Bank in New York City. In addition to using PCs for business management, such as handling inventory for office supplies, processing mail, and conducting online communications, also produced and published documents, reports, and other business-related media for Deutsche Bank.

Gained LAN experience with Military Sealift Command performing various assignments, including supply management, using Supply Management 5 (SM5) for ordering and keeping inventory of ship's supplies, and employing the Haystack system to check on the availability of supplies from the Fleet & Industrial Supply Centers (FISC). Received OJT training in Turboprep to evaluate supply and other reports. Trained by the *Kanawha's* LAN Administrator in the creation of Microsoft Outlook email accounts for new crewmembers. As part of LAN training, studied Global Operating System Upgrade Windows Server 2003 LAN Manager Course, to the degree of being able to assume the duties of a LAN administrator. The Basic Communications Course reading materials also provided enhanced understanding of PCs.

Operate shipboard IBM-based computer systems, applying extensive education, experience, and knowledge of Windows and Internet environments. Employ proper computer-related protocols, including rules for Internet access and usage and security awareness, such as hacking and viruses. Use the Global Operating System Upgrade Windows Server 2003 LAN Manager Course handbook as a guide in working with the specific LANs used by MSC, including hardware, software, and associated protocols. Experience includes reading manuals and troubleshooting network connectivity issues. Applied proficiency in Microsoft Office Software, including Word, Excel, and PowerPoint, as well as Outlook and Internet Explorer for email and internet access. Skills include standard computer diagnosis and maintenance, such as disk defragmenting, installing, downloading and removing programs and files, and using security and antivirus software.

Honors & Awards:
- Second On-the-Spot Incentive Award for Outstanding Performance, 12/2010
- Academic Achievement, Penn Foster Career School, 94% overall rating, 01/2010
- Earned "Qualified" status 4 times to become 2nd RET three years in a row, 2007 to 2010
- Captain's Letter of Recognition and Recommendation, 11/2009
- SCO's Letter of Recognition and Recommendation, 07/2009
- On-the-Spot Incentive Award for Outstanding Performance, 07/2009
- Bonus/Merit Award, Supply/Utility, 05/2009
- Awarded/Certification Citing Completion/Local Element CMS Training, 02/2009
- Special Recognition, Most Outstanding Team Member, 12/2008
- Awarded/Certification Citing Completion/STE Operator-Training Course, 2008
- Awarded/Citation for Excellence in Interpersonal Relations, Pitney Bowes, 04/2003
- Academic Honors: completed coursework in accelerated time; hired immediately by Pitney Bowes, 09/2000

EDUCATION

Penn-Foster Career School, Scottsdale, Arizona
Graduated: 01/2007
Major: P.C. Maintenance & Repair
Degree: Career Degree
Point Grade System: 44.5 Continuing Education Units (CEUs), 10 Contact Hours
GPA: 94 out of 100%
Honors: Academic Honors

Queens College, Flushing, NY
Graduated: Attended 1994 to 1995
Major: Attended for Computer Imaging and Assisted Design/Drafting, among other course studies
Degree: No Degree

Springfield Gardens High School
Springfield Gardens, NY 11413
Diploma, 1994

Supervisor Quotes and Rating Team Commentary:

"Mr. Smith has demonstrated to me his desire to learn and his willingness to work hard and to perform his job to the best of his ability. I feel that he will be an asset to the Radio Electronics Community and should be select and promoted to 2nd Radio Electronics Technician at the earliest opportunity." – Mr. Smith, Ship's Communication Officer, USNS *Kanawha* (T-AO 196), Military Sealift Fleet Support Command, Letter of Recommendation, 2009

"Mr. Smith has been assigned to the USNS *Kanawha* (T-AO 196) for two consecutive tours. During that time, Mr. Smith has distinguished himself as an industrious and motivated worker. He performs all his duties with dispatch and dedication. Mr. Cherenfant has expressed a desire to cross-deck to the Communications department. He has, on his own time, sought out the Ship's Communication Officer, Mr. Van Sant, to arrange |

International Résumés

The international résumé, as previously defined, is a résumé used outside the U.S., in countries where a traditional curriculum vitae isn't required. Each year, more countries switch to the standard résumé format because, like U.S. employers, foreign countries find themselves with greater numbers of people applying for jobs, and the human resources offices don't want to read through long, detailed CVs. Currently, Australia, most Asian and African countries, and several European and Latin American countries now use some variation of the résumé format.

The international résumé is structured much like a U.S. résumé, with some minor differences. Some countries require personal information, and in most cases they like to see the education come before the work history.

Other things to be careful of when preparing a foreign résumé are paper size and differences in language. Many countries require an A4 paper size, which is longer and narrower than the standard letter size used in America. And because different countries spell words in different ways, always remember to spell check using the dictionary made for that country—for example, be aware that Australia, Asia, and Europe use different spellings, such as 'colour' for 'color,' and 'standardise' instead of 'standardize.'

On the next pages you'll see an example of a typical international résumé. Notice where the education section is, and that the spelling is in the Australian style.

NAME

145 Lake Drive • City, Region, Australia • phone # • name@aol.com

EXECUTIVE MANAGEMENT: Innovation, Development, Quality, Product Engineering

Talented and accomplished Engineering Management Professional with extensive international background in solution development, profitability growth, cost control, program management, and organisational leadership. Adept at establishing, improving, and directing technical initiatives and business units. Excellent customer relations, technology, and resource management skills.

Engineering Operations • Product Development • Strategic Planning • Quality
Customer Relations • Problem Solving • Program Development • Six Sigma
Cost/Budget Control • Intellectual Property Management • Partnerships

---

EDUCATION

BS in Mechanical Engineering, University of Auckland

PROFESSIONAL EXPERIENCE

CORPORATION 1, Sydney, Australia   1999 – Present
Engineering Group Manager (2013-present)
Oversee technical cost reduction activities for this $22.3B global supplier of mobile electronics and transportation systems. Develop and lead solutions for warranty analysis and parts returns. Direct investigations of No Trouble Found (NTF) warranty returns. Supervise staff of 3 engineers. Administer budget of close to $500,000.

- Produced >$130M in savings for GM and >$140M in savings for Delphi by delivering more than 400 solutions.
- Improved acceptance rate from 20% to 70% by standardising idea submissions process. Achieved 100% success rate for ideas placed into production.
- Designed successful pilot program to analyse all returned parts.
- Created program to implement state-of-the-art testing and detection equipment.
- Identified need for industry's first ballistic testing for vehicle front end heat exchangers and led development of testing protocols and procedures.
- Earned Excellence Award for facilitating compressor plant startup project.

Systems Manager - Special Project (2007-2013)
Initiated and managed advanced technology engine program from inception through to prototype delivery. Oversaw business, technical, and intellectual property management. Administered $1M budget. Coordinated activities of virtual team of 45 persons from global internal and external organisations. Created concept system with demonstration hardware and production plans.

- Delivered prototype that produced no vibrations and near-zero emissions, using combination of automotive and jet engine technologies.
- Developed highly successful project management technique that cut costs 75%.
- Project resulted in 1 omnibus patent, 42 ROI technologies/products, and sale of concept to business incubator company.

NAME • Page 2

(Corporation 1, continued)

Director of Engineering, Asia-Pacific (2005-2007)
Stationed in Tokyo, managed product engineering teams in India, Japan, and Australia; managed joint ventures in South Korea & China. Administered $11M budget. Created, manned, and managed staff of 4 teams totaling 23 engineers. Developed processes and procedures, as well as developmental training programs. Coordinated joint ventures with Korea and China. Led teams that successfully developed new systems and won major system bids.
- Facilitated $25M in new revenue by leading successful bid for HVAC project.
- Established Customer Engineering Center in Japan from scratch.
- Implemented regional Technical Organisation to support customers in Asia.
- Accelerated Korean JV Technical growth by negotiating a novel agreement that supported engineering growth without changing the engineering cost structure.
- Developed a CAD-detailing company in Romania in only 4 weeks. Program dramatically reduced CAD bottlenecks and improved efficiency.
- Recipient of the HVAC Pioneer Award from the company.

Technical Representative (2001-2005)
Selected to represent company to clients and resolve ongoing customer issues.
- Led 4-person team that improved quality 400% and saved $250,000 per year.
- Increased company's rating from 'Average' to 'World Class' for technology.
- Facilitated an additional $750,000 in net profit through increased quality.
- Earned Trade Secret Award for developing a highly lauded innovation.

Technical Representative (1999-2001)
Co-chaired product design team that delivered $150M in revenue and drove quality rating from Average to World Class.
- Improved efficiency and reduced costs by streamlining vehicle assembly line.
- Increased annual profits $2M for division and led key cost-saving initiatives.

TRAINING & DEVELOPMENT

Training in Six Sigma, Design for Assembly, and Program Management

TECHNICAL SKILLS

MS Office, CAD systems. CFD, computer modeling, Windows, Macintosh

Special Situations

So far in this chapter we've dealt with the most common résumé and CV formats. But what about those special situations, where the normal résumé or CV just isn't quite right, or when a company or academic institution or government agency requires a special document? For example, a résumé for a graduate school admissions package might require the candidate to include non-work and non-school related information, such as volunteer activities. Information technology résumés usually need a special section somewhere on the document detailing the applicant's technical skills.

All these special situations can be easily handled by simply adding sections to the résumé. The trick is knowing where to place them. For instance, in the IT field, where you place your technical skills depends on the type of position you're searching for. A hands-on position, such as a programmer, software engineer, PC support technician, or network engineer requires the technical skills be on page one, right before the employment history. A person seeking a managerial or executive position in technology should place their skills on page two, after the education section.

On the following pages you'll see examples of different résumés. Look through them, and see how the sections are arranged to best suit the professional needs of the candidates.

IT EXECUTIVE

123 7th St., Apt XYZ

Pembroke, NJ 123345   name@yahoo.com

Tel.: (555) 555-555

Cell: (555) 555-555

IT EXECUTIVE • CHIEF INFORMATION OFFICER • IT DIRECTOR • VICE PRESIDENT

Talented and accomplished IT Executive and CIO with proven ability to successfully direct information technology, telecommunications, and support services operations. Expertise in overseeing technology improvement initiatives and aligning technology services with business goals. Experience with leading enterprise-wide implementations. Previous background in consulting, project management, and business development.

IT Operations • Strategic Planning • Business Process Automation • E-Commerce
Business Continuity • Solution Development • Compliance • CRM • Sales Management • P&L
Budget Administration • Leadership • Long-term Planning • IT Security

PROFESSIONAL EXPERIENCE

BIG LIFE INSURANCE COMPANY, INC., New York, NY   1999 - Present
Chief Information Officer / Senior Vice President (2004-present)
Oversee all IT operations for $200 million insurance company with 300 employees in 7 locations, supporting 1,200 external sales agents. Administer $10 million technology budget. Supervise staff of 30, plus 20 onshore and offshore contract personnel. Develop and implement corporate IT strategy, 3-year system maintenance plan, and policies/procedures. Manage project portfolio. Play active role in corporate operations management and the development of new products and services.

- Saved $1.5 million in capital investments and grew sales conversions 10%. Led team that re-engineered enterprise sales process and implemented new sales system.
- Facilitated >10% annual sales growth during period where industry average is < 4%
- Saved $150,000 by introducing new a HR infrastructure and automating payroll.
- Increased website traffic more than 300% by recommending utilization of search engine marketing (SEO) and website optimization processes.
- Improved Help Desk service levels 15% via implementation of call center technology.

Vice President, Information Officer (2000-2004)
Managed technology support, telecommunications, VoIP, LAN/WAN, Internet/Intranet, client-server systems, and enterprise application architecture development functions. Member of company's Steering Committee and Strategy Committee. Formulated annual IT operating plan and 3-year system maintenance plan. Managed $10 million budget. Oversaw offshore application development. Negotiated vendor contracts and license/maintenance agreements.

- Saved $500,000 in support expenses by implementing lights-out data center operations.
- Directed implementation of VoIP system and other technologies for distributed call center across all company locations, reducing annual telecom costs by $130,000.
- Delivered $800,000 in annual savings by negotiating offshore development agreement.

(Big Life Insurance Company, continued)

Director of e-Commerce (1999-2000)

Managed IT/telecom operations and oversaw e-business functions. Created corporate e-commerce strategy. Supervised staff of 7 and administered $5 million budget. Directed technology support services. Served as Project Director for mission-critical initiatives.

- Planned and led on-site and off-site call center infrastructure implementations.
- Facilitated data warehousing projects and Internet/Intranet development projects.
- Coordinated development and management of company website.
- Supported digitization of >5 million paper files to eliminate physical storage necessity.

A FINANCIAL FIRM, LLP, New York, NY   1994 - 1999

Manager, PeopleSoft and Data Warehousing Service Lines (1998-1999)

Senior Consultant, PeopleSoft and Data Warehousing Service Lines (1996-1998)

Served as Engagement Manager and Project Manager on large-scale implementations. Carried out the design and execution of custom systems development projects.

- Completed package implementation and systems integration project for global financial services firm. Supervised internal and client IT teams.
- Managed design and implementation of data center for startup telecom company.
- Carried out enterprise business re-engineering project and data warehouse implementation for global professional services company.
- Served as Team Leader for information warehouse design and development project.

Supervising Associate & Office Technology Manager (1994-1996)

Managed daily technology support for 6 corporate legal office locations supporting 700 associates in US. Carried out long-term technology planning and acquisition. Created and managed $2 million budget. Served as Project Manager.

- Oversaw development and implementation of reporting, IT, and telecom infrastructures.
- Developed and implemented the technology infrastructure for a data processing facility.

CAREER NOTES: Previously held positions of **IT Support Services Technician II** (1994) and **IT Support Services Technician I** (1994) with BIG BANK.

EDUCATION

MBA in Information Systems, FORDHAM UNIVERSITY, New York, NY
BA in Economics, FORDHAM UNIVERSITY, New York, NY

TECHNICAL SKILLS

MS Office, Access, Project, PeopleSoft, Crystal Reports, Crystal Info, Lotus Notes, ARCServe, Oracle RDBMS, Citrix, TEDS PRP, Genelco Life Support Plus, E.Piphany Service Center/Analytics, EPAM Website Content Management System (CMS), Hyperion

IT TECHNICIAN

Address here
City, State, Zip

Phone Number Here
Email Address Here

Help Desk Support • IT Administration • IT Support • Technical Services • IT Associate

SUMMARY OF QUALIFICATIONS

- Adept at supporting hardware, software, and network systems.
- Hold A+ and Network+ certifications.
- Familiar with providing telephone-based and desk-side user support.
- Well developed abilities in database management and network backup services.
- Proven ability to resolve hardware and software issues as first line of support.
- Excellent analysis, problem-solving, customer service, and reporting skills.

TECHNICAL SKILLS

Operating Systems:	Windows 98-2003, DOS, Mac OS
Networking:	LAN/WAN, Ethernet, TCP/IP, ISDN, wireless, PING, NETSTAT, IPCONFIG, fiber optics, backup and recovery
Applications:	MS Office, Visio, antivirus software, firewalls, Ghost, Remedy
Development Tools:	Javascript, HTML, XML, Flash, Dreamweaver, Director, 3D Studio Max, Photoshop CS2, Illustrator, Premiere, Cool Edit Pro, Paint Shop Pro
Hardware:	PC / server assembly & repair, routers, switches, hubs, peripherals

PROFESSIONAL EXPERIENCE

IT ASSISTANT, COMPANY NAME, City, state   2006 - Present
- Provide 1st-level telephone and deskside support for over 1,500 end users. Respond to 60 calls per day, on average. Track issues. Support Windows and Macintosh environments.
- Reset passwords and update profiles. Monitor licensing and report on changes for desktop software. Update training requirements for new users and new software.
- Improved cost control by implementing licensing database to track expiration dates.

IT ASSISTANT, COMPANY NAME, City, state   2005 - 2006
- Managed foundation's website. Revised content and layout.
- Updated and maintained 40,000-record membership database.
- Provided technical support, including password resets. Responded to inquiries.
- Held responsibility for network risk management, including daily server backups.
- Carried out desktop publishing, designed programs for 100 lectures per year, created event posters for distribution, and designed lecture hand-out covers.

IT ASSISTANT, COMPANY NAME, City, state   2004 - 2005
- Managed all facilities-related functions, including help desk and customer service.
- Set up and maintained client database. Scheduled and tracked work orders.

EDUCATION

BSc in Media Technology, w/Honors, The University of Lincoln, Hull, NE (2004)

CERTIFICATIONS & TRAINING

Certifications: MCSA (in progress), A+, Network+
Training: Project Management, Multimedia Production, Professional Management

CONSTRUCTION SUPERVISOR

9725 NW 52nd St., #319 • City, State 11111 • (111) 222-3333 • name@yahoo.com

SUMMARY

Talented and accomplished Project Management professional with international experience in planning, cost management, design, and construction. Proven ability to complete multi-million dollar projects on time and within budget. Familiar with commercial and government sectors. Able to oversee projects from inception through scope determination, resource management, and completion. Adept at cost control, forecasting, and troubleshooting. Expertise in contract administration, negotiations, bid preparation, estimates, RFPs, purchasing, documentation, and punch list management.

PROFESSIONAL EXPERIENCE

CONSTRUCTION, INC., Miami, FL   2003 – Present
Cost & Schedule Manager, Contract Administrator, Estimator
Perform contract management, project management and scheduling, and project estimation for commercial and government clients nationwide and globally. Additionally provide engineering, documentation, and regulatory assistance. Coordinate project teams up to 50 persons, including subcontractors, domestically and overseas.

Selected Projects
US Army Corps of Engineers, Transatlantic Programs Center
Developed indefinite delivery quantity contracts for design-build/construction-related services, valued at up to $1.5B. Performed full range of planning, engineering, and design to support construction, repair, restoration, and operation services in Africa, Asia, and the Middle East.
- Played a major role in the preparation of a successful RFP. Delivered estimates, schedules, and contract administration. Developed standards for document control and program planning.
- Prepared procedure specifications and templates, facilitated control and progress reporting. Aided in integrating additional satellite programs for client.

Aviation Department
Managed a $29M project involving extension and modification of bridges and terminal access road extensions. Project included underground utilities, dewatering systems, and landscaping. Oversaw cost and schedule development, payment requisition, change order management, negotiations of claims, and contract administration of subcontractors. Coordinated field activities.
- Supervised construction of a $30.4M, seven-story parking garage. Prepared project estimate for bid, direct total project life cycle for 804,000 sq. ft. structure.
- Created a $16.4M bid estimate, budget, and schedule for a 155,000 sq. ft. cargo facility.

Department of Transportation
Directed $25M project involving expansion and renovation of major highway, and included construction of bridge and three access ramps, and renovation of nine bridges and eight ramps. Oversaw all financial and field management aspects of project, coordinated subcontractors, and
- Completed project ahead of schedule and under budget.
- Played a key role in achieving $600,000 savings for project, by reducing project length.
- Project earned State Quality Award for major interchanges in 1998.

CONSTRUCTION SUPERVISOR **Page 2**

COMPANY 2 Caracas, Venezuela 1999 – 2003
Contract Administrator/Scheduler/Cost Engineer

- Managed multiple construction projects for Venezuelan Oil Industry.
- Directed construction of pipelines, stations, and substations as part of $186 million Apure expansion project. Served as Contract Administrator, overseeing entire contract process from bid package preparation to final award. Assisted with qualification/selection of construction and inspection consultants and contractors.
- Provided schedule development and management for $127 million project involving design of 70-acreCardon Oil Refinery industrial park with 20 major industry sites, and expansion/renovation of large dock facility.
- Carried out cost engineering for $23 million gasoline receiver station expansion/renovation project. Performed earned value management, prepared weekly cost/performance updates, conducted trend forecasting, and oversaw subcontractor payment requisition process.

COMPANY 3, Caracas, Venezuela 1997 – 1999
Contract Administrator

- Held full responsibility for all payment requisitions and change orders with ownership and subcontractors for this $285 million, two-year project involving construction of eight-kilometer section of Caracas subway system.

COMPANY 4, Caracas, Venezuela 1996 – 1997
Assistant Project Engineer

- Scheduled design, procurement, and construction; managed procurement, and provided assessment analyses for project involving installation and upgrade of computerized control systems for twin 56-story skyscrapers in Caracas.

ADDITIONAL EXPERIENCE

Research/Grant Assistant, **COMPANY 5**, Miami, FL (1995)
Assistant Engineer, **COMPANY 6**, Venezuela (1994)

EDUCATION

MS in Construction Management, School 1, Miami, FL
BS in Civil Engineering, School 2, Maracaibo, Venezuela

PROFESSIONAL DEVELOPMENT

Project Management Professional Certification (in progress)
Post Graduate studies in Construction Management
Training in Systematic Planning of Industrial Facilities, Organization, and Management

COMPUTER SKILLS

MS Office, PowerPoint, Project, Primavera, P3E, Suretrak, Open Plan, Timberline, Prolog

SENIOR ATTORNEY, JD

36544 Summitville St. • City, CA 90210 • (555) 555-1212 (c) • (555) 555-1212 (t) • name@yahoo.com

PROFILE

Highly talented and accomplished Counsel with extensive corporate litigation background. Special expertise in managing complex litigation, regulatory compliance, intellectual property, class actions, Chapter 11 filings, and contracts. Adept at supervising outside counsel. Proven ability to plan and lead defense in high profile cases, represent employers before state and federal courts and commissions, and manage all aspects of corporate legal issues. Superior presentation and business leadership skills.

PROFESSIONAL EXPERIENCE

GENERAL COUNSEL, FIRM 1, City, NJ   2002 – Present

Supervised defense and prosecution of litigation matters involving class actions, contract disputes, and intellectual property. Supervised all outside litigation counsel. Planned and led defense of 280 product-related liability matters with potential exposure of more than $2B. Transferred product liability and wrongful death cases from 20 jurisdictions to U.S. District Court for District of New Jersey.

- Oversaw defense strategy for multiple Attorney General investigations and actions involving alleged violation of consumer fraud/ unfair competition statutes.
- Directed response to investigation by U.S. House Committee on Energy and Commerce that included corporate testimony before Subcommittee on Oversight and Investigation.
- Responsible for regulatory oversight on aspects of new product development.
- Negotiated and drafted celebrity endorsements agreements and manufacturing agreements.
- Acted as corporate spokesperson on high profile, international media events.

ASSOCIATE, BIG LAW FIRM, Woodbridge, NJ   2000 – 2002

Key member of commercial litigation team, responsible for all facets of complex cases, including false advertising, patent infringement, contract disputes, class action litigation, and wrongful death.

- Conducted trials, depositions, and motion practice in state and federal court.

ASSISTANT DISTRICT ATTORNEY, DA OFFICE, City, State   1998 – 2000

Presented over 100 felony cases to grand jury, including high-profile homicide, arson, attempted murder, and others. Managed caseload of ninety misdemeanor cases from inception to trial.

- Prosecuted numerous trials as first chair.

ADDITIONAL EXPERIENCE

JUDICIAL INTERN, US DISTRICT COURT, DISTRICT OF NJ, City, NJ (1997 – 1998)

EDUCATION

Juris Doctor, UNIVERSITY LAW SCHOOL, City, NJ
BA in Sociology, BIG COLLEGE, City, NY

BAR ADMISSIONS

New York, New Jersey, U.S. District Court (District of New Jersey)

LEGAL INTERN

3428 Long Rd. • City, OH 12121 • (555) 555-1212 • name123@yahoo.com

Talented and accomplished Legal Professional with extensive professional and academic training

- Presently completing Juris Doctorate requirements.
- Notary Public and Legal Counsel trainee.
- Outstanding research and presentation abilities.

- Experience in Corporate Law.
- Familiar with financial law.
- Excellent communication skills.

EDUCATION

Juris Doctorate, Big College of Law, City, OH (in progress)
BBA in Accounting and Business Law, Big State University, City, TN

PROFESSIONAL EXPERIENCE

COMPANY 1, City, OH   2007 – Present
Legal Counsel Intern
Provide support for team of attorneys, including General Counsel, and carry out special projects as assigned in areas of contract review, documentation preparation, and transactions.

- Serve as Credit/Debt Agreements Compliance Officer. Review contracts and documentation and ensure compliance with credit and debt agreements. Provide analysis and recommendations to management regarding validity of proposed actions in accordance with covenants.
- Prepare and deliver required notifications to lending institutions.
- Organize, compile, and/or draft required document for transactions as Secretarial Administrator for 32 subsidiaries, totaling over $400 million in annual revenues.
- Carry out initial due diligence for company's divestitures. Work in conjunction with external financial advisors to evaluate and approve confidentiality agreements with potential buyers.
- Compile data for due diligence team. Draft schedules for purchase agreements.
- Draft confidentiality and security agreements, promissory notes, and other documents.

Legal Systems Administrator
Created database to track and administer stock options. Maintained corporate secretarial books and database, prepared reports for management. Carried out daily administrative functions to support Vice President, General Counsel, and Secretary.

- Prepared legal documentation and correspondence pertaining to mergers, acquisitions, stock option agreements, and litigation. Tracked corporate trademarks.

LICENSES AND CERTIFICATIONS
Notary Public, State of Ohio

COMPUTER SKILLS
Windows, Word, Excel, Access, PowerPoint, eCounsel, Secretariat, Lexis/Nexis, Westlaw

CHAPTER 5: THE COVER LETTER

What would you think if a plumber or a salesman or a lawyer handed you a business card, and when you looked at it, there was no phone number? Or the name was missing? Or it had no company name? Or it contained all sorts of spelling mistakes? Would you contact that person to do work for you? Of course not. You'd probably toss it away and laugh about how unprofessional the person was.

Forgetting to send a cover letter with your résumé is just as unprofessional.

Remember, your résumé is your marketing tool—it sells you. Omitting a cover letter when you submit a résumé is like sending out bad marketing materials. It says to the reader, "This person either doesn't know the correct way of applying for a job or they're too lazy to bother doing it the right way."

Not the kind of first impression you want to make.

Surveys of human resource professionals and hiring managers show that more than 50% of them consider the cover letter as important as the résumé when they're deciding who to interview. *More than 50%.* Think about that. If a really good résumé is producing, on average, 30 interviews per 100 résumés sent out, forgetting to use a cover letter—or sending one filled with mistakes—could be lowering that number to only 15 interviews per 100. If you're looking for a job, that's a big difference! Can you afford to take that chance?

In this chapter, we'll examine strategies for creating better cover letters, and look at a few cover letter samples, so you can get an idea of how to prepare a strong letter.

Writing a Cover Letter

What is the purpose of the cover letter? In a nutshell, the cover letter is your introduction to the reader. It has to let the reader know what you can do for them, what your experience is, what kind of job you're looking for, and why the reader should look at your résumé. All in one concise page.

Sounds easy, right? Tell me if this letter looks familiar:

Dear Sir/Madam:

I am writing to express my interest in the position of Salesman, advertised as being open with your company at this time. I have six years of sales experience, and I'm really good with customers because I'm friendly and pleasant.

I've broken all sorts of sales records at my current job, which I'm only leaving because my new boss and I don't get along well. Last year I won Salesman of the Year, and this year I'll probably win it again.

I'm available for interviews, and look forward to hearing from you about this job.

Regards,

John Smith

John Smith

Does it sound like a lot of the cover letters you've read, or perhaps written? That's too bad. It's a classic example of a letter that won't work. Here's why:

1. **Addressed to no one.** Whenever possible, use the name of the person you're writing to. If you don't know it, insert a generic but appropriate title, such as Dear Hiring Manager or Dear Human Resources Professional.

2. **The first sentence is *boring*.** Like any piece of writing, you want your letter to capture someone's attention right away and make them want to keep reading. Remember, the person you send this to has to read dozens of letters each day for that one position—and they may be reading for several positions at once. Boring letters don't stand out.

Of course, that's not to say you need to start your letter with a sentence that reads like something out of an adventure novel, either. I once had a client whose letter began with "I am a tiger in the boardroom." Not only is that sentence inappropriate for a business document, it doesn't make sense. Is he aggressive? Violent? Dangerous? Camouflaged? It tells the reader nothing about his skills, and, even worse, sounds rather silly.

3. **Hello, Mr. Obvious.** "I'm really good with customers because I'm friendly and pleasant." Why put something like this in a letter? If you're a salesperson, you're expected to be friendly and pleasant, and to be good with your customers. This would be like a plumber saying "I know all about wrenches," or a doctor saying "I know how to cure sick people." Don't waste time on the obvious; grab peoples' attention with *special achievements.*

4. **Too casual.** The entire tone of the letter is too friendly. You're not writing to a friend or a relative; you're writing a business letter to a potential employer. Save the casual tone for the water cooler, after you get hired.

5. **Mr. Negative.** A sure-fire way to get your application tossed in the trash is to say something negative about a current or past company or supervisor. People read that, and immediately believe you'll end up doing the same about their company if they hire you. There's no reason to tell any prospective employer why you're leaving your job or what kind of problems you're having there unless someone specifically asks during an interview. Even then, try to say as little as possible and put a positive spin on things.

6. **Waiting by the phone.** Look at the last paragraph again. The applicant has said they'll be waiting for a call. That's fine, and it happens sometimes. But in the real world, a hiring manager can forget to make a call. Or get so busy they have to put a call off for a day. Or two. And in the meantime, they end up hiring someone else. Why? Because that other person didn't wait for a call. They picked up the phone two or three days after sending in their résumé and letter, and followed up. Let the reader know you'll be actively following up with a call in a few days.

TIP: If you have a contact number for the person you send your résumé to, always follow up within 2 weeks.

Now that we've gone through some basics, let's look at another letter. Same client, but this is the letter I wrote after creating a new résumé for him.

Dear Hiring Manager:

I am an award-winning and experienced Sales Professional with a history of exceeding all assigned sales goals. In my current position of Sales Representative I have earned multiple awards for sales and consistently ranked Number One in my division. Now I would like to bring my talents and expertise to work for your company as your new Sales Executive.

My sales background has provided me with the excellent people and communication skills necessary to succeed in this highly competitive business. I am able to establish rapport with my customers, as well as communicate with individuals in all levels of business and management, and I'm adept at working with clients to determine requirements and develop effective solutions. Some of my major accomplishments include:

- Currently ranked Number One in Nation for Sales Achievement.
- Earned Salesman of the Year Award 8x (from 2007-2015).
- Ranked Number Two in Nation for Sales Achievement in 2013 and 2014.
- Exceeded goal by 300% in 2015, 278% in 2014, and 150% in 2013.
- Earned Best in Class awards each year my entire time with the company.
- Met or exceeded sales quota every month since 2001.

In addition to my sales skills I have experience in customer service and support, as well as staff management and training. I am able to manage daily operations, coordinate assignments, and prepare all necessary reports and documentation.

The accompanying résumé provides greater details of my accomplishments and demonstrates what I have to offer. I will call your office in a few days to inquire about the possibility of a meeting.

Thank you for your time and consideration.

Sincerely yours,

John Smith

John Smith

See the difference? Now the letter is exciting, filled with specific achievements that capture the attention, and much more businesslike in tone, without being boring.

Whenever you write a cover letter, you should go back and examine it sentence by sentence and ask yourself, "Is this information important? Does it grab or hold the reader's attention, or is it just fluff? Does it make me sound like a viable candidate?" Most importantly, is it true? If the answer to those questions is 'No,' then go back and re-write.

TIP: The only thing worse than no cover letter is a bad cover letter!

I've already mentioned that the cover letter is your introduction to your résumé. In order to get someone interested in your résumé, here are the key things your cover letter needs to do:

✓ Focus on what you can do for the company, not what your personal goals are. Remember, the prospective employer is always thinking about how you can help them, not how they can help you. Show them you can make them money or cut their costs or improve their efficiency, and they'll be much more interested in interviewing you.

✓ Demonstrate that you've done your research. Not every company is the same. Do your research on a company before you apply to it, and then mention the skills and achievements in your background that correspond to what they need. In fact, if you're aware of a specific need the company has, mention how your skills and experience would be valuable in resolving their problem.

✓ Provide specific accomplishments to show what you can do. Anyone can say they're good at sales; but not everyone knows to place bullets in their letter validating what they've accomplished in the sales field.

✓ Sound enthusiastic. Don't tell people you want a job. They already know that. Instead, tell them you're excited by the possibility of bringing your skills and achievements to work for their company.

✓ Follow-up. Don't forget to say you'll call or email in a few days. The only time you shouldn't do this is if the advertisement specifically states No Follow Up Calls, or if no contact information is provided.

✓ Remember the KISS rule: Keep It Short and Simple. Never let your cover letter get longer than 1 page. Remember, people don't have much time to read your letter, and a document that goes on and on will end up in that round basket next to the desk.

✓ Avoid talking about money. Save the salary conversation for the interview, unless the ad specifically states you have to list a salary requirement. Even then, try to stay vague, or indicate a range and then say you're willing to negotiate. The last thing you want to do is price yourself out of a job before you even have an interview.

The Parts of the Cover Letter

Now that you know what a cover letter needs to include, how do you set your letter up so it looks professional, is pleasing to the eye, and easy to read? Let's examine the basics of the cover letter format.

1. **Contact information.** This should match the name and contact heading of your résumé's first page. Think of everything as a matching set.

2. **Opening paragraph.** Two or three sentences that introduce you, indicate what type of position you're interested in, and very briefly show why you're qualified.

3. **Middle paragraph.** This is where you show how you can help the company. A couple of sentences about your previous job titles or key skills, followed by a short list of major accomplishments.

4. **Third paragraph.** A good place to talk about other skill sets you have. Again, keep it brief.

5. **Closing paragraph.** Once more, summarize why you're the best candidate for the job and indicate that you'll be contacting the person to set up a personal meeting.

Take a look at the following examples:

IT PROJECT MANAGER

6301 Parkway, 906 • Abilene, TX 12345
555-555-5555 • name@email.com

April 10, 2015

Hiring Agent Name, Title
Company Name
Address
City, State Zip

Dear Hiring Manager:

Consistently contributing to profitability and revenue growth through effective program and project management is just one of the many ways I have served a pivotal role in the success of my current and previous employers. With a strong background in international project and program management, engagement leadership, consulting, and sales & pre-sales engineering, I bring to the table a consistent and award-winning record of success. Interested in joining your organization in a management role, I have included my résumé for your consideration.

My positions in the past have included IT Project Manager, IT Program Manager, and Technology Manager. Among my accomplishments with employers such as EDS and Siebel Systems, I have:

- Planned and led complete life cycles for development and implementation projects ranging up to $50M, and I've provided proposal assistance on deals as large as $500M.
- Slashed project costs at EDS by up to 50% by developing offshore resource partnerships.
- Saved $6M at Siebel through utilization of offshore and best shore resources.
- Earned Siebel's CEO's Circle Award and ISS Global Competency Division Award.

I'm adept at building and leading cross-functional teams, performing gap analyses, risk management, change management, forecasting, pricing, and best practices implementation, and managing client training activities. I'm able to incorporate ITIL and Lean Six Sigma methodologies to enhance productivity and quality, and I have special expertise with CRM and ERP systems.

The accompanying résumé will give you an idea not only of my past achievements but of my potential for making a significant contribution to your company. I look forward to speaking to you regarding this role, and I will call you next week to inquire about the possibility of a meeting.

Sincerely,

IT Project Manager

SENIOR POLICE OFFICER

10719 Dr. • City, FL 12345 • (555) 555-5555 • (555) 555-5555 • name@aol.com

December 2, 2015

Hiring Agent Name, Title
Company Name
Address
City, State Zip

Dear Hiring Manager:

I am an experienced Law Enforcement professional, with more than 20 years on the job, including time with City PD and the County Sheriff's Department. My expertise, together with my knowledge of airport security regulations, qualifies me uniquely for the position Security Chief at your airport.

My ability to work as a team player, effectively manage programs and personnel, and penchant for detail, together with my comprehensive background in law enforcement, have contributed to my successes in my chosen field. I am highly familiar with all aspects of airport police functions, including applicable state and federal laws. Some of my key accomplishments include:

- ✓ Coordinating the implementation of a new computer system for the department.
- ✓ Supervising house arrestees as part of the house arrest unit.
- ✓ Guarding the safety of court personnel while with the judicial services bureau.
- ✓ Earning the 2010 Deputy of the Year award from the County Sheriff's Office.
- ✓ Receiving numerous commendations from the public for my excellent service.

I am an effective organizer and planner with superior decision-making skills. My outgoing and friendly nature allows me to interact well with other staff members at all levels and I pride myself on bringing the right measure of enthusiasm into the equation.

The accompanying résumé can give you an idea of my potential for making a worthwhile contribution as a Security Chief. I look forward to meeting with you to discuss this opportunity further, and will contact your office in a few days to arrange a personal conversation.

Thank you for your time and consideration.

Sincerely yours,

Senior Police Officer

HOTEL EXECUTIVE

285 St., Suite #3 • City, MA 02127 • (555) 555-5555 • name@email.net

March 27, 2014

Hiring Agent Name, Title
Company Name
Address
City, State Zip

Dear Hiring Manager:

I am a highly experienced hotel and resort management professional with extensive financial and operations management skills I am adept at increasing profits, revenue, and market share, and at introducing improvements to customer service and efficiency. My current position involves general management of one of City's most exclusive hotels, where I have produced dramatic profit increases. Now I would like to bring my experience and expertise to you as your new Hotel Manager.

My background in hotel and resort management has provided me with the excellent leadership and communication skills necessary to succeed in this competitive and fast-paced industry. Among my career accomplishments, I have:

- Increased sales, occupancy, and revenue by updating policies and procedures.
- Negotiated profitable contracts with corporate accounts and service providers.
- Earned General Manager of the Year four times during my career.
- Delivered more than $3M in revenue growth in the past 2 years.
- Facilitated the successful opening of two new hotels in Massachusetts.

In addition to my management skills I also possess extensive experience in sales and marketing, at both the local and national levels. I am dedicated to providing the highest levels of customer satisfaction and service at all times, and am constantly looking for ways to improve overall service and profits.

My enclosed résumé provides greater details of my background and what I have to offer. I will call your office in a few days to inquire about the possibility of a meeting.

Thank you for your time and consideration.

Sincerely yours,

Hotel Executive

Advertised Jobs vs. Cold Calling

In the course of your job search you'll find yourself applying not only to advertised positions, but also to companies who aren't openly hiring, but where you hope to find a job anyhow. It's necessary to adjust your letter to match these different circumstances. Luckily, this is as easy as changing a sentence in the first paragraph. Here are two examples, one formatted for an advertised job, and one for a letter sent out cold.

I am an experienced Law Enforcement professional, with more than 20 years on the job, including time with City PD, and the County Sheriff's Department. My expertise, together with my knowledge of airport security regulations, qualifies me uniquely for the position Security Chief at your airport, advertised as open at this time.

I am an experienced Law Enforcement professional, with more than 20 years on the job, including time with City PD, and the County Sheriff's Department. I believe my expertise, together with my knowledge of airport security regulations, qualifies me uniquely for a senior security position at your airport.

See how simple that is?

TIP: The cover letter can—and should!—be customized to match the position and company you're applying for. Just remember to never let it get longer than one page.

Some final cover letter advice

While the style of your cover letter should never be too casual or friendly, it doesn't need to sound like it was written in 1960, either. Business writing today allows for the use of contractions and buzzwords, especially in correspondence, so don't be afraid to occasionally use I'm or it's. Just don't get carried away.

Always keep things positive. Putting negative information about a previous employer in a cover letter can come back to haunt you someday. Always try to put a positive spin on things. For instance, instead of saying, "Took over a poorly run department and created profitability," you could say, "Turned around an underperforming department and delivered major profit growth." Remember, you never know who'll see your cover letter. It might even be your boss from three jobs ago!

Printing your letter. Just like with the résumé, the cover letter should be printed on plain white laser printer paper, or, if you want to get a bit fancier, plain white résumé paper. If you use résumé paper, be sure to buy a fine linen type, with 25% cotton, so you don't get fiber marks on the paper.

CHAPTER 6: OTHER COMMON JOB SEARCH DOCUMENTS

When people think of applying for a job, they usually think about writing a résumé and cover letter. But, while these two documents are definitely the most important tools in your job search arsenal, they aren't the only ones. Job hunters today need to be armed with a variety of career assistance tools in order to maximize the effectiveness of their search. In this chapter, we'll look at some of the more common ones, and show you when to use each one.

1. The Thank You Letter

Perhaps one of the most over-looked tools available to you. Almost everyone knows to send a résumé. Most people know to use a cover letter. But more than half the job seekers out there today forget to send a thank you letter after a telephone or personal interview. And in many cases, it costs them the job. The thank you letter is essential for three reasons:

1. It shows you have the business sense and good manners to thank someone for taking the time to speak with you. This can go a long way in an era where business etiquette is falling by the wayside. Just like being on time, shaking hands, and dressing appropriately are important, so too is making a good impression by saying thank you with an official piece of correspondence, whether it be by email or hard copy.

2. It cements you in the mind of the interviewer. Think people don't notice when you send a thank you letter? You couldn't be more wrong. The letter helps you stand out, by reminding interviewers you were there and that you're still interested in working for them.

3. It's another chance to sell yourself. A good thank you letter not only says 'thank you,' it reiterates a couple of your key skills so they see again how you can help the company. In fact, after you've had the interview, you should have a better idea of how your skills match up to what the company's looking for, so you can use the thank you letter to give a more focused idea of the benefits to hiring you than you did in your original cover letter.

On the following page is a typical thank you letter like the one I provide for all my clients. Notice how easily you could adapt it to any job sector and interview situation.

NAME

8726 Drive • Big Time Old Village, MD 12345 • Tel.: (555) 555-5555 • name@peoplepc.com

---

November 9, 2015

Person's Name
Person's Title
Company Name
Address
City/State/Zip

Dear [Insert Name Here]:

It was a pleasure speaking with you on Monday. I would like to take this opportunity to thank you for the time you spent with me, as well as to express my appreciation for the information you offered. I'm still very interested in the Sales Manager position, and I am convinced more than ever it is the right job for me. I feel my background and qualifications prepare me well for just the sort of challenges and responsibilities we discussed.

The position, as you described it to me, would combine my strong skills in account management, territory penetration, and negotiations, allowing me to make the same valuable contributions to your company as I've made to my past employers, where I've consistently increased revenue by opening new sales territories and negotiating profitable agreements with new and existing accounts.

Again, thank you for considering my qualifications. I enjoyed our talk, and am available at any time to provide you with any more information you may need. I look forward to hearing your decision.

Sincerely yours,

Name

Final thoughts about thank you letters

Although the thank you letter is important, don't get carried away when writing it. The best thank you letter is a short note, perhaps half the length of your cover letter. It's a reminder, not a place to tell a story. Keep it short and simple!

The thank you letter should be sent 1-3 days after your interview, and if you interviewed with more than one person, send each of them their own personalized letter. Unlike the cover letter, where you might not know the person's name when you send it out, address each thank you letter personally. I always tell my clients to get business cards from everyone you speak with, or jot down their names and titles during the interview, so you don't forget someone later.

Of course, it goes without saying that you should proofread the thank you letter just as carefully as you do your resume, cover letter, and any other documents. You've gotten this far; don't do anything to ruin that good impression you've made!

2. Biographies

Two of the hottest trends in the business world today are executive biographies and networking biographies. While both of these are very popular, especially among managers, executives, and corporate officers, they're radically different documents and shouldn't be confused with each other. Let's take a look at each one:

Executive Biography

Executive biographies (sometimes called personal biographies or career summaries) have been around for decades. You've probably seen them if you've ever read a press release about a corporate officer being promoted, or skimmed through the pages of a company's prospectus or annual report. Originally only corporate officers—CEOs, CFOs, Presidents, COOs—used them, often in place of a résumé. Today, more and more executives and even mid-level managers are using them as backup information to their résumés, or as marketing tools. On the next page is an example of a corporate biography. (In fact, it's mine!)

GREG FAHERTY, CPRW

Founder and Senior Writer, www.a-perfect-resume.com

Greg Faherty is the Founder of **www.a-perfect-resume.com**, a highly successful résumé preparation firm servicing U.S. and international clients. In addition, he provides expert résumé services to several major Internet-based résumé companies and has been published in newspapers, career books, and on-line markets.

Through **www.a-perfect-resume.com**, Mr. Faherty provides professional résumé services for all industries. A Certified Professional Résumé Writer (CPRW), he has developed a recognizable presence in one of the fastest-growing industries in the world today.

Mr. Faherty's writing skills and knowledge of the résumé industry enable him to supply clients with a full range of writing services, including résumés, cover letters, thank you letters, executive biographies, CVs, international résumés, and more. In addition, he also provides proofreading and copy editing services to a wide range of clients.

Prior to establishing **www.a-perfect-resume.com**, Mr. Faherty worked in several different fields, including Marketing, Laboratory Management, Quality Control, Photography, Sales, Medical Research, and Medical Equipment Repair.

Mr. Faherty possesses more than 15 years of writing and proofreading experience, including technical writing, instructional manuals, educational materials, employee handbooks, and laboratory procedures, along with other business documentation. He is the author of four elementary-school standardized test study guides, and has contributed published material for companies such as Princeton Review, McGraw-Hill, KidsBooks, and LeapFrog. He's also written several articles on résumés and the art of finding employment., and his works have been featured in *Designing a Cover Letter to 'WOW' Hiring Personnel, 2nd Ed., Cracking the Code to Pharmaceutical Sales,* and *Professional Cover Letter Examples for Managers & Executives.*

A resident of New York, Mr. Faherty holds a degree in Biology from St. Bonaventure University and has completed extensive training and earned numerous awards during the course of his career. He is a member of several writing organizations, including the Professional Association of Résumé Writers and Career Coaches.

Networking Biographies

Over the past five to 10 years, a number of online career networking sites have popped up, including The Ladders, LinkedIn, ZoomInfo, and others. These sites allow people to create an account, post their résumé in a standardized format so that everyone's information page looks the same, and then search the site for prospective business contacts. Unlike job search sites, where you usually just cut and paste your résumé into boxes, these sites have specific requirements as to section length, order of the information, and contact information. When these sites first hit the market, I was one of the first résumé writers offering to re-design people's résumés so they could easily paste their data into the proper categories. Now most major résumé companies offer these services.

3. Personal Profiles

This is a relatively new type of document, and again I was one of the first to offer them. Unlike a résumé, it's meant to be carried around at all times and passed on to prospective clients, business partners, or employers in informal settings, rather than in response to advertised openings. In a way, it's a promotional tool, to be used like a business card but with more information. It's shorter than the average résumé, and not nearly as detailed. In fact, it's more like an outline with a mission statement than a résumé or biography. They're often used by consultants and sales professionals, but you can format one for any career area.

4. Personal Statements

Personal statements are sort of like introductory letters, but they're used almost exclusively as part of the application package when applying as a student for colleges, graduate schools, medical schools, law schools, etc.

The personal statement can be a general statement of your background and what you hope to accomplish in your academic career, or it might focus on a particular aspect of your background or aspirations - depending on what the school wants you to write.

The following personal statement was written as part of an application into an advanced medical residency program.

PERSONAL STATEMENT SAMPLE

Throughout medical school, my residency, and in practice as an Internist I have always had a deep interest in Endocrinology. The vast number of disease states, their respective seriousness, and the fact that so little has been done in this field all struck a chord inside me, and I knew that someday I would have to pursue this further. Endocrinology is an exciting and wide open field, with a chance to improve so many peoples' lives, and I know that I want to be a part of it.

As an Internist some of my most interesting and fulfilling cases involved diabetes, hyperlipidemia, and thyroid disorders. Although only involved in the initial diagnosis and treatment of these patients, I followed their progress and hold a great respect for the physicians managing their care. In today's day and age it is a shame that more is not known about these, and many other, diseases, many relating to the endocrine system. I believe that more time and effort is needed in both research and clinical investigations, and that will take the dedication of doctors such as myself.

I believe that every effort, every small stride forward in Endocrinology will eventually be rewarded not only with a greater knowledge of these diseases but also an improved quality of life for the thousands of patients suffering from them. Although the field is developing rapidly, it is not moving forward fast enough. In the U.S. there are more than 250,000 people suffering from end stage renal disease, and that figure is growing by almost 9% per year. ESRD patients have a mortality rate of greater than 25%, and only have an average lifespan of 10 years after diagnosis. Add to that diseases of the thyroid, parathyroid, pancreas, and adrenal gland and it becomes obvious that there is still so much more work to do, both in the laboratory and the clinical settings.

I plan to complete a fellowship in Endocrinology with attention to clinical research. I look forward to both practicing Endocrinology and participating in clinical trials. I am excited to begin this next phase of my career, and anticipate years of challenges and rewards in the field.

Sincerely,

Name

5. Business Card Résumés

Business card résumés are exactly what the name implies - a shortened version of your résumé printed on a business card you can carry in your pocket and hand to people whenever you think they might be of assistance in your job search. I was one of the first to offer these, and my clients really seem to find them helpful. Like the personal profile, they're not intended to be used when applying for a job; rather, they're another self-marketing tool designed to help you make contacts and spread your name around.

Below is a sample of a business card résumé:

Award-winning Sales Management Professional with more than 10 years of Pharmaceutical Sales experience

John D. Person

3929 South 31ˢᵗ St. • Hopewell Junction, SD 11223
(222) 555-1212 • john@emailaddress.com

Qualifications Summary

➢ 14 awards for Exceptional Sales Performance
➢ President's Club for Sales 10 consecutive years
➢ Produced over $5 million in new revenue (2004)
➢ Able to establish and grow multi-state territories
➢ Adept at effectively penetrating new markets
➢ Extensive knowledge of pharmaceutical products
➢ Superior presentation and communicational skills

Business Card Resume Sample
(Front)

Business Card Resume Sample
(Back)

Reference Page

Up until the 1990s, most people either put their references on their résumé or sent a references page in with the résumé when applying for a job. Today, however, the process is a little different. References are saved for the interview, unless specifically requested in the job ad.

A references page is easy to prepare. First, compile a list of at least three professional (work-related) references, preferably from current or past supervisors. After that, if you want to add a couple of co-workers, business associates, or personal references, you can, but these are secondary in importance. Be sure you know your references will provide good recommendations before you add them to your list. You want people who will praise your work performance.

The format for the reference page is the same as for the résumé or cover letter. The contact information heading and section heading should match the résumé, as should the font.

Here is a sample references page.

Janie V. Name

3428 Mayfield Rd. • City, OH 12345 • (555) 555-1212 • name123@yahoo.com

---

REFERENCES

Bill Smith, Sr. Director of Marketing
Acme Tire Irons
555-555-1212
smith@email.com

Doug Smith, Sr. Director of Sales
Acme Tire Irons
555-555-1212
smith@email.com

Fred Jones, President
Jones Tire Irons
555-555-1212
jones@email.com

CHAPTER 7: SUCCEEDING IN THE ELECTRONIC AGE

Back in the 'stone age' of the 1960s, 1970s, and even 1980s, you only needed one type of résumé: the hard copy. People typed, and later printed, their résumés on nice, white résumé paper and mailed them to companies. The popularity of the fax machine in the 1980's introduced another way to send your resume, and started the movement away from traditional résumé paper, which tended to leave spots and streaks on faxes, because to the high fiber content of the résumé paper.

But once the internet exploded onto the scene, it forever changed the way people distributed their résumés. Now people email résumés, post them online, create résumé web pages, and even send specially formatted résumés designed for database storage and sorting. If you're job hunting today, you need to have your résumé ready to send in whatever format the company wants it in—scannable, text, HTML, or just plain old Microsoft Word.

Note: Here are two important résumé format DON'Ts to avoid whenever sending your résumé to anyone:

1. NEVER send a PDF. Yes, they're secure documents because no one can change the data on them and they don't usually carry viruses. BUT human resource offices and recruiters HATE to receive them. Why? Because it means opening a new program, Adobe Acrobat, in order to read your one document. Also, most databases aren't set up to store and read PDF files. And since HR offices usually store résumés in databases... well, you can imagine what happens when a PDF résumé arrives in email. That's right, it ends up in the 21st Century trash bin in someone's computer. Bye-bye.

2. Don't use a non-standard file type. Never use any file type except MS Word (.doc, .docx) or rich text format (.rtf) when saving your résumé on your computer or sending it to someone. Why? Because more than 90% of HR offices and recruiters use Microsoft Office on their computers. That means if you send a file in AppleWorks or MS Works or NotePad or WordPerfect or some other program, it most likely will open up wrong on the recipient's computer. And by wrong I mean with its format all jumbled and mixed up. Or maybe it won't even open at all. I can't count how many times I receive documents that can't be read by my computer's software. And you know what happens if someone can't read your résumé, right?

Yep. Garbage time.

So do yourself, your job search, and your friendly HR representative or recruiter a favor: Only send your résumé in the type of file the ad requests. If no specific format is requested, use either Microsoft Word (the ones that end in .doc or .docx) or .RTF-type files. You can find both of those in the **Save As** function in your word processor, which gives you options for how to save documents.

TIP: Only MS Word (.doc, .docx) and Rich Text Format (.rtf) are universal to all word processing software. Never use anything else!

Now that we've cleared that up, let's look at some special résumé file alternatives, and when each should be used.

ATS Formatted Résumés

ATS stands for Automated Tracking System or Applicant Tracking System. These are general terms for the database or parsing software systems that recruiters and HR offices use as storage areas for all the résumés they receive. You might also see the term Scannable Résumé used. The ATS résumé is a designed so that all databases can read it, store it, and reproduce it without any formatting issues occurring due to unrecognized graphics or fonts. In essence, it is a simplified version of the standard résumé. On the next page is an example of an ATS formatted résumé:

Web Developer

36 Hemlock St. • City Name, State 00000 • (555) 555-5555 • name@email.com

SUMMARY

More than 10 years of experience in Information Technology. Extensive application and web development experience. Highly knowledgeable in e-commerce integration and support. Excellent project management and analysis skills. Familiar with training and mentoring personnel. Hard working, detail oriented, and able to multi-task effectively. Outstanding communication skills. Fluent in French.

TECHNICAL SKILLS

Operating Systems: Windows 95-2003, HP-UX, VAX/VMS, Macintosh, DOS, Novell Netware

Languages: HTML, Visual Basic, COM, C, Cobol, ASP, ActiveX, JavaScript, Jscript, VbScript, Cascading Style Sheets, XML, XSL, CGI-BIN, Perl, .Net programming (ASP, ADO, C#), SQL

Tools and Databases: Access, MySQL, SQLServer, ADABAS, Posgrio, Oracle, ERWin, ODBC, OLE, Ingres, RMS, NATURAL, MS Certificate Server, MS Transaction Server, MS Index Server, FrontPage / FrontPage Server Extensions, HotDog, Intranet web component delivery, MS Biztalk, Commerce Server, MS MapPoint, Visio Architect, EDI, WDSL, MS Office, Project, Visio

Networking: LAN/WAN, TCP/IP, FTP, SMTP, firewalls, routers

EXPERIENCE

COMPANY NAME, Prince Albert, SK, 2000 – present
Co-Owner / Web Developer
- Co-founder of website development company, responsible for all technical aspects of business. Clients primarily small businesses and private individuals.
- Work with clients to determine requirements. Analyze systems and evaluate software.
- Carry out all design and development, create all graphics and databases.
- Completed work for more than 40 clients to date.
- Designed and launched company's website, www.canadianvirtual.com.

COMPANY CANADA LTD., Prince Albert, SK, 1996 – present
Systems Analyst and Intranet Architect
- Developed business websites and applications. Performed all requirements gathering and analysis, prepared documentation, and carried out all project phases.
- Acted as technical information resource to technical and business representatives.
- Conducted web publishing, Intranet use benefits, computer, Intranet design, and development training for technical and non-technical persons and classes.
- Created and implemented desktop and web applications. Installed and maintained web server, end-user development tools, and web data integration tools.

EDUCATION & TRAINING

BS in Mathematics, University of Waterloo, Waterloo, ON
Enterprise Web Development with Active Server Pages
Intranet and Web Development

Notice there is very little use of bold, no italics, and the only graphics are the lines beneath the contact information. Also, a sans serif font, Arial, was used. For ATF formatted résumés, the only fonts you should use are Arial, Calibri, and Verdana. All of these are sans serif fonts, which means they have plain letters with no ornate loops or little tails. These fonts are the easiest for a computer to read, and come out the clearest when scanned.

TIP: NEVER use a table, section break, or multiple columns in ANY résumé. Why? Because when a document is saved into a database, those sections lose their formatting, the content inside them gets repositioned through the résumé, and the document ends up being impossible to read.

HTML and XML Résumés

With so many people creating web pages for their pets, hobbies, and photographs, it was only a matter of time before people started posting their résumés on custom webpages. In order to create a résumé web page, you first have to convert your résumé into an HTML or XML format. Most word processors today can handle this easily. The new résumé won't look pretty in your word processor, but it will look just fine on the new web page. If you're not computer savvy but want a web page résumé, most résumé companies today can create one for you for a nominal fee.

Plain Text / Ascii Résumés

Sometimes you'll see companies asking you to send in a plain text version of your résumé. A plain text, or ascii, file is a type of file that contains no formatting whatsoever. No bold, no underlines, no graphics of any kind. The margins are also different; a plain text file is usually only 65 characters long. When you convert a regular document into a plain text file, your computer automatically resets the margins and also changes the font to Courier New, which is the industry standard for all ascii files.

You might be wondering why you need a résumé in this format. There are three reasons:

1. It's the best format if a company uses an older style database that can't read even an ATS formatted resume.

2. Ascii files typically don't carry viruses, making them safe alternatives for companies.

3. An ascii file is the best kind of file for cutting and pasting.

That last reason is probably the most important for a person who's sending out their résumé. Often you'll find yourself cutting and pasting your résumé into the body of an email, or into a form on a corporate website or online posting site such as Monster.com or HotJobs.com. In all these cases, if you cut and paste information from your regular résumé, you'll find that the format gets corrupted when you paste it. Bullets can turn into strange-looking groups of symbols, and the ends of sentences can get lopped off or bounced onto new lines. It's always better to cut and paste from your ascii version, in order to avoid most of those problems.

On the next page, you'll see a résumé done in the plain text format.

Web Developer
36 Hemlock Street
City Name, State 00000
(555) 555-5555
name@email.com

Summary
More than 10 years of experience in Information
Technology. Extensive application and web
development experience. Highly knowledgeable in e-
commerce integration and support. Excellent project
management and analysis skills. Familiar with
training and mentoring personnel. Hard working,
detail oriented, and able to multi-task effectively.
Outstanding communication skills. Fluent in French.

Technical Skills
Operating Systems:
Windows 95-2003, HP-UX, VAX/VMS, Macintosh, DOS,
Novell Netware

Languages:
HTML, Visual Basic, COM, C, Cobol, ASP, ActiveX,
JavaScript, Jscript, VbScript, Cascading Style
Sheets, XML, XSL, CGI-BIN, Perl, .Net programming
(ASP, ADO, C#), SQL

Tools and Databases:
Access, MySQL, SQLServer, ADABAS, Posgrio, Oracle,
ERWin, ODBC, OLE, Ingres, RMS, NATURAL, MS
Certificate Server, MS Transaction Server, MS Index
Server, FrontPage / FrontPage Server Extensions,

HotDog, Intranet web component delivery, MS Biztalk,
Commerce Server, MS MapPoint, Visio Architect, EDI,
WDSL, MS Office, Project, Visio

Networking:
LAN/WAN, TCP/IP, FTP, SMTP, firewalls, routers

Professional Experience
Company Name, Prince Albert, SK, 2000 - present
Co-Owner / Web Developer
* Co-founder of website development company,
responsible for all technical aspects of business.
Clients primarily small businesses and private
individuals.
* Work with clients to determine requirements.
Analyze systems and evaluate software.
* Carry out all design and development, create all
graphics and databases.
* Completed work for more than 40 clients to date.
* Designed and launched company's website,
www.canadianvirtual.com.

Company Canada Ltd., Prince Albert, SK, 1996 - 2000
Systems Analyst and Intranet Architect
* Developed business websites and applications.
Performed all requirements gathering and analysis,
prepared documentation, and carried out all project
phases.
* Acted as technical information resource to
technical and business representatives.
* Conducted web publishing, Intranet use benefits,
computer, Intranet design, and development training
for technical and non-technical persons and classes.

```
*  Created and implemented desktop and web
applications.  Installed and maintained web server,
end-user development tools, and web data integration
tools.

Education & Training
*  BS in Mathematics, University of Waterloo,
Waterloo, ON (1996)
*  Enterprise Web Development with Active Server
Pages (1998)
*  Intranet and Web Development (1997)
```

Notice the bullets have been changed to asterisks. This was done after creating the ascii file, as most bullets don't transfer to the ascii format. Other differences include omitting page breaks or page headings. That's because in a database, the resume is all one long page.

To create an ascii file, open your standard résumé and then do a 'Save As' using the plain text option. After you save it, close it and then open it again. This time you'll see it as the plain text version. Go through it and correct any formatting issues, including line breaks and bullets. Then resave it. Next time you need to cut and paste, you'll be all set!

TIP: It's not necessary to create and save a plain text version of your cover letter because you can easily cut and paste from the original MS Word document, since there are usually no formatting changes that need to be made.

CHAPTER 8: BUILDING A GREAT RÉSUMÉ

1. Creating Exceptional Bullets

Up to this point, we've focused on how to format your résumé to meet the needs of your job search. But one of the most important parts of creating an effective résumé is the way you use the correct words to describe what you've done. Remember, your résumé only has 30 seconds or so to impress the reader and make them want to read the entire document. In order to do that, you need to grab their attention.

*TIP: The way to grab a reader's attention is by using **action verbs** in your bullets.*

Remember those pesky action verbs we talked about in Chapter 3? Well, they're so important to creating a good bullet point we're going to review them again. It's always best to begin a bullet point or sentence with an action verb. However, just as action verbs work better than passive words to start a bullet, some action verbs work better than others. Look at the two sample bullets below. Which one grabs your attention more effectively?

- Put together sales strategy that led to $3M in new sales after first year.
- Produced $3M in new sales in only 1 year by creating new sales strategy.

If you said bullet number 2, congratulations. You picked the bullet most human resources professionals would consider more effective. Why? Both begin with an action verb, but bullet 2 not only uses a better action verb, it places the most important part of the bullet in the beginning.

TIP: Always place the most important piece of information at the beginning of a bullet.

You next question is probably, 'How do I know what's the most important piece of information in each sentence?' Well, here are some simple rules you can follow:

Quantifiable results always come first. Anytime you can lead off a sentence with a dollar amount or percentage, that's going to be important. Look at these examples:

- Saved $200,000 by eliminating excess inventory.

- Delivered 52% decrease in corporate spending by re-working annual budget.
- Achieved 18% improvement in efficiency through new training programs.
- Produced $5M growth in revenue by acquiring new clients.

Notice any similarities in those bullets? They all begin with an action verb, followed by a quantifiable result. But they all have one more thing in common, as well. *How* the person produced the result comes *after* the result.

Results before Processes. Unlike standard business writing, where you describe what you did, and then what happened after you did it, in résumé writing it's more important to list what happened - *the result* - before what you did - *the process*. Think of it as a math equation:

Action Verb + Quantifiable Result + Subject + Process = A Good Bullet.

Look at this example:
- Produced $5M growth in revenue by acquiring new clients.

Produced is the action verb, *$5M growth* is the result, *revenue* is the subject, and *acquiring new clients* is the process.

Sounds easy, right? Well, go back and take a look at your résumé. How many of your bullets or sentences are formatted correctly? I'll bet not as many as you thought. Before you send that résumé out, you need to change those bullets so they work *for* you, not against you.

TIP: Action verbs and quantifiable results make résumés interesting to read. Interesting résumés get interviews. Boring résumés end up in the trash!

2. Gathering Your Skills

Creating good bullet points for your accomplishments is a major part of writing a résumé. But it's not the only part. You also need to show people what your skills are, and that you have the right ones for the job. A good way to figure out what your key skills are is to read several job postings in your field, and see what skills they list as requirements. The ones that match yours are your key skills. Once you've done this, then you have to figure out where to put them on the resume so they grab the reader's attention. The best place is right in the beginning of the résumé, in the Summary section. Here are some good examples of summaries that highlight the candidates' skill sets effectively:

Strong background in Regional & Branch Management, Underwriting, and Sales. Award-winning sales professional with consistent record of producing dramatic increases in revenue. Adept at originating, underwriting, and approving loans, managing sales professionals, and promoting products and services. Strong customer service skills, able to work with clients to meet all financial requirements. Expertise in data analysis and reporting. Highly knowledgeable in all mortgage and loan products and regulations.

- Several years of experience in Logistics, Purchasing, and Supply Chain Management.
- Proven ability to reduce costs, improve efficiency, and increase sales and profitability.
- Special expertise in planning, logistics, vendor negotiations, AP/AR, and product pricing.
- Adept at directing process improvements, technology implementations, and strategic planning.
- Excellent leadership and problem solving skills. Multi-lingual. Multiple certifications in field.

QUALIFICATIONS SUMMARY

Talented and award-winning maintenance and facilities operations management professional with civilian and military experience. Proven ability to increase productivity and profitability. Expertise in supporting production schedules, training employees, and motivating personnel. Highly adept at formulating and implementing process improvements, managing logistics, and negotiating agreements. Excellent leadership, turnaround, and organizational skills.

Areas of Expertise

Maintenance Operations • Property Management • Materials Management
Analysis • Strategic Planning • Process Improvement • Planning & Scheduling
Supply/Inventory Control • Policy/Procedure Design • Budget/Cost Control
Logistics • Vendor Contracting • Relationship Management • Compliance

The nice thing about a résumé is you can play around with different formats for your Summary, and see which one works the best for you. No matter what format you use, however, the Summary should always contain a basic description of your professional skills, so whoever reads it instantly gets a good idea of who you are and what you can do.

TIP: The Summary should focus on professional skills, not personal qualities. Leave out anything that sounds like this: pleasant personality, able to work well with others, friendly demeanor, aggressive, well-mannered, excellent communicator, good business sense, etc. *These are personality traits, not professional skills, and they don't belong in your résumé. In fact, it would sound unprofessional to list them.*

3. What Order Should My Information Be In?

This question refers to the order of the sections on the résumé, and the simple answer is, whatever order best displays your skills and what you have to offer. For recent graduates, this might mean placing the education section before the employment, while the opposite would be true for anyone who's had more than a year or two of experience. In general, I'd stick to one of these basic formats:

For recent graduates:
Summary of Qualifications
Education
Work Experience
Training
Computer Skills
Languages
Other Information

For people with more than 2 years of work experience:
Summary of Qualifications
Work Experience
Education
Training
Computer Skills
Languages
Other Information

There are some exceptions to the rules, of course. (There always are!)

For instance, hands-on technical professionals might want to place their technical skills in between the Summary and the Work Experience sections. Likewise, someone who's had a lot of military experience might want to place that before their Education section. The nice thing about a résumé is that whenever you need to, you can create a new section for particular information.

TIP: Make sure all your section headings match; they're equally important to the eye, and when they don't match, the résumé looks sloppy.

4. How Far Back Should The Résumé Go?

This depends on your situation. Most résumé experts agree that somewhere between 10 and 20 years is best. But if your first job out of college was very important, it's okay to go back a little further. Anything further back than 25 years should be omitted from the résumé, because showing a date that far back will be more detrimental to your résumé's effectiveness than the experience will be of benefit.

You might be asking why this is. Well, it's a sad truth that most employers are looking for people within a certain age group, that being the 21 to 50 year-old range. There are several reasons for this. People in that age range are expected to be more energetic. Studies show that people are less likely to purchase products or services from people who look 'old.' Companies are also afraid of hiring older employees because they want to get as many years of service out of a new hire as they can, not bring someone on board who's going to retire in three or four years.

Of course, in the United States it's illegal to discriminate based on age; nevertheless, résumés that indicate a person might be in an older age group, either through employment dates or education dates, generally do not perform as well as résumés where earlier dates are omitted. And since your goal is to get an interview, why take chances?

There are a couple of ways to get around showing your age on a résumé. First of all, only recent graduates should put a graduation date in their education section. Second, omit earlier positions, especially if they aren't relevant. After all, if you've got several years of experience in your field, there's no need to waste valuable résumé space on that retail sales job you had in high school, or that job you had at the car wash when you were 21.

There's a third method, too, when you have older information you simply can't leave off the résumé. In the following example, the client had previous experience in sales he wanted to include, but the dates of the employment went further back than he wanted to show. Here's how I resolved that situation:

CAREER NOTES: Previously held **Senior Sales Executive** position with ACME TOASTER SALES, in Wichita, KS. Earned multiple sales awards, including Salesman of the Year and President's Club.

I placed that simple addition at the end of the employment section. Notice we didn't give it a section heading of its own; instead, we made it an addendum of sorts, indicating the experience is there but without mentioning the employment dates were from more than 30 years ago. The reader has no way of knowing how long the person was with the company.

TIP: Never go back more than 25 years on a résumé; 10-15 years is best in most cases.

5. How much is too much?

You've figured out the order for your sections. You've put together your content and created your bullets, each one beginning with a beautiful action verb to grab the reader's attention. You've identified your key skill sets and listed them in the Summary.

But do you have enough information in the résumé? Or do you have too much? Either of these issues will negatively impact the résumé's performance.

How can you tell when enough is enough?

I can say from experience this is an area where most people have a problem. The average résumé is two pages long. For entry level résumés, or people who've only held one or two jobs their whole career, a single page is often sufficient. On rare occasions - very rare! - a résumé will end up three pages in length. Only CVs or federal résumés should ever be longer than three pages.

Here are some ways to tell if your résumé is the right length. Does it go back far enough, or too far? Did you limit the résumé to your major accomplishments and job functions, or did you also include every minute detail of your daily responsibilities? Take a look at the following examples, and compare them to your own résumé.

1. Information Overload. This is the first page from a 6-page résumé a client sent to me for an evaluation:

I am *seeking* a challenging professional career in the security department for BAE Systems. I plan to bring my leadership and values that the Marine Corps instilled in me to the security department, and to make any mission a success. With team orientated security officers working together any mission will be accomplished with the right leadership and dedication. I have been deployed to Iraq three times and being a combat veteran I know what it is like to work in a stressful environment, and I never let anything get in the way of a mission. I made each and every mission a success, and I will bring that mentality to the security department.

Professional Experience
United States Marine Corps
July 2002 – July 2006

Military Police-Patrolman
Worked in the Provost Marshals Office (PMO) Armory was held accountable for over 150 weapons, thousands of rounds of ammunition, and other controlled items.
- Worked as the MCAS New River Provost Marshals Office Desk Sergeant, my duties included
  - Managed a computer log of all Military Police activity on base.
  - Dispatched different Military Police Patrolman to different activities on base.
  - Conducted background, vehicle, and personal record checks.
  - Used NICE and MDI security systems to manage different tasks.
    - Monitor access to the flight line.
    - Monitor alarm activations.
    - Monitor and control CCTV security cameras.
Enforced Military, Federal, and State Laws, Rules, and Regulations.
Has a vast knowledge of paperwork that pertains to the Military Police field.
Wrote many Military Police reports ranging from theft (government to civilian) to security violations.
Was the Main Gate Non Commissioned Officer In Charge.
Performed a variety security checks throughout MCAS New River, Camp Geiger, Camp Devil Dog and Stone Bay.
Performed Flight Line Security on MCAS New River.

- Performed searches (vehicle, personal, living quarters, and buildings).
- Performed walking patrols at recreational facilities, and living quarters.
- Counseled junior marines on their job performance.
- Supervised the duties many junior Marines.

Vast knowledge of Weapons, Convoy Operations, and Security Operations.
Performed Base Security

- Entry Control Point (ECP) Security
- Interior security.
- Flight line security.
- Perimeter Security.

Performed security for Explosive Ordinance Disposal (EOD), Convoy's, and VIP's, and Main Supply Rout (MSR) Patrols.
 Executed maintenance on vehicles and weapons.
- Supervised Pre/ Post Combat checks.
- Security Vehicle Commander.
- Command Operations Center Duty Non Commissioned Officer (supervisor).
- Trained Many Marines on Crew Serve Weapons and Convoy Operations.

Here's how the same information looked after being revised:

SUMMARY

Talented and accomplished security and law enforcement professional with military and civilian experience. Adept at establishing and managing teams, overseeing critical initiatives, and coordinating responses in threat situations. Multiple certifications and security clearances.

PROFESSIONAL EXPERIENCE

United States Marine Corps, US/Overseas   2002 – 2006

Military Police–Patrolman
Served as Provost Marshals Office Desk Sergeant. Oversaw armory, patrol dispatch functions, security systems, documentation, reporting, main gate entry/exit, and perimeter security. Maintained computer logs. Conducted background, vehicle, and personal records checks. Investigated security breaches and violations. Carried out perimeter, flight line, and interior security patrols. Trained junior Marines.

- Selected to lead Explosive Ordnance Disposal activities.
- Provided special security for VIPs, convoys, and supply route patrols.
- Supervised pre and post-combat weapons and security checks.
- Served as Security Vehicle Commander and Command Operations Center Supervisor.
- Conducted extensive weapons and convoy operations training classes.

What was once a confused jumble of information taking up an entire page is now concise, easy to read, and takes up less than a half page. The final résumé ended up being pared down from six pages to two, and it included more accomplishments than the original.

TIP: Omit the obvious. There's no need to tell people you answered phones, went to meetings, sent out emails, or any of the other minute, everyday details common to most jobs. Stick with the major responsibilities, and then go right to the accomplishments.

2. Wide Open Spaces. It's important to have some white space on the résumé, so people can see where one section end and the next begins. But sometimes people go overboard in an attempt to make their résumé look longer than it really is, like in this next example, which continues on to the next page in exactly the same manner as the original I received from the client:

OBJECTIVE

A job in the field of dental office management.

EXPERIENCE

March 2005-Present
Orthodontics
Some City, NJ
Office Manager
*   Processed payroll using QuickBooks.
*   Marketing attend marketing events, financial plans-arranging and presenting the financials of all cases-all aspects of customer service-Insurance coordinator-all aspects of Human resources-Interviewing, hiring, firing, grievances, office policy administrator,

coordinating marketing projects and staff meetings, advertising, direction and placement of ads and ad dollars.

I persuaded the Dr. to purchase and participate in Staff Driven Practices which more than doubled revenue and number of active patients. Collections- able to keep accounts receivable at less than 2%. Analyzed credit card vendor offerings and negotiated with present vendor to lower the rates.

Oversaw the renovation and construction in doubling square footage of office. Worked with contractors, vendors and municipality in all aspects of application and renovation. Computer coordinator- 1 server and 9 workstations.

Point person for all hardware and software issues, overseeing all daily functions, installation, updates and troubleshooting all problems. Programs include but not limited to Innovative Software, Vistadent, QuickBooks and all regular Microsoft applications including Word, Excel, Powerpoint.

Responsible for all outgoing correspondence to other doctors. Responsible for all patient-related correspondence, letters to general dentists, oral surgeons, responsible parties, insurance companies etc.

1998–2005
Dentists Office
Some City, NJ
Receptionist/Dental Assistant
* This was a typical receptionist, patient care coordinator position.
* Recall coordinator.
* Inventory control, OSHA compliance
* Assist Dr. with many dental procedures, sterilize instruments, operatory maintenance.

EDUCATION

1994   City College   New York, NY

*   B.A., Psychology.

1991   Community College   Brooklyn, NY

*   A.S., Biology

SKILLS

*   Honest, reliable, articulate, Microsoft Word, Powerpoint, very responsible.

After reading that résumé, can you see any reason for it to be 2 pages? I couldn't, either. The client was trying to make up for lack of information by using huge sections of white space on the paper, and by providing long explanations for common, basic responsibilities. In this case, after gathering more information and doing some major re-formatting, I put together the new resume you can see on the next page, which ended up getting the client three interviews within the first two weeks she used it.

Things you should notice on the new resume are that there's still plenty of white space, both between the bullets and between the sections, but the résumé is easier to read and fits nicely into a one-page format.

NAME
203 Road • City, NY 12345• Tel: 555-555-555 • name@optonline.net

Talented administrative/office management professional with background in healthcare

SUMMARY OF QUALIFICATIONS

➢ More than 10 years' experience in healthcare office management.

➢ Special expertise in human resources, office technology, and customer relations.

➢ Proven ability to facilitate dramatic revenue increases through business development.

➢ Adept at improving operations, productivity, office organization, and cost control.

➢ Excellent problem-solving, communications, inventory control, and compliance skills.

PROFESSIONAL EXPERIENCE

ORTHODONTICS, Some City, NJ   2005 - Present

Office Manager

Oversee office administration, including filing, phones, customer service, marketing, insurance coordination, collections, human resources management, advertising, banking, payroll, vendor relations, and office equipment. Interview, hire, and train administrative staff. Administer advertising budget and place ads. Coordinate insurance policy programs, staff meetings, and correspondence.

• Improved efficiency by updating AP/AR, collections, financial reporting, and payroll functions.

• Increased collections by implementing Vanco system to manage recurring payments and by introducing payment incentives that resulted in 20% of patients paying in full, upfront.

• Reduced accounts receivable to between 0.5% and 2%, far below industry average.

• Lowered staff insurance costs by negotiating better rates with providers, and by changing plans.

• Slashed expenses by negotiating better rates with corporate credit card vendors.

• Helped increase revenue 40% by recommending participation in Practice Management Program that introduced new marketing and management techniques.

• Increased customer retention by hosting special events and creating new customer correspondence.

• Coordinated office renovation/construction project that doubled square footage of office.

• Maintained computer systems. Served as point person for all hardware and software issues. Performed troubleshooting. Worked with vendors on software installation and testing.

DENTISTS OFFICE, Some City, NJ   1998 - 2005

Receptionist & Dental Assistant

Served as Receptionist, Patient Care Coordinator, Recall Coordinator, and Dental Assistant. Managed office banking, insurance programs, and collections. Scheduled appointments. Set up payment plans.

• Carried out inventory control and monitored processes for OSHA compliance.

• Assisted with various dental procedures. Sterilized instruments and maintained operating rooms.

EDUCATION

BA in Psychology, City College, New York, NY

AS in Biology, Community College, Brooklyn, NY

COMPUTER SKILLS

MS Office, Innovative Software, Vistadent, QuickBooks

Summing it all up

So what have we learned about putting together a winning résumé? An effective résumé has a good balance between white space and content, includes all the pertinent information without going overboard, generally stays between one and two pages, includes a Summary section, uses action verbs to create interesting bullets, and places the remaining sections in the order that best displays the person's qualifications and experience.

If you're saying "Wow! I never knew there was so much to just writing a résumé," now you understand why more than 90% of the résumés arriving in Human Resource offices or recruiter offices end up languishing in a file cabinet, or worse, taking up space in the trash. Writing a résumé isn't easy. Writing a really good, effective résumé is even harder. That's why human resource personnel appreciate a superior resume so much - it makes their job easier, because they can quickly find a candidate's skills and match them to a job.

TIP: It's not the person with the best qualifications who gets the interview, it's the person who's résumé best showcases their qualifications.

It's always good to try and create your own résumé - and by following the lessons in this book, you'll have a better chance of preparing an effective résumé. But remember, if you don't feel you can talk about yourself adequately, or if you're not great at crafting concise, action-oriented sentences, or if you just don't have the time to do it the right way, then by all means go out and hire a professional to prepare your new résumé. The money you spend will be more than worth it when you get that new job or that promotion you've been seeking.

CH. 9: I HAVE MY RÉSUMÉ, NOW WHAT?

If you've made it this far in the book, congratulations! Either you've taken the wisdom, hints, tips, and lessons from the previous chapters and crafted a new résumé for yourself, or you've purchased a new résumé from a certified professional résumé writer. Regardless of your choice, you've got a résumé in your hands that hopefully displays your talents and accomplishments in the best possible way, and now you're ready to start using it.

So how do you do that?

If it's been a while since the last time you looked for a job, things might have changed a bit. The electronic age - email, job boards, résumé posting - has given people new ways to get their information out to employers and head hunters. But in the end, it all comes down to one simple rule:

The more résumés you send out, the better your chances for getting interviews.*

Using the résumé.

The only thing that's really changed is how you get the résumé out to people. In the BTI (Before the Internet) days, job hunters only had a few options. Respond to ads in the newspaper, either by fax or by mail. Print and mail copies to companies 'cold;' that is, without knowing if there were any job openings. And finally, sign up with a recruiter or head hunter.

Once the internet showed up, it opened new doors for job seekers. Now you can go directly to a company's website and see what jobs are available. Instead of signing up with one or two recruiters, you can use dozens of recruiters, even hundreds, all at once. You can post your résumé online, at career sites like Monster.com and HotJobs. You can create a web page for your résumé. You can view newspaper and periodical ads from all over the country with just a click of the mouse.

However, in the end, it still comes down to how much effort you're willing to put into your job search. It's not enough just to stick your résumé on Monster.com and then sit back and wait, or send it to some recruiters and let them do all the work for you. Remember, you're no longer competing against the people who live around you for that job; you're competing with the entire world! HR offices and recruiters used to get dozens of résumés for each job opening. Now they get hundreds.

Hundreds.

Every day. From people who live locally and people looking to relocate. From people who are out of work, looking to change jobs, or even trying to change careers. Some of those people will have better credentials than you, or more experience. Some might even have better résumés, depending on who wrote yours, and theirs.

Besides, even the best-written résumé isn't going to get you an interview every time. You might not be the right person for the job. A really, really good résumé might get you an interview one out of four times, or one out of six.

That's only 25-30 interviews for every 100 résumés you send out. And yet, some people only send out two or three résumés and then declare their job search a failure.

TIP: Finding a job **is** *a job.*

I tell my clients they should send a minimum of 15 résumés per week. *Minimum.* More if they're in a popular field such as sales, IT, administrative support, or business management. And with all the options out there, sending out that quantity shouldn't be hard to do. Here's a quick checklist of a good job search strategy:

1. Read all the local and regional newspapers every day. Search those want ads, and apply for every job that meets your search criteria. As hard to believe as it is, more than 50% of people still find their next job through a newspaper. And don't forget, you can check those want ads online. No more going to the library and reading all the papers!

2. Make a list of all the companies in the area where you want to work that have positions similar to what you're looking for. Find out the name of the HR Manager, or the department head for the area you want to work in, and send them a copy of your résumé and cover letter.

3. Use the internet. Do a Google or Yahoo search for the types of jobs you're interested in. Be sure to do it by geographic region. For instance, "Pharmaceutical Sales+New York." Unless you're in a highly specialized field, you should find lots of job openings.

4. Find employment sites catering to your career path. There are specialized sites out there for almost anything, whether you're a nurse, a physicist, an electrician, or a teacher. Sign up, and search their want ads daily.

5. Post your résumé on all the major job sites. Although only about 5% of the workforce finds their jobs through Monster.com, HotJobs, and other sites, that's an average, and not the same for every job type. Besides, you never know. That 5% might end up including you.

6. Distribute your résumé. There are lots of sites on the internet where, for a small fee, they take your résumé and email or fax it to dozens, even hundreds, of companies or headhunters in your geographic area. Sure, it costs more than doing it yourself, but it saves you time. (Note: A lot of résumé companies offer this service as well, and if you are getting your résumé done by a professional, why not let them distribute it or post if for you?)

7. Networking. Another great way of finding a job. Talk to people you know in the industry. Pass out your résumé or business card. Go to local business association meetings. Bring up your job search to people you meet at parties. Tell friends to ask around for you.

8. Online networking. No, I'm not talking about social media sites like Facebook or Snapchat. But there are networking sites out there devoted to helping people find jobs. TheLadders, LinkedIn, and BizJobs.com are just a few of these. Some require a fee to enroll, others are free. In all cases, you need to post a version of your résumé formatted to their specific content styles. Again, this is something a good résumé writer can provide for you.

9. Job and employment fairs. Make a list of all the ones in your area and attend as many as possible. Bring lots of résumés and pass them out to as many company representatives as you can. If you can't attend a particular fair, find out what companies will be there and send them your résumé. Odds are, they're looking to hire people.

Using the above strategies, you should easily be able to put out 20-40 résumés a week.

TIP: Have a way to track the companies and jobs you apply to; the last thing you want is for some HR representative or recruiter to get 10 copies of your résumé in a week. Remember, a happy recruiter or HR rep is your best friend!

CH. 10: INTERVIEWING

It's finally happened! After writing the résumé and cover letter, and sending them out, success! A company just called you to arrange an interview.

You've got your foot in the door. Don't blow it now.

Just because a company wants to talk to you doesn't mean you've got the job. It only means you've made it through the first cut. You've impressed them on paper; now you have to do it in person, or over the phone. You're not competing against as many people, but the ones left in the game are all your equals. So it's up to you to make sure you're as prepared as possible. This chapter will look at how to do that.

1. Do Your Homework.

As soon as you find out you've got an interview scheduled, get online or go to the library and find out everything you can about the company, especially as it pertains to the type of work you would be doing. What products do they sell? Who do they sell to? Has their business been going up or down lately? Do they have new products or services coming out? Look for press releases. Check the company's website. Try to figure out what it is in your background that piqued their interest.

After you've done your homework, put together some facts about yourself you think will be important to them. If they've got new products coming to market, and you're good at leading product deployments or opening new sales territories, be prepared to bring that up in the interview. If you're an IT specialist with expertise in manufacturing systems, be ready to ask them what systems they use and discuss how you improved system efficiency at your last job. Even if you're just starting out in the work force, let your interviewer know that your academic background has you up to date in the latest theories, procedures, or data in your field, and how you're looking forward to using that knowledge while you learn the company's methodologies.

2. The Pre-Interview.

Often a company will conduct a pre-interview over the phone. While it might not be possible to prepare adequately for a surprise call, don't despair. Unless it's a previously-scheduled session, no one's expecting you to have notes and questions ready. But there are certain rules of phone etiquette you should follow.

First off, make sure you can converse freely with the person. If you're in your office or cubicle, and there's a chance someone in your company might overhear a conversation you'd rather keep private, simply ask the interviewer if you can call them back in a few minutes, or whenever you know you'll have privacy. That might mean using your coffee break or lunch break to go outside and call them back on your cell phone.

Likewise, don't take the call if you're in a loud, noisy environment. Find a spot where there are no noisy machines, people yelling, dogs barking, or babies crying. Think about how important this call is to your career, and treat it accordingly.

The same rule applies when someone calls you to schedule an interview. Always conduct yourself professionally. First impressions count.

3. Appearance is Everything.

Just as the first time you speak to someone you create a verbal first impression, so too do you create a visual first impression when you arrive for the interview. And appearance is more than just how you dress. It encompasses everything about you: timeliness, manner of dress, physical attitude (body language), and manner of speech. All these things combine to create that all-important first impression in the interviewer's mind.

Here's a list of things to be aware of to maximize making a positive first impression.

➢ **Arrive on time.** Do whatever it takes to accomplish this. Get up early. Map out your route ahead of time. Have alternate routes in mind in case there's a traffic jam or bad weather. Don't end up in a situation where you have to rush through getting dressed, eating breakfast, or finding the building. Stressful situations can lead to all sorts of negative consequences in addition to being late—imagine you're interviewing someone, and they arrive with a crooked tie, or unkempt hair, or food stains on their shirt. Is that how you want to be remembered?

➢ **Dress appropriately.** This might seem obvious, but too many people make the mistake of dressing too casually for an interview. For any type of corporate position, from secretary to CEO, the ONLY appropriate attire is a suit for a man and either a business suit or conservative dress for a woman. Even if the company doesn't require that type of dress code for its employees, it sets a professional tone to the interview and lets the interviewer know you're serious. There are exceptions to this rule, of course, but they're very rare, and it's better to err on the conservative side than appear too casual. And take care of the little things when you dress for your interview—make sure your shoes are buffed, your hair neatly combed, and your clothes wrinkle-free.

➢ **Be prepared.** Bring extra copies of your résumé, along with any other documentation that might be important, such as reference pages, a portfolio if appropriate, letters of reference, and business cards. Be ready with all the information you'll need to fill out an employment application. Make sure to have some paper or a pad so you can take notes during the interview. You should also have your pre-prepared questions with you.

➢ **Bring a good attitude.** From the moment you step into the building to the moment you leave, be polite and friendly with everyone, even if you've already had a bad day, or a bad week. Greet the receptionist and HR people warmly— they often have more influence than their job title might imply. Making small talk with interviewers is fine, but keep it to a minimum. Stick to business as much as possible. There's time to become friends after you get hired.

➢ **Body language.** During the interview itself, maintain interest at all times and appear confident. Smile. Make eye contact when you talk to people. Have your résumé memorized so you don't have to refer to it when you answer questions. Avoid negative body language—don't cross your arms over your chest, don't tilt back in your chair, and don't stare into space while others are speaking.

➢ **Practice.** Before your interview, practice answering those questions the interviewers are likely to ask. If you still don't feel prepared, sign up for interview coaching sessions, or have a friend or business associate practice with you.

TIP: Whether it's breakfast or lunch or just a good snack, be sure to eat something healthy before your interview. Not only will you have more energy and think more clearly, you'll also avoid those embarrassing stomach growls during the interview. Of course, don't overeat, either, or you might find yourself dozing off, which never makes a good impression!

4. Getting Through the Interview.

Although it's impossible to predict everything—or anything—you'll be asked during an interview, you can make some pretty accurate educated guesses. It's almost guaranteed an interviewer will ask why you're interested in the job, why you're qualified for it, and why you want to work for that particular company. You'll probably be asked to discuss specific accomplishments in your career, and at some point someone will ask you to describe your best and worst qualities. Interview coaching is a big business these days because more than ever people need to perform as well as possible in their interviews. In order to help you prepare for your interviews, I've prepared a list of basic questions frequently asked during interviews. While not all of these might apply to your particular situation, enough of them will so that it should be a helpful tool for you.

- Tell me a little about yourself.
- What qualities do you possess that make you the best candidate for this job?
- What do you consider your greatest strengths?
- Name one or two of your weaknesses.
- Where do you see yourself in five years time?
- Why do you want to work for our company?
- Name three ways in which you helped your last company.
- What aspect of your current or last job do you dislike most?
- Tell me about a difficult decision you had to make, and how your decision turned out.
- What type of work environment do you prefer - individual or group?
- Have you ever had problems with a previous co-worker or manager?
- How well do you handle criticism?
- Describe your ideal manager?
- How would your previous co-workers describe you?

The most important thing to remember is whenever you answer any question in an interview, *always put a positive spin on it.* You never want to say anything negative about yourself, your former co-workers/managers, or previous companies. Even if you're asked a negative question, keep your answer positive, like in this example:

Question: Name one or two of your weaknesses.

Answer: This is something I've thought long and hard about. I believe my two biggest weaknesses are that I tend to work too hard, and I sometimes expect others to have the same level of dedication to perfection that I have. While this has been a benefit to past employers in that I've always performed at a superior level, I have to remember that it's also important to sometimes step back and take a breath.

5. Keeping Quiet.

During a first interview, there are certain things you should ask, but also certain things you shouldn't. Among the no-nos are: anything having to do with benefits, vacations, sick days, etc. You shouldn't discuss those types of details until someone makes you a job offer, or at asks you what type of benefit package you are looking for.

It's also usually not a good idea to bring up salary until the end of the interview, after you have a feeling for whether or not you're still interested in the job and if the company is still interested in you. Even then, keep it general. You can ask about the salary range, but don't try to pin people to a specific number until they offer you the job.

Also, be sure to listen intently when your interviewer is speaking, and don't interrupt.

6. After the Interview.

The interview is complete. You've answered all the questions asked of you, and even asked a few of your own. Now what?

First of all, thank everyone who interviewed you for taking the time to speak to you. Shake hands. Be sure to get the business cards of everyone you speak to. At this point, assuming you have a good feeling about how the interview went, it's okay to ask questions like, "Will you be interviewing more candidates?" or "How do I compare to the other people you've spoken with?" or "When will you be making a decision about the position?" You might not get a definitive answer, but sometimes you will.

Within a day or so following the interview, prepare a thank you email or note and send it to each person you spoke to. As I mentioned earlier, the note should be short, indicate you're still interested in the position, and list one or two facts that will remind the person about you and your qualifications.

7. Getting What You're Worth.

Congratulations! The company you interviewed with has just offered you the job. But don't celebrate just yet. There's still some work to be done. You need to hammer out the details now—what's the salary? What are the benefits? What are the prospects for growth within the company?

While that last one might be difficult to get a definitive answer for, you can make sure about the first two.

Before entering into any negotiations, you need to have a good idea of what your needs and wants are, and how far you can deviate from them. Here are some facts you should be aware of for your role or employment level:

1. How much you *need* to make.

2. How much you *want* to make.

3. What the average salary is for people with your job and your experience.

4. What type of benefits package you need - vacations, healthcare, retirement, etc.

With that information in hand, you can ask about the salary and benefits package the company is offering. Usually you'll have a fair idea of the range they're looking at beforehand, as it's a topic that often comes up during interviews, when they'll either ask you for a salary range, or indicate one, for the position. Then it's just a matter of trying to get the best total package you can. Sometimes this might mean making concessions—fewer vacation days for more salary, lower salary for better healthcare - but always have a final goal in mind.

Most importantly, *never* accept a job offer before knowing the salary and benefits.

CH. 11: FINAL THOUGHTS

Now that you've completed all the lessons, let's sum up the key points of this book.

- ✓ It's not the candidate with the best qualifications who gets the most interviews, it's the candidate whose résumé best displays those qualifications.
- ✓ The résumé is a business document designed specifically to detail a candidate's background and accomplishments without providing excessive details.
- ✓ Professionally-prepared résumés perform better. For a person to create their own résumé, they need to have a strong grasp of the English language, the ability to render their experience in concise, accurate terms, and a familiarity with the current résumé standards and format.
- ✓ Cover letters, thank you letters, and alternative résumé formats are just as important to the job search process as the actual résumé.
- ✓ Finding a job is hard work, and the job seeker today needs to utilize many different strategies, including online posting and distribution, traditional newspaper want ads, networking, career fairs, and extensive research.
- ✓ Professionalism is vital, both in preparing your documents and while going through the interview process.
- ✓ Patience is a virtue; the average job search today takes almost 60 days.

So, what are you waiting for? Get moving and find that new job!

And good luck with your job search!

APPENDIX 1

Sample Résumés

On the following pages, you'll find a variety of sample résumés. Every effort has been made to provide as wide a representation of skills and business areas as possible, but in order to include every job category out there, this book would need to be a couple of thousand pages long! Instead, I've tried to touch on the main job sectors and employment levels. Most everyone should be able to find one that comes close to their personal needs. If not, feel free to contact me at **sales@a-perfect-résumé.com** and I'll be glad to help you, whether you're just looking for a sample or if you need a detailed critique of your résumé.

ACADEMIC OFFICER, PH.D.
2206 Drive • City, MD 12345 • 555-555-5555 • name@aol.com

Talented and accomplished Academic Officer and Business Management professional

PROFILE

Extensive background in Business Operations and Management. Proven ability to successfully direct programs as a business owner, as well as a Chief Academic Officer, Department Head, and Director. Special expertise in program development, administration, strategic planning and management, and business financials. Familiar with developing policies and procedures, establishing relationships with government agencies, and conducting performance assessments. Able to recruit and develop personnel. Consistent record of reducing costs.

Operations Management • Strategic Planning • Change Management • Organizational Development
Performance Assessment • Budget/Cost Control • Grants/Funding • Relationship Management
Service Delivery • Capacity Building • Conflict Management • Organizational Effectiveness

PROFESSIONAL EXPERIENCE

COMPANY 1, Adelphi, MD   1990 – 2015
Independent Consultant
Provide consulting services in areas of strategic planning, training, organizational development, program management and evaluation, technical assistance, and alternative dispute resolution. Clients include Dept. of Energy, Dept. of Agriculture, Howard University Hospital, Howard University Leadership Academy, District of Columbia Public Schools, Dept. of Employment services, and several other government groups and companies. Oversee business operations and finances.
- Designed and delivered group training programs in areas such as organizational effectiveness, service delivery, capacity building, coaching, supervision, communication skills, diversity, conflict management, program design, change management, and many others.
- Planned and conducted needs assessments, workplace training, interventions, and strategic planning sessions. Designed programs. Evaluated organizational performance levels.
- Prepared strategies for improving processes, collecting data, and enhancing performance.

UNIVERSITY 1, Washington, DC   2000 – 2006
Dean, Faculty, Academic & Student Affairs
Chief Academic and Student Affairs Officer. Directed educational aspects of academic departments and student support programs. Managed development and execution of policies and standards, programs, and budgets. Oversaw admissions, records & registration, advisory and career services, and library. Managed budgets. Developed strategic plan. Supervised staff of 9. Administered $9M budget.
- Curtailed spending and supplanted budget with external funding for academic programs.
- Improved academic standing and revenues by introducing on-line degree program.
- Revised curricula to meet changing student and market demands and introduced new courses.
- Achieved 10-year re-accreditation from Middle States Commission on Higher Education.
- Enhanced student performance and retention by developing and implementing processes for student learning outcomes assessment and institutional effectiveness.

UNIVERSITY 2, Bowie, MD   1991 – 2000
Chairperson, Dept. of Communications (1980-2000)
Managed all academic functions for department, including quality, instruction, policies, personnel, financials, support services, recruiting, and retention for newly-created department. Represented department to school administration. Administered $500,000 department budget. Supervised 12 instructors and 5 support staff.

- Established department, developed all academic and student policies and procedures, and played key role in university's academic strategic planning process.
- Reduced expenses and supplanted budget with $100,000 in government contracts.
- Improved quality by organizing and leading faculty and staff development workshops.
- Developed and managed undergraduate and graduate degree programs.
- Maintained all required accreditations and continually assessed programs to identify improvements.
- Successfully obtained external funding to construct radio & TV studio, and speech laboratory.
- Sat on multiple commissions and task forces relating to policy, direction, and academics.

ACADEMIC EXPERIENCE

UNIVERSITY 3, Washington, DC   2006 – 2015
Associate Professor, School of Communications
Instruct graduate and undergraduate courses in Communication Theory, Introduction to Communication, Interpersonal Communication, Intercultural Communication, Organizational Communication, Principles of Speech, and Conflict Management. Member of Comprehensive Committee and Dissertation Committee.

- Updated Intercultural Communication, Communication Theory, and Conflict Management courses.
- Oversee accreditation activities and ensure compliance with regulatory agency requirements.

EDUCATION

Ph.D. in Human Communication Studies, Howard University, Washington, DC
BA in Sociology & Psychology, Howard University, Washington, DC

CERTIFICATIONS & TRAINING

Alternative Dispute Resolution Certification, Better Business Bureau

ADDITIONAL INFORMATION

Computer Skills: MS Office, SPSS
Presentations & Publications: Complete list available on request

ADMINISTRATIVE ASSISTANT
380 Road • City, NY 12345 • 555-555-5555 • name@yahoo.com

Administrative Assistant • Data Entry • Office Assistant • Database Administrator

SUMMARY OF QUALIFICATIONS

➢ Talented and accomplished Administrative professional with extensive experience.
➢ Background in customer service, business operations, and hospitality industry.
➢ Expertise in administration, bookkeeping, data entry, documentation, payroll, and computers.
➢ Excellent data management, software, human resources, and organizational skills.
➢ Adept at communicating with customers and improving customer satisfaction.
➢ Able to support sales efforts through phone support and RFP preparation.

PROFESSIONAL EXPERIENCE

COMPANY 1, City, NY   2007 – Present
Legal Administrative Assistant, O'Connell & Aronowitz, PC (2007-present)
- Provide administrative support for several attorneys in fast-paced legal office setting.
- Prepare drafts, legal documents, correspondence, and other business documents.
- Transcribe documents, correspondence, reports, dictation, and other materials.
- Serve and deliver files to courts and attorneys.
- Manage correspondence, deliveries, phones, and filing.
- Carry out receptionist duties as needed.

COMPANY 2, INC., City, NY   2003 – 2007
Office Manager / Front Desk Coordinator
- Managed office operations, served as receptionist, and carried out bookkeeping, payroll, payroll tax processing, and AP/AR for financial planning company.
- Reviewed, verified, and distributed $500,000 to $1 million in commissions per year.
- Processed $15,000 to $20,000 in payables, and up to $800,000 in receivables, per month.
- Improved efficiency by acting as computer technician/help desk support specialist. Implemented company's first standardized data backup procedures.
- Maintained marketing materials, set up client files, and managed office inventory.
- Created marketing materials, standardized forms and procedures in key areas.
- Re-organized marketing materials and client files. Established alternate location for old files.
- Slashed costs 25% by negotiating pricing with vendors and identifying alternate vendors.

SELECTED TRAINING & CERTIFICATIONS

Web Pages & Surveys, Integrated Computer Operations, Payroll Management and the Law, Human Resources and the Law, Harassment Prevention for EEO and HR Specialist Tech. Assistance for EEOC, FMLA and Worker's Comp, Employment Law Update, Train the Trainer, Interviewing People, How to Orient People, Developing Your HR, Policy Manual and Employee Handbook, OSHA for HR Managers, Negligent Hiring and Wrongful Discharge, Preventing Workplace Violence, Ethical Decision Making-A Model Approach, Constructive Conflict Resolution

ADDITIONAL INFORMATION

Computers: Windows, Mac OS, MS Office, Publisher, Front Page, PeopleSoft, FileMaker Pro, TEDS Scheduling Software, Active Sync, HTML, QuickBooks Pro, Medlin Payroll Software, Kronos, HRIS systems, Payroll systems,

Languages: Fluent in Spanish

FUNCTIONAL - ATHLETE

1 Drive ▪ City, FL 12345 ▪ (555) 555-5555 ▪ name@aol.com

Proven team leader with exceptional skills in communications, training, and problem-solving

~ SUMMARY OF QUALIFICATIONS ~

➢ Professional athlete with experience in public speaking, community relations, and leadership.

➢ Adept at establishing and growing relationships with clients and business partners.

➢ Proven ability to coach and mentor in group and individual settings.

➢ Excel at decision-making, problem-solving, and public speaking.

➢ Familiar with working and succeeding in multi-cultural work environments.

~ PROFESSIONAL BACKGROUND & ACCOMPLISHMENTS ~

Public & Community Relations

- Hosted charitable event for Cancer Network. Secured appearances by more than 50 celebrity athletes for organization's first-ever Celebrity Golf Classic.
- Serve as celebrity coach at Football Camp for Kids, in TN. Provide athletic coaching and life choices mentoring for disadvantaged inner city youth.
- Defensive Coordinator for Little League Football team. Provided coaching and life skills mentoring for children ages 13 to 15.

Public Speaking

- Guest host on weekly football-oriented radio show and featured guest on weekly sports radio program, providing post-game analysis, expert opinions, and general insights.
- Delivered speeches to groups as part of fund-raising efforts and volunteer programs.

Leadership & Coaching

- Assistant Defensive Line Coach for University. Developed defensive ends. Provided training, coaching, and mentoring for players. Introduced new pass rush drills and techniques.
- Helped one student break school's single-season sack record and helped team achieve first-ever bowl selection. Achieved major increases in overall sack total for defensive line.
- Defensive Line Coach at High School, supervising and training varsity defensive line players.

Business Development

- Identify and acquire clients and carry out sales/marketing of life and health insurance policies. Set up tax-sheltered annuities for customers. Maintain multi-state territory.
- Grew client under management from zero to 30, exceeding personal goals.
- Facilitated fund raising for charity events by leveraging professional athlete status and contacts.
- Carried out promotion and marketing for celebrity golf charitable event.

Athletics

- Played 100 games as Defensive End for Pro Football Team (6 years).
- Mentored new players and assisted both teams in reaching division playoffs.
- Earned NFC Defensive Player of the Week for efforts in playoff win vs. Washington Redskins.

Name • Page 2

~ EMPLOYMENT HISTORY ~

Registered Representative, COMPANY 1, City, FL	2006 – 2008
Graduate Assistant, UNIVERSITY 1, City, FL	2006
Defensive Line Coach, HIGH SCHOOL 1, City, FL	2004 – 2005
Defensive End, TEAM 1, City, NY	2001 – 2002
Defensive End, TEAM 2, City, FL	1996 – 2001

~ EDUCATION ~

BA in Psychology

University of Tennessee, Knoxville, TN

- All Academic Southeastern Conference Honor Roll for GPA
- Starting Defensive End for 2 years; tied for most quarterback pressures in 1 season in school history

~ LICENSES & CERTIFICATIONS ~

Series 6, Series 63

Life Health and Variable Annuities (Florida, Texas, Mississippi, Tennessee, Indiana, Georgia, Virginia)

~ AFFILIATIONS ~

Retired National Football League Players Association

~ COMPUTER SKILLS ~

MS Word, MS Excel, Adobe Photoshop

SENIOR ATTORNEY
36544 Summit St. • City, CA 90210 • (555) 555-1212 • name@yahoo.com

PROFILE

Highly talented and accomplished Counsel with extensive corporate litigation background. Special expertise in managing complex litigation, regulatory compliance, intellectual property, class actions, Chapter 11 filings, and contracts. Adept at supervising outside counsel. Proven ability to plan and lead defense in high profile cases, represent employers before state and federal courts and commissions, and manage all aspects of corporate legal issues. Superior presentation and business leadership skills.

PROFESSIONAL EXPERIENCE

***General Counsel*, Company, Inc.**, Manasquan, NJ   2002 – Present
Coordinated and supervised defense and prosecution of litigation matters involving class actions, contract disputes, and intellectual property. Supervised outside litigation counsel.

- Planned and led the defense of 280 product-related liability matters with potential exposure of over $2 billion. Transferred product liability and wrongful death cases from over 20 jurisdictions to U.S. District Court for the District of New Jersey.
- Oversaw defense strategy for Federal Trade Commission investigation and multiple Attorney General investigations and actions involving alleged violation of consumer fraud / unfair competition statutes.
- Directed response to investigation by U.S. House Committee on Energy and Commerce that included corporate testimony before subcommittees.
- Responsible for regulatory oversight on aspects of new product development that included clinical trials, formula and label review, and FDA and FTC compliance.
- Negotiated and drafted celebrity endorsements agreements, vendor contracts, manufacturing agreements, and other operational documentation.

***Associate*, Big Law Firm**, Woodbridge, NJ   2000 – 2002
- Key member of commercial litigation team, responsible for all facets of complex cases, including commercial real estate, false advertising, professional malpractice defense, patent and trademark infringement, unfair competition, contract disputes, class action litigation, and wrongful death.
- Conducted trials, depositions, and motion practice in state and federal court.

***Assistant District Attorney*, Office of the District Attorney**, City, State   1998 – 2000
- Presented over 100 felony cases to grand jury, including high-profile homicide, arson, attempted murder, and others. Managed caseload of 90 misdemeanor cases.
- Prosecuted numerous trials as first chair, and led pre-trial evidentiary hearings.

EDUCATION
Juris Doctor, Seton Hall University Law School, Newark, NJ (1998)
BA in Sociology, Ithaca College, Ithaca, NY (1993)

BAR ADMISSIONS
New York, New Jersey, U.S. District Court (District of New Jersey)

BUSINESS STUDENT

7 Lane • City, NY 12345 • 555-555-5555 • name@optonline.net

International Management • Sales & Marketing • Business Administration

SUMMARY OF QUALIFICATIONS

- Presently completing Bachelor of Science in International Management.
- Previous experience includes inventory control and project management.
- Training in international business, global e-commerce, marketing, and management.
- Proven ability to improve productivity, quality, and efficiency at every position held.
- Excellent organizational, problem-solving, and strategic planning skills.

EDUCATION

BS in International Management, DOMINICAN COLLEGE, City, NY (in progress)
- Dean's List Student
- Course work includes Intro to Management, Accounting I/II, Principles of Finance, Marketing, International Management, Global E-Commerce, Global Marketing, Business Communications, International Business, Business Law, Business & Society, Macroeconomics, Microeconomics

EMPLOYMENT HISTORY

CENTRAL SCHOOL DISTRICT, City, NY • 2006 - Present
Custodian
Assist with facilities maintenance and upkeep, including classrooms, structures, grounds, electrical systems, heating systems, and panel control room.
- Helped reduce costs by assisting in negotiations with supply vendors.
- Lowered expenses by identifying unused supplies and improving inventory control.

LARGE GYM, City, NY • 2006 - 2007
Gym Facilitator
Managed daily activities at athletic facility. Assisted with business operations management. Conducted daily equipment inspections to ensure regulatory compliance.
- Implemented quality control recommendations to improve customer satisfaction.
- Identified areas for reducing costs that led to increased profitability.

TECHNICAL SKILLS

MS Office, PowerPoint, LAN, Wireless Systems, C++, Java, Windows

LANGUAGES

Languages: Conversational Spanish

Small Business Owner

9 Termasen Dr. • City, NY 11000 • (555) 111-1111

Talented Business Management professional with extensive sales and customer service experience

SUMMARY OF QUALIFICATIONS

- More than 10 years of management experience.
- Familiar with all aspects of business management.
- Adept at planning, promotions, and forecasting.
- Proven ability to lead effective sales teams.
- History of increasing sales and profitability.
- Hard working, able to multi-task effectively.
- Outstanding training, leadership, and communication skills.

PROFESSIONAL EXPERIENCE

CITY DELI, New York, NY   2002 – Present
Owner / Manager
Founded and manage highly successful delicatessen and catering operation. Oversee and assist with all daily activities, including hot / cold meal and salad preparation, opening and closing functions, and customer service. Perform inventory control, ordering, and purchasing. Negotiate agreements with vendors, ensure all deliveries accurate and on time. Hire and train staff.
- Built business from initial start up to >$1M per year.
- Developed and implemented highly effective marketing and promotions campaigns.
- Reduced costs 15% through changes in shift staffing and elimination of overtime.

SALES & MARKETING INC, Tarrytown, NY   1993 – 2002
District Sales Manager (1985 – 1992)
Directed sales management activities for entire New York metropolitan area consisting of eight headquarter accounts covering more than 550 retail outlets.
- Increased sales 10% through effective sales planning and improved shelf presence of product line.
- Introduced 40-plus new products to accounts, maintained 100% product line distribution.
- Consistently achieved or exceeded all sales quotas each year.
- Prepared, presented, and arranged promotions, sold displays / distributions to support promotions.
- Created and designed section layouts (plan-o-grams) for accounts.
- Supervised and scheduled job assignments for retail sales force.

Territory Sales Manager (1983 – 1985)
Carried out sales and merchandising for Rockland and Orange counties. Sold displays to increase sales volume, implemented and maintained section layouts.
- Met all sales objectives, recognized for leading one of company's highest-rated territories.

GROCERY EMPORIUM, Valley Stream, NY   1991 – 1993
Grocery Department Manager
Managed daily operations, scheduled staff assignments, supervised staff. Maintained inventory control system, monitored and approved incoming deliveries. Arranged promotional displays. Worked closely with vendors on promotions and sales.
- Promoted rapidly from *Clerk* to *Dairy Manager* to *Grocery Manager*.

EDUCATION

St. Thomas Aquinas College, Sparkill, NY
B.A. in Business Administration, concentration in Marketing (1980)

CHEF
Contact information here

TALENTED SOUS CHEF / HEAD CHEF WITH EXPERIENCE IN UNITED STATES AND OVERSEAS

SUMMARY OF QUALIFICATIONS

- More than 7 years of professional experience in kitchen management.
- Proven ability to oversee all aspects of kitchen operations and food preparation.
- Consistent record of reducing costs, increasing quality, and improving service.
- Previous positions include Sous Chef, Head Chef, Cook, and Chef de Partie.
- Adept at creating menus, managing purchasing, and supervising staff.
- Excellent creative, administrative, and business skills.

PROFESSIONAL EXPERIENCE

FAMOUS RESTAURANT, Miami, FL   2006 - Present
Head Chef
Oversee all kitchen, catering, and delivery operations for 70-seat restaurant. Supervise staff of 8; carry out all purchasing. Manage $57,000 budget.
- Increased revenue from $6,000 per month to $10,000, in less than 1 year.
- Introduced new items to in-house and catering menus, resulting in sales growth.
- Improved catering revenue 40% through better service and more menu selections.

LARGE RESTAURANT, Istanbul, Turkey   2005 - 2006
Private Caterer
Established and operated high-volume catering business for parties and special events. Hired, trained, and supervised kitchen/preparation/service staff for all events.
- Achieved double-digit growth nearly every month for seven consecutive months.
- Managed all arrangements for parties averaging from 100 to 150 guests.
- Performed all cooking/meal preparation, menu preparation, and service.

FOUR SEASONS RESORT, Caribbean Island   2004 - 2005
Sous Chef
Directed all kitchen Operations, including room service, banquet functions, and 136-seat casual restaurant. Supervised staff of 15. Managed purchasing, service, quality, and inventory control.
- Improved profitability by reducing purchasing and labor costs.
- Increased catering business by placing special emphasis on quality of service and product.

FOUR SEASONS RESORT, Europe   2002 - 2004
Sous Chef Trainee
Managed complete kitchen operations, including ala cart breakfast, gardmanger kitchen, banquet operations, and room service for 273-room hotel. Supervised night chef and kitchen staff.
- Improved cost control by streamlining resource and inventory usage to reduce waste.

EDUCATION

BS in Tourism & Hotel Management, University, School of Tourism & Hotel Management

ADDITIONAL INFORMATION
Computer Skills: MS Office, Internet, Fidelio, POS systems
Languages: Spanish, Italian

Chief Financial Officer

Street
Big City, MA 12345   name@yahoo.com   Tel.: (555) 555-5555
                                                                       Cell: (555) 555-5555

Senior Financial Officer with proven ability to successfully direct financial operations and lead companies through start-up and IPO stages. Special expertise in Private Equity sector.

PROFILE

Consistent record of reducing costs and improving profitability for private equity firms, large corporations, and start-up organizations. Adept at managing investor relations, accounting, tax and regulatory compliance, MIS, portfolio analysis, and treasury functions, in US and overseas. Proven ability to improve efficiency and productivity through technology implementations and automation of processes. Highly familiar with coordinating profitable disposition and purchase of portfolio companies.

Areas of Expertise

Corporate Financial Operations • Strategic Planning • Investor Relations • Due Diligence • Compliance
Accounting • Portfolio Analysis • Treasury Functions • Taxation • Fund Accounting • Audit Support
Administration • SEC Reporting • Corporate Formation • M&A Support • Technology Implementation
Risk Management • General Ledger • Payroll • AR/AP • EBITDA Growth • Process Improvement

PROFESSIONAL EXPERIENCE

COMPANY 1, LP, Boston, MA   1995 - 2008
Chief Financial Officer
Served as CFO from inception to peak of investment period for private equity firm with >$3B in commitments and total corporate transaction investment values of >$10B. Helped build company to 61 employees and offices in US and Asia. Established and directed accounting, treasury, compliance, reporting, risk management & administration, MIS, and more. Supervised 5 accounting and 2 MIS direct reports. Researched and reported transactional tax implications.

Oversaw and approved fund tax and management company tax estimates and returns. Administered Fund and Management Company borrowings, contributions and disbursements. Prepared cash disbursement reports and cash requirement forecasts. Monitored compliance. Liaison to auditors. Tracked EBITDA, valuation multiples, capital structure, and ownership for portfolio company investments.

- Led production of over 500 reports per quarter, including portfolio analyses, capitalization tables, transactions, portfolio company descriptions, financial statements, contributions, and more.
- Dramatically improved accuracy and reduced processing time for cash distribution and bulk distribution processes by designing proprietary program to track disbursements, cash flow, wire instructions, and other actions vital to processes.
- Deferred income tax on $2.1M for 3 years by recommending accrual basis to delay taxation of management fees collected in advance of period earned.
- Coordinated all aspects of disposition of 20 portfolio companies and purchase of 40 portfolio companies. Managed >$3B in cash collected and $3.4B in cash distributed based on transactions.
- Increased efficiency by designing record keeping system to track Deferred Management Fees.
- Improved reimbursement process by designing integrated database to track expenses by deals.
- Reduced tax form preparation times and expedited A/P processing through Lean/Kaizen events.
- Designed all back office systems, policies, and procedures. Staffed departments.

Chief Financial Officer ~ Resume ~ Page 2

COMPANY 2, City, NY   1993 - 1995
Director, Accounting and Reporting
Oversaw key financial operations and transition activities for beverage company with more than $500M in annual net revenues. Key member of transition team during Quaker's purchase of brand name and migration of operations from New York to Chicago. Supervised staff of 12 in cost accounting, internal controls, GL, A/P, consolidations, reporting, and taxes. Prepared and administered multi-million dollar annual budget. Authored and delivered presentations to Audit Committee and IPO underwriters. Reviewed quarterly debt compliance schedules.
- Saved $30,000 per year through effective preparation filing of SEC reports.
- Identified $3.5M in future tax deductions by conducting due diligence for 2 acquisitions.
- Saved $20,000 per year and expedited invoice processing, without sacrificing quality.
- Enhanced efficiency and productivity by designing consolidation and tax accrual spreadsheets, co-authoring "Accounting & Reporting Guide," and coordinating integrated Material Requirements Planning system installation.
- Increased productivity by implementing GL and accounting software.
- Effectively designed cash disbursement systems for 2 subsidiaries.

CAREER NOTES: Previous positions include **Senior Associate of Emerging Business Services Division** at COMPANY 3 and **Manager** at COMPANY 4. Details available on request.

EDUCATION

MS in Public Accounting, City University
BS in Business Management, City College

CERTIFICATIONS & TRAINING

Certified Public Accountant (1990-1994)

TECHNICAL SKILLS

MS Office, Solomon, AccPac, and various other GL and proprietary software packages

PROFESSIONAL AFFILIATIONS

Private Equity Chief Financial Officer Association (PECFOA)
Financial Executives Networking Group (FENG)
Financial Executive Institute (FEI) (membership pending)
Association for Corporate Growth (ACG) (membership pending)

CHIEF TECHNOLOGY OFFICER

1200 Road • City, GA 12345 • 123-555-5555 • name@email.net

Chief Information Officer • Chief Technology Officer • CEO • COO • Senior IT Executive

PROFILE

Talented and accomplished Senior IT Executive and Corporate Officer with extensive experience in directing IT organizations, business and technology operations, financials, and business development. Adept at strategic planning, technology development and deployment, project leadership, process improvement, restructuring, and multi-million dollar profitability enhancement. Proven ability to establish and oversee companies, programs, and mission-critical projects.

IT Governance • Corporate Operations • Business Development • Technology Transformation
Strategic Planning • B2B Technologies • Technology Design & Deployment • Reorganization
Turnaround Activities • System Implementation • Budget/Cost Control • Risk Management
Entrepreneurship • ERP Systems • Negotiations • E-Commerce • Change Management

PROFESSIONAL EXPERIENCE

COMPANY 1, INC., City, GA   2005 - Present
Owner & President
Purchased and oversee multi-million dollar furniture business, including IT functions, business planning and strategies, sales, marketing, financials, product development, vendor relations, and government contracts. Carried out business turnaround. Recruited new management team.
- Grew business from $300,000 to >$2M in less than 3 years.
- Increased profit margins from 12% to >22% by restructuring organization.
- Improved efficiency and productivity by implementing inventory management and controls, customer satisfaction processes, and customer sign-off processes.
- Streamlined workflow by automating design, order entry, project tracking, and more.
- Enhanced market penetration by winning commercial and government contracts.

COMPANY 2, LLC., City, GA   2003 - 2004
Senior Vice President – Information Technology
Recruited by nation's second-largest credit card processor to reorganize Clearing & Settlement Processing operations and create world-class organization. Oversaw all technology operations, including application development, infrastructure, support, maintenance, and project management. Also managed HR, Marketing, Sales, and Customer Service for Columbus location. Supervised 8 direct and 95 indirect reports. Administered $15M budget. Coordinated vendors.
- Planned and led first 2 phases of 3-phase enterprise-wide legacy system overhaul.
- Saved $200,000 (3.5%) through effective project management.
- Turned around under-performing corporate location.
- Enhanced performance levels by implementing QA and testing processes.

COMPANY 3, INC., City, GA   1998 - 2003
Founder & Chief Technology Officer
Established consulting firm specializing in assisting companies with technology and business issues. Directed all technology operations. Served as interim and/or permanent CIO for clients. Investigated and resolved critical problems. Developed strategies. Supervised 150 persons per engagement.
(continued)

Chief Technology Officer • Page 2

(CIO & Founder, Company 3, continued)

- Designed and implemented strategic IT plans, technology assessments, and technology transformations for clients ranging from $60M to $1.4B.
- Managed $75M system re-write for $1.4B travel distribution company. Turned around previously failing project, implemented new timelines and budgets, and met all deliverables.
- Directed design and launch of 64 new customer web sites.
- Helped create and execute IT strategic plan for $1.4B staffing services company.
- Partner at TATUM CIO, group of 100 CIOs. Developed sales and marketing materials, conducted sales calls, and assisted with closing of sales.
- Served as Vice President and CIO at eCompanyStore. Directed all IT operations for $42M company. Planned and led comprehensive SAP implementation. Helped grow business >450% from 2000-2001. Assisted in bringing in $15M in venture capital funding.

COMPANY 4, INC., City, GA   1981 - 1998
Chief Information Officer & Managing Director of Information Technologies (1995-1998)
Oversaw global IT assets and information systems for $15B international air carrier. Supervised 2,200 direct and indirect reports across parent company and 2 subsidiaries. Administered $550M budget.
- Reduced technology costs $120M over 2 years by implementing standardized technology infrastructure. Additionally facilitated $250M in added revenues.
- Delivered $150M in annual savings by introducing e-commerce strategy for all divisions.
- Improved efficiency by restructuring company's IT systems and implementing common processes, as well as leading strategic planning processes.
- Slashed costs $50M by resolving ongoing technical issues.

Director of Marketing Technologies (1994-1995)
Managed marketing-related global IT assets and systems, including sales, reservations, revenue management, fleet, route planning, and consumer affairs. Administered $85M budget and oversaw staff of 200.
- Produced $125M in annual savings and cut staffing costs $25M by implementing company's internet and electronic ticketing systems.
- Facilitated $750M in new revenue while saving company $840M over 3 year period, by launching $18M revenue management system and $50M aircraft routing system.
- Introduced company's first corporate database, resulting in improved accuracy.

System Manager & Manager of Marketing Technologies (1990-1994)
Corporate Forecaster (1984-1990)
Senior Analyst/Senior Programmer (1981-1984)

EDUCATION & TRAINING

BS in Applied Psychology, Georgia Institute of Technology, Atlanta, GA

Executive Management courses, The Wharton School, Philadelphia, PA

CONTROLLER, CPA

Street Address • City, State 11022 • (555) 555-1212 • name@emailaddress.com

PROFILE

Talented and accomplished Finance professional with background in Accounting, Business Finance, and Auditing. Proven ability to oversee all corporate financial operations. Certified Public Accountant with previous experience as corporate auditor. Adept at budgeting, forecasting, business analysis, project management, risk management, and general business operations.

PROFESSIONAL EXPERIENCE

COMPANY NAME, City, CA   2002 – Present
Controller / Project Manager
Manage daily business operations, including finance, human resources, marketing, and on-going projects for $7 million contracting firm. Supervised and trained staff of 10. Oversee accounting, including accounts payable and receivable. Prepare and administer $4M annual budget. Perform forecasting and financial reporting. Prepare and submit project bids, review project plans, and deliver price estimates. Direct complete project life cycles.

- Reduced costs. Selected and approved sub-contractors and negotiated agreements.
- Increased total revenue from $3.5M to $7M by increasing marketing and improving services.
- Streamlined expenses 15% by implementing standardized controls and reducing staff.
- Negotiated new contracts with vendors and service providers to increase profitability.

INTERNATIONAL ACCOUNTING FIRM, City, CA   1999 – 2002
Senior Auditor
Performed financial audits and due diligence of client base consisting primarily of biotechnology and software firms. Ensured compliance with all SEC regulations.

- Ranked Number One in Class for 2001 and 2002.
- Audited internal controls, reviewed finances, and led investigations to support IPO actions.

EDUCATION

BS in Business Administration, San Diego State University, San Diego, CA (2000)

- Emphasis in Accounting. Completed Internship with PriceWaterhouseCoopers in 1999

LICENSURE

Certified Public Accountant (2002)

COMPUTER SKILLS

Windows, MS Office, Lotus Notes, QuickBooks, MasterBuilder, proprietary accounting software

AFFILIATIONS

American Institute of Certified Public Accountants (AICPA)

CONSTRUCTION EXECUTIVE

Avenue ▪ City, Washington 99352 ▪ (555) 555-5555 ▪ name@verizon.net

Construction Management ▪ Site Services ▪ Facilities Management ▪ Field Engineering

Talented and accomplished management professional with international background in site services, field engineering, construction engineering, work control, contractor oversight, and quality control. Highly familiar with acceptance inspection and turnover/startup activities relating to industrial facilities and systems. Superior project management, planning, leadership, and budget control skills.

▪ Service Management	▪ Contractor Oversight	▪ Field Engineering	▪ Quality
▪ Construction Engineering	▪ Budget/Cost Control	▪ Compliance	▪ Automation
▪ Facilities Management	▪ Strategic Planning	▪ Heavy Equipment	▪ Security
▪ Project Management	▪ Document Control	▪ Turnover/Start Up	▪ HVAC

PROFESSIONAL EXPERIENCE

COMPANY 1, INC., City, WA   1996 – Present
Site Services Manager (2000-present)
Direct multiple departments and operations for billion-dollar supplier of construction services for US government. Support industrial nuclear construction for Dept. of Energy. Oversee heavy equipment, light fleet, construction facilities, document and quality control, construction survey, and subsurface investigations, among other areas. Supervise 16 persons in document control, QC, facilities management, equipment management, inspections, and environmental compliance. Administer $2.8M budget.

- Successfully led more than 600 projects per year since 2000.
- Improved efficiency by implementing use of High Definition 3D Laser Surveying technology.
- Achieved equivalent of 56 employee years with zero lost time accidents.
- Consistently maintained work volume while overall construction organization business dropped 70%, by identifying potential markets with other site organizations and offering new services.
- Introduced use of close tolerance survey techniques to detect minor movement in nuclear facilities.
- Reduced costs by negotiating contracts with multiple heavy equipment vendors.
- Effectively managed 200-unit Government Services Administration light fleet pool, including billings, payments, and vehicle maintenance. Reduced fleet 30% with no loss of service to projects.
- Oversaw maintenance for 50,000 sq. ft. in construction, storage, and office facilities across 7 areas.
- Cut costs by closing 35 facilities and eliminating 35,000 sq. ft. of poorly-utilized space.
- Managed procurement, calibration, and failure resolution for measurement and test equipment.

Project Control Engineer (1998-2000)
Carried out work breakdown structure management, cost analyses, accrual processing, and management reporting for Spent Nuclear Fuels Project Office. Facilitated on-going project involving removal of weapons-grade nuclear reactor fuel assemblies from underwater storage basins.

- Improved efficiency by developing SQL-based interface that reduced keyboard entry volumes.

Project Control Systems Administrator (1998-2000)
Selected to take over and development and administration of cost and performance measurement system project. Performed system development, modifications, data evaluation, configuration management.

- Turned around failing project. Eliminated scope creep and cost overruns, implemented functionalities, and completed data transfers. Coordinated 40-person team.

(Company 1, continued)

Construction Technology Engineer (1996-1998)
Oversaw development, maintenance, and technical improvement for multiple automation and software development projects. Evaluated new technologies. Identified areas for field services improvement. Performed technical training.

- Selected and implemented barcode scanning system for construction craft time distribution data management. System deployed to 450 personnel at 7 project office locations.
- Managed modifications to craft payroll system to facilitate batch loading of field data.
- Led implementation of equipment calibration tracking system and welder qualification database.

COMPANY 2, City, WA   1990 – 1996
Construction Engineer
Managed and/or carried out construction engineering, field engineering, work planning, contract management, software development, security system configuration management, document control, and other projects/activities for Dept. of Energy. Lead Field Engineer for projects involving tank farm construction, building construction, salt well tank upgrades, alarm system implementation, and more. Performed inspections, testing, system start-ups, design modification, and more. Recruited and supervised up to 26 contract employees.

- Managed field engineering, testing, and start-up of new fire alarm system for 275 facilities.
- Directed construction of 8-million-gallon radioactive waste storage tank farm.
- Oversaw construction of nuclear materials packaging and evaluation facility, including security systems, instrumentation, electrical systems, HVAC, and fire detection systems.
- Supervised installation of specialized monitoring systems for radioactive waste storage tank farm.
- Led installation of alarm and security systems for plutonium finishing plant.

EDUCATION

Graduate, Electronics Technician Program, Missouri Institute of Technology/DeVry Institute

PROFESSIONAL DEVELOPMENT

Training: The Kerzner Approach to Project Management Excellence, Project Planning, Safety Leadership, Change Impact and Claim Management, Writing Project Scopes, Construction Quality Management for Contractors, Proposing Client Solutions, Total Quality Management, Configuration Management

Inspection Certifications: Electrical, Instrumentation, Fire Detection, Nondestructive Leak Testing

TECHNICAL SKILLS

MS Office, Access, Project, Visio, SQL Server, Lotus Notes, Primavera Project Planner (P3), Visual Basic, Allen Bradley Programmable Logic Controllers

ADDITIONAL INFORMATION

Security Clearance: Dept. of Defense Secret Security Clearance

Affiliations: Project Management Institute (PMI)

DENTIST

5138 address street		Cell: (555) 555-5555
Major City, CA 12345	name@yahoo.com	Tel: (555) 555-5555

SUMMARY

Talented and accomplished general dentist with comprehensive background in restorative, surgical, and diagnostic dentistry. Award-winning academic background and five years of professional experience. Expertise in periodontal and periapical surgery, extractions, endodontics, and more. Outstanding research abilities. Excellent patient care, analysis, and business skills.

EDUCATION

University of Southern California, City, CA
Doctor of Dental Surgery (2000)
- Completed Internship in Oral Surgery at County Hospital
- Elective concentration in Implant Dentistry
- Ranked in 95th Percentile. Dean's List Student.
- Recipient of Award of Excellence in Dental Education
- Outstanding Preclinical Tutor Award

California State University, Northridge, CA
B.S. in Chemistry (1995)
- Dean's List Student
- Sigma Xi Research Award; CSU Foundation Scholarship recipient
- Completed graduate course work in Chemistry (1995-1996)

PROFESSIONAL BACKGROUND & ACCOMPLISHMENTS

- Founded and operate three successful dental practices since 2002, including rural practice.
- Provide complete dental services, from general dentistry to oral surgery.
- Conduct surgical procedures such as periodontal surgery, periapical surgery, vestibuloplasty, implant placement, and tori removal. Perform endodontic and restorative procedures.
- Carry out surgical extractions and removal of impacted third molars.
- Hire, train, and supervise associate dentists, dental assistants, and administrative personnel.
- Manage billing, purchasing, leasing, quality and safety, and general finances.
- Achieved revenue increases for all locations on consistent, year-to-year basis.

EMPLOYMENT HISTORY

Owner/Dentist, **Dental Group**, City, CA	2004-Present
Associate Dentist, **Dentist 1**, City, CA	2002-2003
Associate Dentist, **Dentist 2**, City, CA	2001-2002
Associate Dentist, **Dentist 3**, City, CA	2001-2002

TECHNICAL SKILLS

Word, Excel, billing programs, dental practice management software, Internet

EDITOR

Some Ave. • City, State 12345 • (555) 555-5555 • name@hotmail.com

Business Management • Editing/Publishing • Sales • Marketing • Customer Relations

~ SUMMARY OF QUALIFICATIONS ~

- Talented Business Management Professional with additional skills in Sales and Editorial operations.
- Proven ability to produce major increases in sales, profitability, and customer satisfaction.
- Adept at improving efficiency and productivity through effective utilization of technologies.
- Strong background in retail includes store management, sales, and customer service.
- Hard working, detail oriented, and able to multi-task effectively. Excellent problem-solving skills.

~ PROFESSIONAL EXPERIENCE ~

COMPANY 1, city, state   2005 – Present
Co-Founder & Editor-in-Chief
Established and manage specialty press publishing company. Designed and implemented all business practices and procedures. Recruited, trained, and supervise staff. Oversee all business operations.
- Edited 3 annual volumes of fiction, quarterly print magazine, and several websites.
- Achieved exceptional reputation for quality and performance in highly competitive market.
- Grew business to profitability during period of extreme industry downturn.
- Frequently represent company at industry events and deliver presentations on publishing and writing.

COMPANY 2, city, state   2000 – 2005
Assistant Manager
Directed daily operations for technology, cellular, satellite retail establishment. Managed sales, ordering, inventory, account management, and customer service.
- Consistently met or exceeded assigned goals in sales while minimizing shrinkage.
- Recognized for achieving exceptional levels of customer satisfaction.

COMPANY 3, city, state   1997 – 2000
Data Entry Clerk
Carried out data entry for 2 separate agencies. Performed extensive fact checking.
- Improved efficiency and productivity by assisting with office conversions to paperless filing systems.

CAREER NOTES: Previously drove Military Transport Vehicle for AIT Base in Ft. Huachuca (1994-1997).

~ EDUCATION & TRAINING ~

Extensive course work in English & Journalism - University of Michigan and Mott Community College

~ COMPUTER SKILLS ~

MS Office, web development, publishing software

Electrician

29 Wildwood Court • City, NY 12345 • (123) 456-7890 • name@yahoo.com

Talented Electrical Site Superintendent and Electrical Oversight Manager

• 15-plus years of professional experience.	• Expertise in site evaluation and monitoring.
• History of completing projects ahead of schedule.	• Adept at installation and decommissioning.
• Superior record of site safety and quality.	• Excellent team building and leadership skills.

PROFESSIONAL EXPERIENCE

VERY LARGE POWER PLANT, City, CT   2009 – Present
Electrical General Foreman (2005-present)
Contracted through electrical union to oversee electrical subcontractors and electrical craftsman in decommissioning of nuclear power plant. Plan, organize, and facilitate electrical planning, site planning, daily job scheduling, and site safety. Manage the removal of telephone, computer, and all electrical power cables from 160 volt down. Supervise 6 to 90 electricians on multiple projects.

- Delivered six million man-hours with no lost-time accidents since initiation of decommissioning.
- Delivered dramatic cost savings by planning, designing, and leading conversion of permanent generators into mobile generators to provide temporary power during back out procedures.

Foreman / Planner / Electrician (1999-2004)
Oversaw and carried out all electrical shutdown of buildings, and assurance of building readiness for demolition. Provided contracted services for several electrical contracting companies/union. Led the installation of temporary power, light, phones, and computers to facilitate migration/relocation of active areas during backing out of electrical and underground conduit systems.

- Improved efficiency and productivity by reviewing plans and blueprints and identifying ways to reduce man-hours by streamlining/adjusting project plans and activities.
- Enhanced safety by ensuring all personnel properly training and certified in appropriate government and safety procedures. Maintained compliance with all OSHA regulations.
- Recognized for preventing any unscheduled interruption of critical systems.
- Completed more than 378 work plans on or ahead of schedule per year.

ENGINEERING COMPANY, City, CT   2005 – 2009
Foreman
Supervised crew of 12 as Night Foreman at Millstone Point nuclear power plant. Led modification of motorized valves. Maintained electrical systems. Ran crew that laid out electrical distribution panels and installed all electrical for construction of office building and laboratories for pharmaceutical firm.

PREVIOUS EXPERIENCE

Owner, Name & Son Electrical Contractors, City, CT   1999 – 2005

TRAINING & EDUCATION

Licensed Master Electrician, State of Connecticut
OSHA Training; CPR Training

TECHNICAL SKILLS

MS Office, Internet, blueprint interpretation, job/safety inspections

IT EXECUTIVE

Address • City, FL 12345 • (305) 555-1212 • name@email.com

SENIOR TECHNOLOGY EXECUTIVE
Vice President, Chief Information Officer, Executive Director

Extensive record of success in the management of corporate IT operations. Consistent history of directing successful department and program operations. Proven ability to reduce costs, increase efficiency, and improve profitability. Special expertise in lowering capital expenditures through upgrading of existing systems, providing effective technology solutions, and performing strategic planning. Outstanding problem solving skills.

Core Competencies:

Strategic Planning • Contract Negotiations • P&L Management • Cost Control
Productivity Improvement • Feasibility Studies • Project Life Cycle Management
Vendor Relations • Capital Purchases • Budget Administration • Team Building

PROFESSIONAL EXPERIENCE

COMPANY NAME, City, FL   2005 – Present
Director of Information Technology
Oversee IT operations for a large non-profit organization, including re-alignment of technology and business strategies, capital purchases, project planning and implementation, and more. Supervise 6 direct and 79 indirect reports. Manage support for 270 end users.

- **Saved $670,000 in labor costs and reduced order-to-fulfillment times 50%** by implementing a program to automate mail processing.
- **Increased efficiency** and streamlined functions by re-organizing purchasing function and integrating purchasing, manufacturing, and distribution departments.
- **Improved inventory control accuracy** by migrating legacy system to MS Dynamics.
- **Grew revenue 21% ($500,000)** by developing effective e-commerce strategy.
- **Reduced training costs 10%** by introducing webinar program.

COMPANY NAME, City, FL   1996 – 2005
Director of Management Information Systems
Managed all information and technology operations for 362-bed acute care facility, including data center, MIS, telecommunications, PBX, and Biomedical departments. Supervised up to 44 persons. Administered a $3.5M budget. Prepared strategic information management plan. Oversaw all network and desktop support, upgrades, help desk operations, and projects.

- **Delivered $2M in savings** by migrating from an analog to a digital telecom system.
- **Recovered $1M in unbilled revenue** by identifying a flaw in the billing system.
- **Reduced expenses $400,000** by consolidating data center operations for 2 hospitals.
- **Saved $110,000** per year in telecom costs by implementing site-to-site VPN solution.

EDUCATION

BS in Health Services Administration, Florida International University, Miami, FL

TECHNICAL SKILLS

MS Office, Project, Visio, Flash, MS Dynamics, SharePoint, RTL Lawrence, Systems Security & Disaster Recovery, Network Support & Integration, Technology Infrastructure

GRADUATE STUDENT

12 Drive • City, NY 12345 • (555) 555-5555 • name@yahoo.com

Masters in Forensic Psychology with professional background in counseling

~ SUMMARY OF QUALIFICATIONS ~

- ➢ Extensive academic training in psychology and forensic psychology.
- ➢ Professional experience in peer counseling, education, and assistance.
- ➢ Clinical background in drug & alcohol rehabilitation setting.
- ➢ Expertise in research, data management, and report preparation.
- ➢ Hard working, detail oriented, and able to multi-task effectively.
- ➢ Excellent problem-solving, communication, and counseling skills.

~ EDUCATION ~

MA in Forensic Psychology (2015)
JOHN JAY COLLEGE OF CRIMINAL JUSTICE, New York, NY
- **Course work:** Psychology & Law, Psychopathology, Psychology of Criminal Behavior, Psychology of Terrorism, Psychology of the Victim, Personality Assessment 2 & 3 (MMPI-2 and Rorschach testing), Key Concepts in Psychotherapy, Advanced Psychology of Personality, Crisis Intervention, Alcohol & Drug Use, Research Design and Methods.

BA in Psychology, minors in Business & Education (2013)
STATE UNIVERSITY OF NEW YORK, Albany, NY
- Courses included Abnormal Psychology, Sexual & Physical Abuse, Sensation & Perception, Childhood Behavior, Theory & Practice of Peer Counseling, Industrial Organizational Psychology.
- Completed training program in peer hotline counseling. Responded to calls and provided education on multi-cultural and diversity issues, crisis management, alcohol & substance abuse, STDs, rape, eating disorders, suicide, and more. Provided information on outside resources.
- Served as Research Assistant for Anxiety Disorder Laboratory. Conducted telephone interviews, prepared subject files, and entered data into SPSS database.
- Graduated Cum Laude; Dean's List student.

~ EXPERIENCE ~

Extern, COMMUNITY HOSPITAL, City, NY   2007
- Completed externship at hospital's New Directions Inpatient Unit.
- Participated in morning review and treatment team meetings. Conducted biopsychosocial interviews.
- Facilitated/co-facilitated group therapy sessions. Researched and assisted with patient aftercare.
- Developed familiarity with psychopharmaceuticals and treatment usage. Observed psychiatric assessments and pre-admission inquiries. Assisted with preparation of individual treatment plans.
- Observed patients in mental health unit and ran current events group.

~ COMPUTER SKILLS ~

Connections, Outlook, Lewis Live, Word, Excel, PowerPoint, SPSS, PsychInfo, Internet

GRAPHIC DESIGN MANAGER

12345 Street Name • Big Town, VA 12345 • 123-456-7890 • name@companyname.com

Senior Graphic Designer • Creative Director • Graphic Design Manager

PROFILE

Highly accomplished, nationally-recognized Creative Director and Senior Graphic Designer with proven ability to facilitate corporate success, consistently meet all client demands, and deliver creative solutions in branding, marketing, promotions, and strategic advertising. Experienced at supporting large corporations, government agencies, and non-profit organizations. Adept at building and leading effective teams. Excellent presentation, negotiation, relationship management, and problem-solving skills.

Areas of Expertise

Graphic Design Management • Solution Design • Corporate Branding • Project Management
Production Management • Logo Design • Page Layout Design • Trade Show Display Design
Team Building • Budget & Cost Control • Identity Design • Email Marketing • Leadership

PROFESSIONAL EXPERIENCE

COMPANY 1, Big City, VA   2000 - Present
Creative Director / Owner
Established and manage design studio and advertising agency servicing client base that includes The White House, Dept. of Education, Dept. of Labor, American Insurance Assoc., Piedmont Foundation, Kingdom of Saudi Arabia, Arthritis Foundation, Sky Jet, Qorvis Communications, and many others. Oversee all business operations. Supervise senior-level freelance creative and design specialists, copywriters, and print production houses on projects. Administered budgets as large as $500,000.

- Achieved profitability in first year and grew sales by expanding services offered to include marketing campaigns, identity design, email marketing, and brand development.
- Recognized by First Lady Laura Bush as instrumental in "...the creation and completion of the brochure about UNESCO called Forging a New Partnership of Hope."
- Worked with office of First Lady Laura Bush on creating and producing brochure to assist US government communicate national goals as returning member of United Nations Education Science and Cultural Organization (UNESCO).
- Designed and product national public service ad campaigns to help rebuild relationships between US and Saudi Arabia. Ads ran in all major newspapers and magazines, including New York Times, Washington Post, USA Today, People, and Newsweek.
- Designed all conference materials for Secretary of Labor Elaine Chao's highly acclaimed 'Children in the Crossfire' campaign to prevent and rehabilitate child soldiers.
- Completed projects for HUD, FHA, National Council for Advanced Manufacturing, GenePool Creative, The True Studio, The Washington Health Club, and others.

COMPANY 2, Herndon, VA   1997 - 2000
Art Director
Oversaw all design, conceptualization, and project management activities for full-service advertising agency specializing in strategy planning, branding, research, media planning, creative development, PR, and direct response advertising. Supervised up to 4 pre-press production assistants and coordinated project teams. Worked on campaigns and projects as large as several million dollars.

- Created print and collateral materials for Fortune 500 companies.
- Co-designed ADDY Honorable Mention-winning Tiger Talk Phone Cards for ExxonMobil.
- Created winning logo for Amtrak's Pacific Surfliner brand. Campaign increased ridership 15% by rebranding to target college students and young adults.
- Earned recognition on multiple occasions for innovation and creativity.
- Completed projects for Dynacorp, EDS, GTSI, Litton/PRC, Marriott, Qwest Communications, and US Postal Service, among others.

PREVIOUS EXPERIENCE

COMPANY 3, Plano, TX   1995 - 1997
Still Image Production / Photographer
Supported success of B2B marketing communications by producing, managing, performing, and editing photography for internal marketing campaigns. Cataloged images and created image libraries. Published image libraries to corporate broadcasting sites. Produced and edited >100 images per day.

EDUCATION

Associates of Visual Communications, The Art Institute of City, City, State
- Course work included Corporate Identity, Advertising, Desktop Publication, Packaging Design, Trade Show Design, Typography, and Photography

TECHNICAL SKILLS

Windows, Mac OS, MS Office, Photoshop, Illustrator, InDesign, Quark Xpress, Acrobat, QuickBooks Pro

ADDITIONAL INFORMATION

Portfolio: www.companyname.com

Community Involvement: Production of charity event marketing/promotions

HOME CARE PROVIDER

344 Street ▪ City, NY 12345 ▪ 555-555-5555 ▪ name@yahoo.com

Experienced residential care provider seeking to transition into home care provider position

SUMMARY OF QUALIFICATIONS

➢ Several years of experience as residential counselor in long-term care environment.
➢ Able to care for disabled patients according to home care regulations.
➢ Familiar with administering medications and implementing behavioral plans.
➢ Adept at maintaining clean, safe conditions for clients.
➢ Hard working, detail oriented, and able to multi-task. Excellent communication skills.

PROFESSIONAL EXPERIENCE

HEALTH CARE ORGANIZATION, City, NY   2005 – Present
Residential Counselor
Monitor and care for clients at long-term care facility. Responsible for up to 10 clients.
• Implement and document client behavior plans and ensure compliance at all times.
• Administer medications and work with clients on independent living and social skills.
• Help develop and implement recreational plans for individuals and groups.
• Carry out training and mentoring of newly-hired home care workers.

PREVIOUS EMPLOYMENT

Counselor, HOSPITAL 1, City, NY   2004
Counselor, HOSPITAL 2, City, CT   1990 – 2003

CERTIFICATIONS & EDUCATION

Home Care Medicine Administration
SKIP (Patient Handling)
General Studies, Gateway Community College, New Haven, CT

COMPUTER SKILLS

MS Word, data entry systems, Internet

HUMAN RESOURCES MANAGER, SPHR

1941 Boulevard, #5 ● City, MN 12345
555-555-5555 ● name@hotmail.com

SUMMARY

Seeking **Human Resources Director or Manager** position where 10+ years of experience will add value. Track record of routinely implementing human resources goals and strategies, along with increasing employee performance and retention by resourcefully balancing human resources.

PROFILE

- Strong **human resources** background includes improving benefits and health programs, employee relations, compensation, benefits, training, EEO, FMLA safety programs, and compliance.
- **Improved recruiting and retention** at Company 1 by working with managers on recruiting, advertising, interviewing, and offers.
- Cut workers comp claims 80% in 60 days as **HR Manager** (2004-2005). Increased retention by updating compensation for 150 positions as **HR Manager/Generalist** (2001-2003).
- Met 100% of goal for reduced absenteeism and developed effective management training program in 60 days, as **Senior HR Generalist** (2005-2006).
- **CEO said**: "With our growth came the challenge of goals, employee relations, coaching and counseling, training, recruiting and hiring top performers for a variety of positions. Lori successfully met that challenge and worked very closely with our upper management team." (2005)

EXPERIENCE

Senior Human Resources Manager: COMPANY 1, City, MN (2006-2008).
Oversaw HR operations for engineering, planning, and design services company. Actively involved in long-range HR planning and budget development. Managed compliance, 401(k) plan functions, employee relations, compensation, benefits, recruiting, retention, and other activities. Supervised HR specialists.

- Implemented compliance with all legal employment requirements, including EEO/AAP, OSHA, FMLA, ADA, HIPPA, and more, for headquarters and all branch offices.
- Updated and maintained job descriptions for all positions within company.
- Improved recruiting and retention by working with managers on recruiting, advertising, interviewing, and offers. Also led recruiting of interns and recent graduates.
- Assisted with college career fail program management each year.
- Increased employee satisfaction by designing and updating Benefits and Wellness program.
- Directed 401(k) program. Worked closely with 401(k) Board of Trustees and plan administrator to improve communication of information to employees. Held quarterly and one-on-one meetings.

Sr. Human Resources Generalist/Manager: COMPANY 2, City, MN (2005-2006).
Knowledgeable with employee relations, training, coaching and counseling. Supported corporate and branch offices. Supervised Human Resources Staff.

- As the senior HR professional, worked with upper management on strategic planning and related issues for this firm, with 260 employees in 24 locations nationwide. Reported to the CFO.
- Created policies and procedures to enable 25% growth in staffing, to 325 by end of 2006.
- **Organized and improved** employee relations, performance management, coaching and counseling efforts. Developed online employee handbook accessible to all 24 branches.
- Developed and led training on executive leadership, sexual harassment and other issues.

Senior Human Resources Manager: COMPANY 3, City, MN (2004-2005).
Planned and supervised all HR for this manufacturer. Managed employee relations, coaching and counseling, critical hiring, monthly training, benefits administration and company safety program, for 200 employees in three locations.

- **Formalized and greatly improved all HR policies and procedures**, including explanation and documentation of employee conduct, to improve staff performance and avoid litigation.
- **Increased employee Benefits/Wellness and Retention** by developing new Wellness Program that met employee, management, and company needs. In regards to Retention, developed system to meet with supervisors, managers, and employees monthly to recognize outstanding staff performance.
- Created and delivered leadership training for 10 upper managers that met all goals.
- **Reduced workers compensation claims 80%** in 60 days while managing safety committee.

Human Resources Manager/Generalist: COMPANY 4, City, MN (2001-2003).
Provided wide range of HR services for this firm, with 225 employees in MN and CA. Served on executive management team. Played key role in strategic planning. Supervised team of two employees.

- Planned and managed policies, procedures, employee handbooks, coaching/counseling, and safety committee. Met or exceeded all performance goals. Ensured compliance with all employment laws.
- Rapidly recruited and hired nearly 100 employees, from entry- to executive level.
- Maximized performance, retention and corporate profits by researching and updating compensation guidelines and job descriptions for 150 positions in 60 days.

Human Resources Generalist/Recruiter: COMPANY 5, City, TX (2000-2001).
Handled projects to fill positions nationwide in HR and recruiting role.

- Met aggressive quotas for placing 10-20 candidates per month.

Human Resources Recruiter/Generalist: COMPANY 6, City, MN (1999-2000).
Provided wide range of placement/HR efforts. Maximized performance levels by creating rewards and recognition programs. Recruited qualified candidates to fill positions from entry-level to executive.

Human Resources/Corporate Recruiter: COMPANY 7, City, MN (1997-1999).
Supported rapid growth at more than 45 locations by designing and setting up corporate relocation process. Also created effective training programs for employee and managers.

EDUCATION/TRAINING

- Senior Professional in Human Resources (SPHR), Society for Human Resource Management (SHRM)
- Seminar, 'Latest in Benefits & Wellness Programs'
- Seminar by Donald Trump, 'How to Become a Great Leader'

ADDITIONAL INFORMATION

- **Professional memberships**: SHRM and TCHRA.
- **Computer skills**: MS Office, Access, PeopleSoft, Ceridian. Lotus Notes, and Restrac.
- **Volunteer work** includes Big Brothers/Big Sisters and American Cancer Society.

INTELLIGENCE OFFICER

Drive ▪ City, PA 12345 ▪ 555-555-5555 ▪ name@comcast.net

SENIOR SECURITY MANAGEMENT PROFESSIONAL
Security Chief – Intelligence Officer – Data Management Director – Security Director

Award-winning security professional with several years of military experience in intelligence gathering, analysis, and distribution. Active Top Secret / Sensitive Compartmented Information (TS/SCI) security clearance. Adept at preparing and delivering briefings, reports, presentations, and analysis summaries. Proven ability to improve operations, documentation, procedures, and team performance. Expertise in supporting and facilitating classified and high-profile military initiatives. Excel at building and leading top-performing teams. Excellent problem solving skills.

Core Competencies:
Security Operations – Force Protection – Strategic Planning – Compliance – Data Management
Scheduling – Problem Solving – Analysis – Security Audits & Evaluations – Information Security

PROFESSIONAL EXPERIENCE

MILITARY AGENCY, US / Germany   2005 – Present
Officer In Charge, Anti-Terrorism / Force Protection (2008-present)
Administer key intel support for leadership and personnel on all Antiterrorism Force Protection issues. Core member of Threat Working Group, Force Protection Working Group, and Squadron Anti-Terrorism team. Conduct analysis and research to provide critical intelligence support. Assist with audits and facilitate compliance with Unit, DoD, and Inspector General-level requirements.
- Provided vital intelligence support for Crisis Action teams overseas.
- Led unit to the Commander in Chief's Installation Excellence Award.

Officer in Charge (2007-2008)
Performed research, analysis, and dissemination of source intelligence. Prepared and delivered intelligence briefings. Authored weekly intelligence summaries with detailed threat analyses. Selected as Lead Briefer. Upgraded office network, computers, and connectivity. Falcon View expert. Managed COMSEC handling and storage security. Expertise in satellite communications utilization.
- Prepared 90 summary reports that played major role in facilitating decision-making process.
- Furnished situational awareness for overseas actions and helped guarantee aircrew safety.
- Led the creation of more than 40 intelligence briefs and maintained 100% compliance.
- Recognized for superior performance and rated as Extraordinary Systems Officer.

Intelligence Officer (2006)
Senior Intelligence Officer who provided vital intelligence to support Operation Enduring Freedom and Operation Iraqi Freedom missions out of Germany.
- Prepared and delivered over 100 pre-mission briefings for crews.
- Developed Escape and Evasion kits and Evasion Plan of Actions for combat missions.

Officer In Charge, Intelligence Mobility (2006)
Supported safety of $3.9B in assets. Managed airlift planning and scheduling, aircrew training, and combat tactics. Coordinated integration of intelligence. Monitored mobility readiness of 15 intelligence personnel for global deployability. Carried out control operations for 1.5 million sq. ft. base. Presented daily summaries and briefings on global military, political, and humanitarian developments. Led monthly tests of Deployable Intel Support Kits. Managed $123,000 annual budget. Supported $400,000 in computer equipment.
- Improved efficiency and system reliability by planning and coordinating exchange of secure telecom equipment, and by replacing outdated COMSEC equipment.
- Served as Purchase Card Billing Official for all squadron funds.

(Military Agency, continued)

Officer In Charge, Intelligence Systems (2005-2006)
Researched and analyzed intelligence data. Prepared reports. Supported over 4,900 personnel and $5.2B in equipment. Presented briefings and conducted debriefings. Assisted with management of $200,000 Automated Data Processing Equipment account. Provided intelligence for Presidential missions. Maintained worldwide deployability for wartime and contingency taskings. Managed planning, crew training, scheduling, and base operations. Conducted control operations. Served as Computer Systems Security Officer and maintained satellite communication equipment. Maintained 30 computers. Developed pre-inspection processes.

- Updated COMSEC procedures to ensure 100% compliance.
- Improved efficiency by upgrading computer equipment, office network, and connectivity.
- Led implementation of new intel systems to replace outdated equipment.
- Acted as temporary Squadron Security Manager. Handled security clearance processing for personnel. Maintained all COMSEC materials.

EDUCATION

MBA (Magna Cum Laude), Touro International University, Cypress, CA (2006)
BA in Political Science (Magna Cum Laude), Howard University, Washington, DC (2004)

PROFESSIONAL DEVELOPMENT

Air and Space Basic Course
T-Tail Intelligence Formal Training Unit
Intelligence Officer Course
Supervisor Safety Course
Department of Defense (DoD) Government Purchase Card
SORTS Data Handler
Security Manager Training
Air Force Training Course (Train the Trainer)

AWARDS & RECOGNITION

Outstanding Unit Award
National Defense Service Medal
Global War on Terrorism Service Medal
Training Ribbon
Company Grade Officer (CGO) of the Quarter (2006)
Outstanding Unit Compliance Inspection (UCI) Performance (2006)
Image Award (2006)

ADDITIONAL INFORMATION

Security Clearance: Active Top Secret / Sensitive Compartmented Information (TS/SCI)
Affiliations: Volunteer Victim Advocate, Sexual Assault Response Program
Technical Skills: MS Office, Deployable Intel Support Kit (DISK), Secure Telephone Equipment (STE), OMNI Secure Terminal, Communication Security (COMSEC), FalconView

INTERIOR DESIGNER
Address • Phone • email • website

Visionary designer with proven ability to transform spaces into
beautiful, functional, emotionally-pleasing environments

PROFILE

Creative designer with impeccable style and an eye for detail. Special expertise in interior design and redesign, space planning, and product selection that meet any and all customer styles and desires. Skilled at determining needs and developing innovative designs. Adept at researching materials and implementing cost-effective solutions to ensure compliance with project budgets. Multiple certifications, including NCIDQ, Certified Redesign Specialist and Certified Staging Specialist.

Core Competencies:

Interior Design/Redesign ~ Home Staging ~ Project Management ~ Negotiations
Space Planning ~ Painting ~ Window Treatments ~ Construction ~ Green Planning
Problem Solving ~ Budget & Cost Control ~ Customer Relations ~ Merchandising

PROFESSIONAL EXPERIENCE

COMPANY NAME, Salt Lake City, UT   1991 – Present
Owner / General Manager
Manage company specializing in interior redesign, home staging, garden design, relocation/move-in services, and color consultation. Maintain customer base in Utah, Rhode Island, Massachusetts, New Hampshire, Vermont, Connecticut, Washington, and Israel. Instructed interior design and gardening classes and workshops.

- Planned and completed redesign of living room, office space, foyer, bedrooms, and closets for client. Project included pain selection and reorganization of spaces with focus on elegance, comfort, and family-friendly environment.
- Carried out home staging for 2,000 sq. ft. residence that included design and construction of bathrooms, remodeling of living spaces, and repainting of interior and exterior. Residence sold in less than 6 weeks.
- Staged client's home in preparation for sale. Project included remodeling, plus purchase of new furniture and decorations while remaining within client's budget.
- Worked with high-profile landscape architects in Boston, creating home gardens and public landscapes throughout New England.

COMPANY NAME, New Hampshire / Vermont / Israel   1991 – 2005; 2009
Owner / Designer
Designed complex, artistic gardens and landscapes for commercial and residential customers. Managed complete project life cycles, from design to post-planting maintenance. Prepared technical drawings. Purchased all plants and materials. Supervised contractors. Exhibited at Vermont Flower Show.

- Lectured on horticulture and garden maintenance at schools, clubs, and on radio.

COMPANY NAME, Concord, MA   2003 – 2005
Design / Sales Associate
Designed closets and custom workstations for customers of boutique company. Additionally created floor and window displays for furniture and organization products.
- Maximized space utilization for customers through effective space organization.

COMPANY NAME, Cambridge, MA   2001
Design Intern / Assistant Photo Stylist
Worked closely with senior designer / business owner on design creation and interior redesign activities. Staged rooms for before and after photography of high profile residential and commercial renovation and design projects.

CAREER NOTES: Previously held positions of **Interior Designer** with **COMPANY NAME, Interior Designer/Assistant Project Manager** for **COMPANY NAME**, and **Interior Designer** at **COMPANY NAME**. Projects included construction of Sloan School of Management at MIT, and creating open concept space plans for large companies.

ADDITIONAL EXPERIENCE
Horticulture Staff Member, UNIVERSITY NAME (2010-2011). Maintain gardens and plantings at visitor center and greenhouse.

Design Assistant, COMPANY NAME, Wethersfield, CT (2009). Arranged flowers for special events. Set up store displays. Performed furniture refinishing.

EDUCATION
BFA in Interior Architecture, Rhode Island School of Design, Providence, RI
Extensive coursework in Interior Architecture, Color Theory, Art, Architecture, and Furniture History

CERTIFICATIONS
Certified Staging and Redesign Specialist, The Academy of Staging and Redesign
NCIDQ (Certificate Number 4668), National Certification for Interior Design
Massachusetts Certified Horticulturist

PROFESSIONAL ORGANIZATIONS
National Certification for Interior Design (NCIDQ)
Certified Staging Professionals
Color & Paint Professionals - International
Feng Shui Resource Exchange for Designers, Home Owners, Architects, &Builders
Interior Redesign, Decorating, and Real Estate Staging Professionals
NAPWL National Association of Professional Women in Landscape
Real Estate Staging Association-National

INTERNATIONAL CURRICULUM VITAE
Address • City • Country • Phone • Email

EXPERIENCE INFORMATION TECHNOLOGY EXECUTIVE

Talented and accomplished IT Executive with international experience in design, implementation, and management of infrastructures, enterprise architectures, information systems, and EDA tools. Proven expertise in directing security, network/system administration, helpdesk operations, telecom systems, ERP systems, and internal development functions. Adept at managing multiple teams across worldwide locations. Excellent problem solving, leadership, and negotiation skills.

EDUCATION
INSTITUTO SUPERIOR TÉCNICO / UNIVERSIDADE TÉCNICA DE LISBOA, Portugal
MBA in Electrical & Computer Engineering – Telecommunications & Electronics (1986)

KATHOLIEKE UNIVERSITEIT LEUVEN, Belgium
Bachelor's in Artificial Intelligence and Techniques for Automated Analogue Design

PROFESSIONAL EXPERIENCE
COMPANY 1, City, Portugal   2008 – 2015
Corporate Director of CAD & Technology / IT Infrastructure (2010–2015)
Director of Information & Design Support Systems (2009–2010)
Oversaw global security, network/system administration, helpdesk, infrastructure, and VoIP for this $105M semiconductor design IP company. Took on CAD and IT Infrastructure responsibilities in 2007. Supervised 30 engineers in Portugal, Poland, China, Belgium, and France. Administered $750,000 budget. Negotiated contracts with hardware, software, and service providers.

Operational Improvements:
- Evaluated and selected Electronic Design Automation (EDA) software tools.
- Led development/customization of >100 silicon process nodes design kits.
- Worked with engineering design to develop analog/mixed-signal design flow.
- Improved productivity by developing software tools to automate design flow.
- Enhanced efficiency by implementing process-oriented methodologies and facilitating successful ISO9001 certification of CAD processes.

Selected Achievements:
- Lowered EDA costs $500,000 by implementing usage control and optimization.
- Reduced infrastructure costs $1,400 per workstation by implementing open source/Linux environment and migrating engineering infrastructure to Linux.
- Grew infrastructure to keep pace with corporate growth across 7 global regions.
- Directed the Lisbon facilities, including all maintenance contracts.

International Curriculum Vitae • Page 2

(Company 1, continued)

Hardware Description Language Consultant (2008-2009)

Developed analog/mixed-signal Hardware Description Language (HDL) IP core models.

- Set up company's Verilog HDL (VHDL) modeling environment, which improved product quality and faster delivery of models to clients.

PREVIOUS EXPERIENCE

UNIVERSITY 1, City, Portugal   2007 - 2008

Assistant Professor

Instructed Computer Architecture and Operation Systems for telecommunications and informatics students. Developed and implemented UNIX/Linux Operating Systems curricula.

UNIVERSITY 2, City, Portugal   2005 - 2007

Research Assistant

Managed and administered computing infrastructure for CAD/CAM laboratory at national institute's Electronics department. Developed software for various research projects.

TRAINING & PROFESSIONAL DEVELOPMENT

Structured Project Management
Leading Organizations
Leading People
General Management

TECHNICAL SKILLS

Applications: MS Office, OpenOffice, NeoOffice, Exim, Glassfish, Oracle e-Business Suite, SAS, SQL Server, System Architect, CAD applications
Operating Systems: Windows, Linux, UNIX, Mac OS
Development Tools: C/C++/C-shell, Lisp, Java, Perl, Python, PHP, MySQL, Electronic Design Automation (EDA) tools (Cadence, Synopsys, MentorGraphics, Mathworks, Verilog)
Networking: VoIP, DHCP, LDAP, TCP/IP, basic network infrastructures & protocols

ADDITIONAL INFORMATION

Affiliations: IEEE
Languages: Portuguese, Spanish, English, French, Italian

INTERNATIONAL RÉSUMÉ

Street ▪ Milan, Italy 12345
Tel: +55 555 55 55 555 ▪ name@gmail.com

Java Architect ▪ IPTV Architect ▪Java Development ▪ Java Programming ▪ Project Manager

PERSONAL

Nationality: Italian
Marital Status: Single Male
Available for Relocation: Yes

QUALIFICATIONS

- More than 9 years of experience in project management and software development.
- Adept at directing complete software development life cycles.
- Excellent technical skills, including broadband, interactive TV, video-on-demand, entertainment services, video delivery platforms, set top box systems, and access systems.
- Able to liaison with operations, sales, customer service, QA, and other business units.
- Expertise in release management, quality methodologies, and distributed infrastructures.

PROFESSIONAL EXPERIENCE

COMPANY 1, Milan, Italy   2004 – Present
Project Manager
Oversee design and implementation of mobile services and platforms, videoconference applications, and home medical monitoring systems for company specializing in software development and system integration. Hire, train, and supervise team of 6 developers. Oversee complete software life cycles. Set schedules. Communicate extensively with clients and serve as liaison between clients and business groups. Direct design and development of enterprise architectures. Monitor projects to ensure client satisfaction.
- Project Manager for large mobile content provider. Direct architecture upgrades and implementations. Manage connections with mobile operators in multiple cities.
- Increased efficiency by re-engineering project management and tool development processes.
- Introduced new tools for software management and software release management.
- Reduced costs by improving productivity of development team without additional staff.

COMPANY 2, Milan, Italy   2003 – 2004
Project Manager
Directed group of 5 developers specializing in architecture design and implementation for IPTV services at major provider of voice, internet, and video services. Coordinated project teams as large as 20 persons.
- Led the development of IPTV software, including front end layer, content management, and backend layer. Integrated system with provisioning, billing, and CRM systems.
- Consistently met all milestones and budgets. Worked with marketing to hit release dates.
- Contributed to major revenue growth by facilitating company's 'triple play' offering.
- Recognized for increasing product expertise for multiple technical departments.

COMPANY 3, Milan, Italy   2001 – 2003
Java Developer
Carried out Java development for this start-up company. Designed B2B and B2C service applications for SMS and WAP-based mobile phones and PDAs.
- Developed chat, forum, poll, and directory services, plus SMS-based news and scheduling for conference attendees.

COMPANY 4, Milan, Italy   2000 – 2001
Developer
- Performed Java development of web applications, including web portals, e-commerce systems, CMS, and others. Served as Linux Server System Administrator.
- Designed and configured local networks and network services, including DNS, FTP, and NIS.
- Created internal project management web site for market research consulting company.
- Built company's network from scratch and carried out several improvements/upgrades.

EDUCATION

Computer Science Degree (BS equivalent), University of Milan, Milan, Italy (in progress)
High School Diploma, Liceo Scientifico Macchiavelli Segrate, Milan, Italy

PROFESSIONAL DEVELOPMENT

Enterprise Javabeans Programming
J2EE Platform
English Language Skills

TECHNICAL SKILLS

Operating Systems: Windows, Linux, UNIX

Applications: MS Office, Project, Visio

Development Tools: Java (ejb, jms, servlet, jndi, jsp, jsf, struts, midlet, awt/swing), J2EE Architecture, JavaScript, JBoss, Sun AS, Resin, Tomcat, Ant, CVS, Apache, Flash, OpenLDAP, XML, XSLT, HTML, MySQL, PHP, .NET, Eclipse IDE, UML, Object-Oriented Programming

Network Protocols: TCP/IP, UDP, SMTP, DNS, http, and more

LANGUAGES

Native Italian, conversational English, basic French

IT PROJECT MANAGER

Street Address • City, VA, 12345 • 123-555-5555 • name@yahoo.com

Project Management • IT Consulting • Senior Technical Lead • Program Management

PMI Project Management Professional (PMP) with 10 year record of proven success in program and project management, IT consulting, business development, technology implementation, team building, and software development. Special expertise in design, development, deployment, and management of J2EE and Web solutions. Adept at managing engagements and projects, leading effective teams, managing client relationships, and resolving technical issues.

Core Competencies:

Project Management • Engagement Control • IT Consulting • Client Relations • Strategic Planning
Software Development • Resource Management • Implementation Management • Forecasting
J2EE/Web Solutions • Budget/Cost Control • Business Development • Problem Solving

PROFESSIONAL EXPERIENCE

COMPANY 1, City, VA   2000 – Present
Program Manager (2005-present)
Key member of team that directs management of $12M National Science Foundation account for $3.4B global provider of management and technology consulting services. Carry out account planning & strategy, business development, engagement control, documentation management, financial administration, P&L management, project management, and staff training.
- Brought in $2.3M in sales by facilitating project wins through business case presentation.
- Increased engagement profitability from 5% to 11% through effective resource leadership.
- Enhanced efficiency by playing a major role in creation of project methodologies, project management planning templates, and on-boarding procedures.

Project Manager / Technical Architect (2007-present)
Hold responsibility for project planning, forecasting, assignments, technical architecture and design, technology product review, resources, client relations, status reports, and financial management. Supervise staff of 21. Manage removal and protection of SSN data in NSF systems and databases. Led the comprehensive evaluation, analysis, definition of roadmap, and cleansing of disparate systems.
- Managed updates of Client Server and J2EE applications using Sybase and Oracle databases to remove/replace/protect SSN data.
- Increased project revenue 37% by identifying additional work and obtaining client approvals.
- Facilitated $1.2M in new revenue by successfully completing implementation of NSF user identifications, leading to proposals for single source user authentication system.
- Member of team that earned Team Accomplishment Award from NSF.

Project Manager / Technical Architect (2006-2007)
Directed Rules Engine project for NSF. Managed evaluation, selection, acquisition, and implementation of COTS rules engine. Supervised staff of 12 and administered project budget. Oversaw complete project life cycle. Provided proof of concept for stakeholders.
- Utilized success of project to increase account penetration and open new opportunities.
- Cut project risk and maximized vendor support by proposing a license acquisition strategy.

Project Manager / Technical Lead (2004-2006)
Led the development and implementation of full cost tracking system for NSF Facilities. Supervised a staff of 9. Managed analyses of user group data and conversions of data.
- Identified a strategy to improve cost tracking while minimizing impact to other applications.
- Recognized for completing project within tight budget scope.
- Improved efficiency by implementing automated training instead of classroom training.

IT Project Manager • Page 2

(Company 1, continued)

Technical Lead / Lead Developer (2004-2006)
Provided technical leadership in developing J2EE application for Defense Contracts Management Agency (DCMA) to serve as interface for all of the agency's reporting tools. Utilized Oracle, Java Struts, JSP, and other technologies to create application. Implemented Cognos security.
- Increased revenue $125,000 for project by recommending new features approved by client.
- Completed a project providing users with integrated reporting management tools.

Lead Developer / Technical Lead (2002-2004)
Carried out project planning, task allocation, requirements gathering, technical architecting and design, implementation, QA, configuration, and support for project to develop application that allowed DCMA users to create learning plans, manage courses and course catalog, and track training. Supervised 5.
- Implemented workflow management and all client-required functionalities.
- Developed successful interfaces with other defense agencies' training applications.

Technical Lead / Lead Developer / Software Developer (2000-2002)
- Led the design and development of an IT Registration application for the US Army.
- Customized Java components for various applications and outside products for US Army.
- Held lead role in designing the prototype of the Army Smart Card application.
- Led the design/development of reports for Pennsylvania's Juvenile Tracking System.

COMPANY 2, City, VA   1998 – 2000
Graduate Assistant
- Played a major role in design and development of a Java-based job scheduling application used by several hospitals.
- Served as Web Application Developer for multiple projects.

EDUCATION

MS in Information Systems, George Mason University, Fairfax, VA
MBA in Marketing, Osmania University, India

CERTIFICATIONS & TRAINING

PMI Project Management Professional (PMP)
Sun Certified Java Programmer

TECHNICAL SKILLS

Java, Java Struts, JSP, Java Servlets, JavaScript, XML, HTML, Perl, SQL, PL/SQL, WebSphere, ATG Dynamo, Oracle 9i/10g, BEA WebLogic, Sun Application Server, Tomcat, JRun, Oracle, SQL Server, MS Office, Access, Sybase, MySql, Project

IT SUPPORT

Address here   Phone Number Here
City, State, Zip   Email Address Here

Help Desk Support • IT Administration • IT Support • Technical Services • IT Associate

SUMMARY OF QUALIFICATIONS

- Adept at supporting hardware, software, and network systems.
- Hold A+ and Network+ certifications.
- Familiar with providing telephone-based and desk-side user support.
- Well developed abilities in database management and network backup services.
- Proven ability to resolve hardware and software issues as first line of support.
- Excellent analysis, problem solving, customer service, and reporting skills.

TECHNICAL SKILLS

Operating Systems:	Windows 98-2003, DOS, Mac OS
Networking:	LAN/WAN, Ethernet, TCP/IP, ISDN, wireless, PING, NETSTAT, IPCONFIG, fiber optics, backup and recovery
Applications:	MS Office, Visio, antivirus software, firewalls, Ghost, Remedy
Development Tools:	Javascript, HTML, XML, Flash, Dreamweaver, Director, 3D Studio Max, Photoshop CS2, Illustrator, Premiere, Cool Edit Pro, Paint Shop Pro
Hardware:	PC / server assembly & repair, routers, switches, hubs, peripherals

PROFESSIONAL EXPERIENCE

IT ASSISTANT, Company Name, City, state   2006 – Present
Provide 1st-level telephone and desk side support for over 1,500 end users. Respond to 60 calls per day, on average. Track issues. Support Windows and Macintosh environments. Reset passwords and update profiles. Support MS Office. Monitor licensing and report on changes for desktop software.
- Improved cost control by implementing licensing database to track expiration dates.
- Administer average of $19,000 per month in Technology Dept. invoices.

IT ASSISTANT, Company Name, City, state   2005 – 2006
Managed foundation's website. Revised content and layout.
- Updated and maintained a 40,000-record membership database.
- Provided technical support, including password resets. Responded to inquiries.
- Held responsibility for network risk management, including daily server backups.

IT ASSISTANT, Company Name, City, state   2004 – 2005
Oversaw all facilities-related functions, including help desk and customer service.
- Set up and maintained client database. Scheduled and tracked work orders.
- Ordered supplies, arranged equipment rentals, prepared files and invoices.

EDUCATION

BSc in Media Technology, w/Honors, The University of Lincoln, Hull, UK (2004)

CERTIFICATIONS & TRAINING

Certifications: MCSA (in progress), A+, Network+
Training: Project Management, Multimedia Production, Professional Management

JANITOR (SENIOR CUSTODIAL)

18 Bigheart Drive • Small City, NY 11111 • (123) 456-7890 • name@aol.com

Highly talented and accomplished Custodial professional with extensive experience managing custodial and janitorial services and teams for public school systems

SUMMARY

20 years of increasingly responsible custodial positions in New York State public school systems. Proven ability to oversee all custodial and maintenance functions and teams at the school level. Highly familiar with building and grounds maintenance. Custodian III eligible. Comprehensive expertise in maintaining buildings, grounds, facilities, and equipment. Knowledgeable in heating / air conditioning / ventilation systems, mechanical systems, and basic plumbing, carpentry, and electrical work. Able to train and supervise effective crews. Award-winning background with excellent communication skills.

PROFESSIONAL BACKGROUND & ACCOMPLISHMENTS

- Served as Head Custodian at Elementary School and High School.
- Trained and supervised teams of up to 10 persons, including Custodian I, Custodial Workers, and Custodial Cleaners. Coordinated day and evening maintenance and cleaning crews.
- Oversaw and performed maintenance of boilers, restrooms, electrical systems, heating / air conditioning systems, and all pumps, motors, and compressors.
- Carried out all daily, weekly, and monthly scheduled equipment and building maintenance.
- Assigned and / or completed necessary electrical, plumbing, and building / grounds repairs as needed, as well as general carpentry, painting, and improvements.
- Managed building security systems, ensuring proper alarm functionality. Conducted safety inspections, fire drills, and police-arranged walkthroughs. Played active role in preparation and practice of bomb threat and bioterrorism drills and procedures.
- Maintained parking areas, including plowing, salting, and other weather-related functions.
- Prepare buildings and grounds for inclement weather conditions and conduct inspections for
- Monitor staff and contracted company work to ensure proper completion of general maintenance and special construction projects.
- Recipient of multiple awards and letters of recognition for Outstanding Performance.

EMPLOYMENT HISTORY

Head Custodian / Custodian II, Elementary School, City, NY (2000-Present)
Custodian, High School, City, NY (1993-2000)

EDUCATION, TRAINING, AND CERTIFICATIONS

- Certifications: Custodian II, Custodian III
- Education: Graduate, Small City High School
- Training: Custodial Maintenance, OSHA Safety Training, Boiler Operator's Workshop, Supervising & Managing People, Facilities Workshop, Asbestos Awareness. Electricity I

AWARDS & RECOGNITION

- Letter of Appreciation for Performance Above Exepectations, Central School District
- Award for Dedication, Commitment, and Performance, Superintendent, Central School District

MEDIA BUYER

3220 Panthers Trace • Decatur, GA 30034 • 404-468-5628 • hillarydukes@gmail.com

Media Buyer • Media Planner • Account Executive • Sales Executive • Account Management

SUMMARY OF QUALIFICATIONS

➢ Talented and award-winning business professional with extensive background in sales, media buying and coordination, and account management.

➢ Proven ability to develop and grow profitable relationships with customers and media outlets.

➢ Consistently enhanced profits through effective negotiation of rates and available space.

➢ Recognized for extensive record of increasing sales and exceeding all sales goals.

➢ Outstanding customer service, problem solving, negotiation, and relationship management skills.

➢ Background includes familiarity with wide variety of industries, from fashion to automotive.

PROFESSIONAL EXPERIENCE

COMPANY 1, City, GA   2006 – Present

Media Coordinator / Buyer, New Strategic Marketing (2008-present)

Purchase media space for in-house advertising agency. Communicate and negotiate extensively with newspapers, radio stations, billboard companies, and direct mail outlets. Utilize research and analysis to maximize space selection while minimizing paid rates. Assist with production of creative art for media spaces. Monitor ads. Provide updates to clients. Evaluate campaign effectiveness. Administer budget ranging from $65,000 to $100,000 for 2 locations.

- Saved $20,000 in 2008 to date, through effective negotiation of rates.
- Recognized for increasing ROI and profitability by improving campaign effectiveness.
- Enhanced ad and campaign success through careful analysis of customer and market trends.

Customer Relations Manager (2006-present)

Dealer Representative for multiple locations, investigating and resolving customer issues as escalation point after sales and service personnel and facility managers. Communicate with customers in person and via phone. Work in conjunction with dealership managers to identify and resolve issues.

- Established policies and procedures to improve customer satisfaction levels.
- Increased profitability by alleviating issues that would have led to lost sales.
- Achieved major increases in customer satisfaction (built one dealership to 'A' level).
- Introduced use of customer satisfaction surveys and new approval process for financial documents.

COMPANY 2, City, GA   2004 – 2006

Inside Sales Representative / Buyer's Remorse Specialist

Carried out inside sales, prospected for new clients, qualified prospective clients, and analyzed declined merchant agreements to determine courses of action and facilitate funding/closing. Renegotiated declined orders with merchants. Managed movement of transactions through entire contract process. Worked with sales representatives, sales managers, and department managers to coordinate sales transactions. Developed effective sales and renegotiation strategies.

- Exceeded all individual and departmental sales goals.
- Produced $1.35M in sales in 2005, $850,000 (170%) above goal.
- Earned Team Award for Outstanding Sales Accomplishments.
- Recovered millions of dollars through effective renegotiation of agreements with customers.

Media Buyer • Page 2

COMPANY 3, City, GA   2003 – 2004
Sales Specialist/Visual Merchandiser
Performed sales and merchandising in retail environment. Developed concepts for floor visuals and set up merchandise presentations to attract customer interest. Assisted with special shows and projects.

- Increased sales by establishing and maintaining client profile system.
- Recognized for delivering superior customer service.
- Earned management recognition for multiple high volume, single-sale transactions.
- Consistently exceeded monthly sales goals by at least 50%.

COMPANY 4 INC., City, GA   2001 – 2003
Sales Associate & Visual Merchandiser
Carried out sales in retail environment. Managed Visual Team. Arranged store and window displays, presentations, and visuals to entice customers. Coordinated special events.

- Earned Outstanding Sales Award and Highest Sales for an Associate Award.
- Exceeded annual goals by as much as 43% and produced $500,000 in sales in less than 1 year (2002).
- Trained new personnel on sales and visual merchandising techniques.

EDUCATION

AA in Fashion Merchandising & Marketing
Bauder College, Atlanta, GA

PROFESSIONAL DEVELOPMENT

Certifications: Certified Customer Relations Manager (Toyota)
Training: Search Engine Marketing, Sales, Merchandising, Customer Relations

ADDITIONAL INFORMATION

Computer Skills: MS Office, QuickBooks, Adobe Reader, various proprietary applications and databases.
Languages: Conversational in French
Affiliations: Dekalb Co. Women of Legacy (United Way program)

REGISTERED NURSE

Street ▪ City, WA 12345 ▪ (555) 555-5555 ▪ Name@hotmail.com

Registered Nurse with extensive healthcare background and experience in public health

Talented and accomplished healthcare professional with 10 years of domestic and international experience as a registered nurse. Special expertise in emergency and critical care, preceptoring of new employees, and coordinating projects. Professional background includes serving as Charge Nurse and Staff Registered Nurse. Proven ability to develop and lead custom healthcare programs. Excellent presentation, training, leadership, documentation, and workflow management skills. ***Core competencies include:***

Emergency Care – Critical Care – Staff Supervision & Training – Triage – Cost Control – Inventory Control
Patient Counseling – Healthcare Support – Pre/Post-Surgical Care – Quality of Care – Compliance

PROFESSIONAL EXPERIENCE

HOSPITAL AND MEDICAL CENTER 1, City, WA   2007 – Present
Staff Registered Nurse, Emergency Dept.
Oversee patient care for 23-bed Emergency Room at Level IV trauma center with daily average of 130 patients, and additional 150 acute in-patient beds. As Charge Nurse, supervise 8 RNs, 3 technicians, and 1 admin. Coordinate department flow, including triage. Set nursing schedules. Manage healthcare support for acute MI, CVA, TPA administration, sepsis, trauma, orthopedic, and psychiatric emergencies. Aid trauma team in evaluation, resuscitation, and treatment. Assist with transfers to Level I trauma centers as needed.

- Work closely with physicians to manage patients. Update physicians on patient status.
- Serve as Preceptor to new employees. Train personnel in triage and critical care nursing, conduct new staff orientation, and provide instruction on computers and medical equipment.
- Assisted in developing new training program. Mapped process for new nurses to move through different departments in ER, and for monitoring nurses' progress.
- Improved workflow and patient care by implementing highly effective standing orders to initiate care prior to patients being seen by physicians.
- Reduced costs by monitoring staffing needs and minimizing overtime and use of agency nurses.

HOSPITAL 2, City, CA   2005 – 2007
Traveling Registered Nurse/Per Diem Nurse
Provided services to Emergency departments at San Francisco General Hospital (27-bed ER, Level I trauma center) and Overlake Hospital & Medical Center (40-bed ER, Level III trauma center). Assisted with all trauma and ER cases, including various disease states, neurological issues, and cardiac emergencies at hospital noted for work in HIV and AIDS sectors.

- Cared for patients with multiple medical problems, including DKA, psychiatric emergencies, substance abuse, and multiple diagnoses. Initiated social worker involvement as required.
- Delivered emergency care and treatment for pediatric patients with medical emergencies and trauma.

HOSPITAL 3, City, Australia   2006
Staff Registered Nurse - Emergency Dept. & Intensive Care Unit
Trained and worked in Intensive Care Unit as Staff RN. Integrated US nursing skills with foreign medical culture. Supported neurological, trauma, post-surgical, and cerebral hemorrhage patients.

- Performed ventilator care, hemodynamic and cardiac monitoring, and titrated medications.
- As ER Nurse, provided care for patients with minor and major medical emergencies.

HOSPITAL 4, City, CA   2000 – 2002, 2007
Traveling Registered Nurse
Carried out patient care in ERs, Cardiothoracic Step-Down Units, and Cardiac Telemetry Units at various hospitals. Worked in small to large facilities in Washington, Virginia, Colorado, and California. Served as Relief Charge Nurse, and preceptor to new employees/traveling nurses.

- Provided post-surgical care and education for coronary artery bypass graft, valve replacement, pacemaker, heart transplant, internal cardiac defibrillator, cardiac catheterization, and electrophysiologic study patients.
- Assisted with discharge planning, coordinated flow of patients in ERs, and set staffing assignments.

MEDICAL CENTER 1, City, NY   1999 – 2000
Staff Registered Nurse - Cardiac Step-Down Unit
Provided total patient care and performed continuous telemetry monitoring.

- Carried out education and care for patients with multiple diagnoses, including cardiac catheterizations, pacemakers, angioplasties, stent placements, and trans-esophageal echocardiograms.

VOLUNTEER EXPERIENCE

- **Sydney, Australia (2006):** Volunteered with AIDS Trust of Australia. Assisted in raising money for HIV/AIDS care. Participated at fund-raising events.
- **Haiti (2005):** Member of Northwest Eye team that carried out cataract surgeries and plastic surgeries for adults and children in rural areas. Co-led setup and organization of pre-op and post-op areas. Worked closely with OR team.
- **Mississippi (1995):** Volunteered in student program to help build residential units in rural areas.

EDUCATION

BS in Nursing, Plattsburgh State University, Plattsburgh, NY 1998

LICENSURE, CERTIFICATIONS, & TRAINING

Licensed Registered Nurse - State of Washington, State of New York
Certification in Intravenous Venipuncture
Basic Life Support (BLS) for Healthcare Providers
Advanced Cardiac Life Support (ACLS) Provider
Trauma Nurse Core Curriculum (TNCC)
Pediatric Advanced Life Support (PALS) (inactive)
Training in: Critical Care, Emergency Nursing, Hemodynamic Monitoring, Cardiac Monitoring, and more

COMPUTER SKILLS

MS Office, Soarian, Picis, Mednet, and other healthcare information systems

OIL/GAS DRILLING SPECIALIST

P.O. Box 1234 • City, WY 12345 • 555-555-5555 • name@aol.com

SENIOR DRILLING MANAGER
Oil/Gas Exploration, Drilling, International Water Resources Development

PROFILE

International experience in oil, gas and water well drilling, environmental preservation, HES programs, and more. Proven ability to direct drilling operations for vertical and horizontal wells up to 16,000 feet. Familiar with planning and leading hazardous waste investigations, water and ground contamination treatment, water disposal system construction, and exploratory projects. Excellent team, program, and project management skills. Certified Water Treatment Specialist and Hazardous Materials Manager. *Core competencies include:*

✓ Program Management	✓ Water Well Drilling	✓ Water Systems
✓ Oil/Gas/Petroleum Drilling	✓ Budget/Cost Control	✓ Balance Drilling
✓ Environmental Remediation	✓ Hazmat Technologies	✓ Mud Drilling

PROFESSIONAL EXPERIENCE

COMPANY 1, City, ND   2007 – Present
Drilling Consultant
Oversee drilling operations for 20,000-ft. Bakken Shale wells with horizontal laterals up to 10,000 ft. Supervise teams of 25 or more, including geologists, drilling engineers, and 3rd-party service providers.
- Successful completed 15 wells in different areas of North Dakota.
- Saved $1M (20%) per well by reducing overall drilling times from 30 days to 20 days.
- Achieved major improvements in worker safety, resulting in reduced costs.
- Met or exceeded compliance expectations, virtually eliminating environmental impact of projects.

COMPANY 2, City, WY   2006 – 2007
Drilling Superintendent
Managed drilling operations for vertical, horizontal, underground, and mine drilling and production operations up to 10,000 ft. in Wyoming and Louisiana. Oversaw rig supervisors for up to 3 rigs simultaneously, on projects averaging $1.5M per well. Directed re-drilling of old fields for enhanced oil recovery purposes. Led development of new drilling techniques. Monitored environmental compliance.
- Identified virgin reservoirs in old fields that delivered up to 300 BBL per day.
- Increased efficiency, reduced drilling times, and cut costs of drilling shallow horizontal drainage wells by managing development of new drilling techniques.
- Significantly lowered accident rates and improved overall operation safety levels.
- Enhanced efficiency by implementing advanced procedures for drilling and production operations.

Oil & Gas Drilling Specialist • Page 2

COMPANY 3, City, WY   2004 – 2006
Owner & Drilling Consultant
Established drilling and completion consulting company. Directed oil and gas drilling operations in Canada and US. Led drilling up to 16,000 ft. Supervised 20 persons per project. Administered project budgets ranging from $500,000 to $2M. Oversaw all business operations and financials.
- Planned and directed oil, gas, and water disposal project across North America.
- Monitored environmental aspects of projects and minimized hazardous discharges and spills.

COMPANY 4, City, WY   2000 -2004
Drilling Consultant & Land Owner Water Well Remediation Manager
Managed CBM gas well drilling and completions to 3,500 ft for Coal Bed Methane wells. Coordinated teams. Designed and constructed produced water disposal systems and led formation protection programs. Oversaw produced water management and well enhancement. Supervised 10-20 persons per project.
- Saved average of $10,000 per well (4%) by implementing new, standardized completion techniques.
- Delivered tens of thousands of dollars in water disposal fee savings by designing and constructing water treatment plants to remove sodium from produced water and allow water discharge to be used for irrigation of agricultural crops.
- Managed drilling of new, higher volume water supply wells for land owners.

EDUCATION

BS in Environmental Engineering
ANDERSEN UNIVERSITY, Sacramento, CA

CERTIFICATIONS & TRAINING

- Certified Water Specialist, Water Quality Association
- Hazardous Materials Management Certificate
- Licensed Water Well Drilling Contractor (CO, MT, ID, OR)

ADDITIONAL INFORMATION

Computer Skills: MS Office, Wellview, Landmark/Dims, WellPro, and others
Languages: Conversational in Spanish

Operations Manager

32nd Street, Apt. 5 • City, NY 12345 • (123) 555-5555 • name@yahoo.com

Accomplished Management professional with background in Purchasing & Operations

SUMMARY OF QUALIFICATIONS

- Highly experienced in Operations Management, Purchasing, and Supply Chain Management.
- Proven ability to reduce costs, improve efficiency, and increase sales and profitability.
- Special expertise in planning, logistics, vendor negotiations, AP/AR, and product pricing.
- Adept at directing process improvements, technology implementations, and strategic planning.
- Excellent leadership and problem solving skills. Multi-lingual. Multiple certifications in field.

PROFESSIONAL EXPERIENCE

COMPANY 1, INC., City, NY   2002 – Present
Procurement /Operations Manager (2007-present)
Oversaw daily operations for $20 million retail/wholesale company with seven department stores. Managed procurement of direct and indirect materials and coordinated service requirements. Monitored open-to-buy for each department, reviewed sales reports, and analyzed business activities. Evaluated inventory and ensured optimal levels for departments and SKUs to avoid overstock and excess demand, and to maintain maximum profit margins. Carried out forecasting of sales and inventory by season, month, and week, based on previous years' data. Ensured vendors complied with terms of purchase orders. Applied necessary adjustments to deal with fluctuating market conditions.

- Increased accuracy of supply chain, inventory management, and distribution.
- Reduced costs by negotiating terms and pricing with vendors, and by arranging freight options.
- Enhanced profitability by implementing creative retail strategies and product positioning.
- Minimized inventory costs by arranging markdown credits with vendors for overstock items.
- Arranged domestic and international logistics of incoming goods and scheduled distribution to retail and warehouse locations.
- Improved accuracy of A/P and billing processes through effective adjustments.
- Monitored progress of return merchandise and authorized payment adjustments. Provided necessary documentation to vendor or factoring firms.
- Facilitated sales and marketing productivity improvements by introducing customer database.
- Determined promotional pricing and select items for placement on advertising materials.
- Directed training of new management personnel. Prepared guidelines and training schedule.

Assistant Operations Manager (2006-2007)
Completed 3-month internship involving rotation through all departments, including POS, warehouses, and receiving. Assisted with planning, scheduling, purchasing, marketing, and accounts payable.
- Performed detailed analysis of each business area and presented recommendations and report to senior management. Majority of recommendations for improvement implemented.

COMPANY 2, City, Turkey   2005 – 2006
Administrative Coordinator / Marketing Representative
Responsible for business operations and business development for residential construction company.
- Managed regulatory issues, business documentation, and customer service.
- Developed and implemented effective marketing, sales, and pricing strategies.
- Performed sales of home improvements and upgrades for the firm's apartments and houses.
- Supervised contractors and vendors in installation of home improvements and upgrades.

Operations Manager • Page 2

ADDITIONAL EXPERIENCE

COMPANY 3, City, NY   2004 – 2005
Contracted Test Engineer
Carry out quality rating of assignments for leading internet search services company. Utilize remote interactive manager to ensure compliance with specific criteria. Evaluate search content responses in instances where automated robot search tools do not work. Identify potential misuse of services, including malicious processes to increase website popularity. Locate and remove spam content and flag pornographic materials.

EDUCATION

Master of International Business, Florida International University, Miami, FL (2001)
BS in Management, Bilkent University, Ankara, Turkey (2000)

CERTIFICATIONS & TRAINING

Certified Purchasing Manager (in progress)
Certified Supply Chain Manager (in progress)
Certificate in Internat'l Business Applications and Marketing, Istanbul Chamber of Commerce, Turkey

TECHNICAL SKILLS

MS Office, StatPro, QuickBooks, Visual Café, Minitab, Print Shop, RPRO, LINDO, SAP, Windows, Mac OS

ADDITIONAL INFORMATION

Languages: Conversational in German and Russian, fluent in English and Turkish
Citizenship: Citizen of Turkey; authorized to work in United States

Paralegal
10608 Ave. N. • Brooklyn Park, NS 55445 • (555) 555-5340 • name@spammail.com

Legal Secretary ~ Legal Assistant ~ Paralegal ~ Law Office Manager ~ Administrative Assistant

• Experience in legal office administration.	• Expertise in document preparation and review.
• Familiar with facilitating case and trial preparations.	• Able to liaison to clients & opposing counsel.
• Certified Notary Public and Spanish translator.	• Superior research, reporting, & business skills.

PROFESSIONAL EXPERIENCE

LAW PRACTICE LLC, St. Louis Park, MN   2004 – Present
Legal Assistant
- Provided administrative support for three attorneys and one arbitrator in personal injury practice.
- Assisted with preparation of files and documents for trials. Performed extensive transcription.
- Reviewed medical documents and prepared summaries for attorneys.
- Communicated with clients, medical providers, and opposing counsel to obtain documentation.
- Worked with attorney on exhibit preparation. Documented exhibits. Ensured all necessary files forwarded to courts and/or opposing counsel and insurance companies.

LAW OFFICE, City, MN   2003 – 2004
Paralegal
- Supported legal collections practice. Carried out general administrative functions.
- Prepared and issued demand letters summonses, complaints, garnishments, and other documents.
- Responded to queries regarding garnishments, summonses, and complaints from garnishees, employers, and debtors. Provided and obtained information for cases.

LAW OFFICE, Minneapolis, MN   2002
Legal Secretary
- Assisted attorneys in preparation of wills, unlawful detainers, correspondence, directives (healthcare, end of life, and others), powers of attorney, and additional documents for court cases.
- Supported five attorneys. Provided information to Pre-Paid Legal Services clients.

CIVIL ACTION GROUP, Bloomington, ID   2001
Process Server Coordinator
- Coordinated assignments for team of 45 process servers. Responsible for 10-state western territory as well as Guam and Puerto Rico. Assigned and scheduled cases.
- Evaluated client requests and prepared estimated price quotes and expected turnaround time.
- Recognized five times for Superior Job Performance. Exceeded all goals.

EDUCATION
AAS in Paralegal Studies (Dean's List student), **College**, Oakdale, MN
BA in English Literature, Political Science concentration, **University**, Ames, IA

LICENSES & CERTIFICATIONS
Notary Public for the State of Minnesota

TECHNICAL SKILLS
MS Office, PowerPoint, Access, WestLaw, Lexis-Nexis, Internet, type 70 wpm, transcription, Internet

PHYSICIAN, MD, Ph.D.

401 Bear Run Drive • City, PA 12222 • (555) 555-1212 • name@usa.net

SUMMARY

Talented and accomplished Internist and Intensivist with extensive clinic and hospital experience in Internal, ICU, and Emergency Medicine. International background in establishing and leading medical programs in areas of outpatient clinics, emergency medicine, and EMS. Familiar with training and supervising medical personnel, students, and EMS professionals. Award-winning record of accomplishments. Research experience. Excellent analysis, reporting, and diagnosis skills. Licensed for New Jersey and Pennsylvania.

LICENSURE

Diplomate in Internal Medicine
Licensed in Internal Medicine, New Jersey & Pennsylvania

EDUCATION

MAJOR HOSPITAL, Trenton, NJ
Chief Medical Resident (2003-2004)
Internal Medicine Residency (2000-2003)

University of Medical Sciences, United Kingdom
M.D. (1998)

Kean University, Union, NJ
B.A. in Honors Biology, emphasis in Molecular Biology (1993)

PROFESSIONAL EXPERIENCE

PRACTICE GROUP, Livingston, NJ   2005 – Present
Emergency Physician
- Fast Track and Emergency Room physician. Perform triage, admitting, and patient care for average of 20 patients per shift in Level II trauma center.

PRACTICE GROUP, Livingston, NJ   2004 – 2005
Hospitalist
- Internist and Hospitalist for private multi-specialty medical group servicing St. Barnabas Medical Center. Provided patient care in ICU and general medical floors.

LOCAL HOSPITAL, Trenton, NJ   2000 – 2004
Chief Medical Resident / Internal Medicine Resident
- Completed Internal Medicine residency rotations, with additional ICU and ER elective rotations.
- Accepted position of Chief Medical Resident in 2003, responsible for resident scheduling, conference coordination, and instruction of medical students.
- Assisted with development of new ICU protocol for waking ventilated patients.
- Conducted study using in-hospital Utstein method to compare efficacy of resident-run resuscitation code teams vs. attending-run teams.

ADDITIONAL INFORMATION

Affiliations: American Medical Association
Awards & Recognition: Resident Recognition Award, Dept. of Medicine (2002, 2003)

SALES REPRESENTATIVE

336 Serenity Lane • City, State 55555 • (555) 555-1212 • name@gmail.com

Insurance Sales • Territory Management • Sales Executive • Regional Manager

QUALIFICATIONS

- Award-winning sales management professional with consistent record of success.
- Proven ability to exceed all goals and to train and lead award-winning sales teams.
- Special expertise in account development, market penetration, and account renewal.
- Background includes several years of experience in medical products/healthcare fields.

SELECTED ACCOMPLISHMENTS

➢ Achieved goal of 97% or better renewal retention rate with Old Insurance Co.
➢ Trained and mentored all staff members to 1 or more sales awards.
➢ Outperformed other districts while managing largest district in state.
➢ Consistently met all sales, renewals, and recruiting goals as Sales Manager.
➢ Earned multiple awards for sales as Sales Representative.

PROFESSIONAL EXPERIENCE

OLD INSURANCE CO. OF AMERICA, City, state   2006 – 2015
District Manager (2015)
Promoted to District Manager position based on past successes with this large insurance company. Tasked with building staff and expanding territory penetration. Managed 4 regions. Supervised staff, set goals, and monitored performance. Developed and implemented new marketing and sales processes. Actively involved in client identification and acquisition.
- Achieved assigned goal of 97% or better renewal retention rate.
- Outperformed other districts while managing largest district in state.
- Recognized for delivering largest numbers and consistent production.
- Increased performance levels by implementing new sales and product training procedures.

Sales Manager (2007-2014)
Conducted 13-week training sessions for new agents. Supported multi-county territory. Recruited staff members. Oversaw all weekly paperwork. Carried out sales and renewals.
- Consistently met all sales, renewals, and recruiting goals.
- Increased sales through account acquisition and growth within existing accounts.

Sales Representative (2006-2007)
Performed sales of insurance products in territory.
- Earned award for selling 100 or more units within 2-week period.
- Achieved Ruby Award for producing 150 units in 2-week time frame.
- Reached promotable level 20% ahead of schedule. Selected for Sales Management training.

EDUCATION

BSBA in Marketing, John Carroll University, Cleveland, OH

TECHNICAL SKILLS

MS Office, Access, SPSS, FrontPage, and proprietary systems

Sales Representative 2

2919 Street • City, MN 12345 • 555-555-5555 • name@comcast.net

Sales & Marketing Management professional with proven record of success.

PROFILE

- More than 9 years of **sales** experience, working with physicians, clinicians, and hospital administrators. Adept at managing accounts and negotiating contracts.
- **Earned multiple awards** for sales and performance in current role, and exceeded all goals.
- **Sales** and **marketing** skills include business development, networking, client service, market research and sales support. Experienced calling on top-level decision makers.
- Medtronic sales rep said: "My territory exceeded plan in all businesses and (Jacqueline) deserves credit for contributing to that success. (She's) become a tremendous asset."

EXPERIENCE

COMPANY 1, INC., Tacoma, WA/Bloomington, MN   2001 – Present
Principle Sales Representative (2009-present)
Manage $8.7M territory for manufacturer of medical and related products. Promoted twice, from Sales Representative to Senior Sales Rep to current role. Supervise 3 clinical specialists. Develop relationships with healthcare professionals. Attend pacemaker and defibrillator implants. Negotiate contracts.

- **Delivered 39% territory growth** from 2006 to 2009 (130% of goal).
- Earned **Pacing Rep of the Region** in 2005 and **CRDM National Rep of the Quarter** in 2007.
- Recognized as **District Representative of the Year** 3x (2002, 2004, 2006).
- Received **President's Club Award** in 2007 while **increasing market share 34%.**
- Awarded Regional Brady Rep of the Quarter.
- Successfully turned around underperforming account within 1 year.

Clinical Specialist/Regional Education Trainer (2001-2005)
Assumed added responsibility as Regional Education Trainer in early 2001. Collaborated and built strong relationships with physicians. Attended implants. Carried out pacemaker and defibrillator checks for clinics. Provide technical, educational, and sales support for customers, and supported 3 sales reps. Conducted in-services for nurses, cath lab personnel, and patients. Performed bi-annual training sessions.

- Helped sales rep achieve Brady Representative of the Quarter.
- Personally sold 15 temporary pacemakers in past year, with 13 more in negotiation.
- Recognized by customers for **superior training abilities.**

CAREER NOTES: Previously held **Account Representative** positions with COMPANY 2 (1994-1995) and COMPANY 3 (1986-1994). Consistently made quotas. Ranked first in sales to new clients. Recruited staff and managed bookkeeping and payroll functions.

EDUCATION

Master of Business Administration, University of Phoenix (in progress).
Bachelor of Business Management: Bethel College (1999).

COMPUTER SKILLS

Word, PowerPoint, Excel, Rumba, Real World, Lotus 1-2-3 and Internet navigation.

TEACHER
Student Rd. • Township, OH 12345 • (555) 555-5555 • name@sbcglobal.net

Talented Educator with Consistent Record of Career Success

SUMMARY OF QUALIFICATIONS

➢ More than 13 years of experience as Montessori teacher/program director.
➢ Proven ability to develop, implement, and lead highly successful programs.
➢ Adept at formulating curricula, lesson plans, and thematic units.
➢ Previous experience as care provider in nursing home environments.
➢ Dependable, caring, and organized. Excellent communication skills.

PROFESSIONAL EXPERIENCE

SCHOOL 1, CITY, OH   2004 – Present
Spanish Teacher / Enrichment Care Program Director / Library Assistant
Instructed classes in Spanish for 4 grade levels (Preprimary, Kindergarten, Lower Elementary, and Upper Elementary), totaling approximately 130 students. Directed Enrichment Care program. Communicated extensively with parents and staff regarding students' progress and program enhancements.

- Improved Spanish curriculum by expanding from 1 resource book to multiple books, videos, CDs, audio tapes, games, storyboards, and more to develop students' listening, speaking, reading, and writing skills.
- Introduced thematic lesson plans and designed and implemented creative study units to enhance students' educational experiences.
- Organized Enrichment Care program registration and accounting procedures to increase efficiency. Coordinated parent communications.
- Designed and edited school newspaper; edited and organized parent and staff handbooks, event programs, staff schedules, and other materials.
- As Library Assistant, oversaw computerized check-in and check-out of books and conducted weekly library classes for students.

EDUCATION

Bachelor of Arts in Spanish
University of Minnesota, Minneapolis, MN

VOLUNTEER/COMMUNITY INVOLVEMENT

Classroom Volunteer, Girl Scout Leader, PTA Member, PTA Vice President.

ADDITIONAL INFORMATION

Languages: Fluent in Spanish
Computer Skills: MS Office, Publisher, WordPerfect, Blackboard

VETERINARIAN, DVM

21 Fake Road Lane ▪ Newberry Beach, NA 12345 ▪ (123) 456-789 ▪ cdogdoc@nomail.com

SENIOR VETERINARIAN: Small & Exotic Animal Care

Consistent history of providing exceptional medical care for animals with life threatening and routine conditions. Outstanding diagnostic skills. Areas of expertise include emergency care, chronic disease treatment, orthopedic and geriatric care, management of infectious disease outbreaks, dental care, and routine surgeries. Excel at fostering strong human-animal bonds and building long-term relationships with clients. Background encompasses work in shelters and adoption centers as well as standard veterinary practices. Experienced at training personnel and providing education for pet owners. ***Professional strengths include:***

Diagnostics – Examinations – Quality of Care – Practice Management – Post-Operative Care
Laboratory Screening – Mass Removals – Staff Development – Regulatory Compliance
Community Relations – Dental Care – Cost Control – Electronic Records – Compassion

PROFESSIONAL EXPERIENCE

SPCA ANIMAL HOSPITAL, City, NA   2012-Present
Doctor of Veterinary Medicine
Acting veterinarian-in-charge for a large shelter organization with two locations. Oversee clinic operations, including shelter and foster pet care, client education, staff training, and cost monitoring. Perform vaccinations, spay/neuter surgeries, dewormings, declawings, flea and tick prevention, microchipping, allergy treatment, mass removals, hernia repairs, cystotomies, dental cleanings, extractions, geriatric laboratory screenings, diagnostic testing, digital radiographies, and more. Actively involved in fund raising and adoption services.

- Identified and resolved cases of vector-borne, zoonotic, parasitic, and chronic diseases.
- Resolved instances of life-threatening malnutrition, neglect, dehydration, and exposure.
- Improved efficiency and quality of care by introducing new procedures.
- Reduced outbreaks of infectious diseases and parasites by emphasizing staff education and implementing fecal examination upon intake for rapid parasite identification.
- Introduced a consulting program to educate adopters on medical conditions.

ANIMAL HOSPITAL, City, NA   2010-2012
Doctor of Veterinary Medicine
Diagnosed and treated small animals and exotics at this full-service facility. Obtained medical histories, ordered radiographs and blood work, and resolved routine and advanced medical issues. Performed general surgeries, diagnostic testing, leptospirosis titers, aerobic cultures, drug monitoring, histopathologies, cytologies, and more. Volunteered to monitor and treat hospitalized and boarded patients on Sundays and holidays.

- Recognized by clients and staff for superior diagnostic and patient care skills.
- Resolved complex cases such as a puppy with Hypertrophic Osteodystrophy, a dog with cervical neck syndrome, and a cat with infectious peritonitis (FIP).
- Played an active role in the development of a special wellness program for puppies.

THE PET HOSPITAL, City, NA   2004-2010
Doctor of Veterinary Medicine
Performed examinations, dental procedures, mass removals, spays, neuters, hernia repairs, declawing, laceration repairs, pyometra surgeries, vaccinations, emergency care, general surgeries, ultrasound-guided liver biopsies, Erechia testing, ACTH Shon tests, post-operative care, C-sections, bloat (gastric dilatation volvulus) surgeries, splenectomies, GI endoscopies, and more. Trained employees in emergency, disease, and internal medicine. Participated in business operations management and identified areas for improvement. Treated wide variety of disease states, including leptospirosis, neoplasias, pancreatitis, and others.

- Treated a pug with short bowel syndrome, requiring major small intestine resection.
- Diagnosed and stabilized a German shepherd with idiopathic pericardial disease and arranged a transfer to a specialized care center.
- Resolved a case of gastric dilatation volvulus in a Great Dane. Diagnosed case, stabilized patient, and performed emergency surgery.
- Served as a disease specialist for local Petsmart and resolved instances of disease outbreak among small mammals, reptiles, and avians.

VETERINARY HOSPITAL, City, NA   2003-2004
Associate Veterinarian
Treated small animals and exotics. Observed and trained under senior veterinarians. Provided emergency on-call services. Conducted routine examinations, disease state evaluations and treatments, and diagnostic tests, including fecal exams, CBCs, chem panels, ACTH Shm, urinalysis, cytologies, radiographs, protein/creatinine ratios, ultrasounds, endoscopies, and more. Performed dental procedures, mass removals, hernia repairs, pyometras, C-sections, bloat surgeries, and abdominal exploratory surgeries.

- Managed the resolution of a case involving a Bassett hound with a necrotic intestine.
- Diagnosed and successfully treated leptospirosis and secondary renal failure in a dog.
- Increased standards of care by training staff on state-of-the-art care practices.

EDUCATION

Doctor of Veterinary Medicine, University School of Veterinary Medicine, West City, NA
Bachelor of Science in Biology, Big University, West City, NA (1999)

LICENSURE

Licensed to Practice Veterinary Medicine (State), DEA License (State)

ADDITIONAL INFORMATION

Training: Continuing education in Abdominal Ultrasound, Pharmaceuticals, Nutrition, Therapeutic Diets, Nutraceuticals, Behavior, Internal Medicine, Radiology, and other areas
Affiliations: American Veterinary Medicine Association (AVMA), Veterinary Information Network (VIN), American Society for the Prevention of Cruelty to Animals (ASPCA)

Web Developer

36 Hemlock St. • Brookfield, NY 00000 • (555) 555-5555 • name at email.com

SUMMARY

Talented and experienced Information Technology professional with background in Web Development and Software Engineering. Multiple certifications, highly adept at web application design. Extensive knowledge in development of interactive websites and e-commerce applications. Familiar with wide variety of programming languages. Hard working, detail oriented, and able to multi-task effectively.

TECHNICAL SKILLS

Languages: ASP, HTML, DHTML, XML, Visual Basic, VBScript, JavaScript, ActiveX, C/C++, Visual C++, SQL, CGI Scripting

Tools: Visual Studio Suite, Dreamweaver / UltraDev, Homesite, InterDev, Windows 2000 Indexing Service, Windows 2000 Scheduler, WinAce, WinRAR, FTP Servers, Visual Studio .NET Suite, PC Anywhere, Exchange Server, Imail

Applications: MS Office, Netscape, Acrobat, Photoshop, ImageReady, IIS, WinZip

PROFESSIONAL EXPERIENCE

COMPANY 1, Brookfield, NY   1999 – Present
SENIOR WEB DEVELOPER
Designed company's original website, using HTML, and proprietary 3rd party software for auction module. Utilized C++ to build additional functionalities into 3rd party package.

- Designed and implemented new site and auction module software, using Visual C++ and DHTML. New auction module was ISAPI extension that required full year to complete. Additionally, entire site now completely based on SQL Server 2000 databases.
- New system reduced overhead, improved response time to client requests, and increased sales $75,000 in first year.
- Developed and introduced innovative data entry system in Visual C++ with flexible, automated features that produced 300% increase in productivity.
- Redesigned auction software to access SQL databases through views and stored procedures for greater efficiency.
- Introduced new database system during update of website. Redesigned database, migrated data, and authored all associated documentation.
- Responsible for all content posting, graphics, and overall layout.

COMPANY 2, Springfield, MA   1997 – 1999
SOFTWARE ENGINEER
Designed enhancements to existing products and developed new products using Visual C++.

- Created advanced charting and graphing capabilities for company's flagship product, Costimator.
- Designed program to back up and restore user files, and then integrated new grid control for Costimator.

EDUCATION

B.S. in Information Technology, concentration in Web Application Development, Capella University

X-RAY TECHNICIAN

Street • City, State, Zip • (555) 555-5555 • name@yahoo.com

Talented x-ray technician with several years of professional experience

- Experienced in wide range of radiology equipment.
- Able to utilize mobile radiography units.
- Well-developed troubleshooting abilities.

- Adept at setting up patients for evaluations.
- Familiar with emergency room procedures.
- Excellent analysis and reporting skills.

PROFESSIONAL EXPERIENCE

HOSPITAL 1, City, LA   2006 – Present
Radiography Technician

- Perform radiographic (non-destructive) evaluations to determine mechanical integrity of structures for oil & gas exploration, refining, storage, chemical, paper/pulp, and power generating industries.
- Utilize mobile radiography units to conduct inspections and data collection.
- Carry out both X-ray and gamma radiographic procedures. Prepare and deliver reports.

PREVIOUS EMPLOYMENT

Programmer, **COMPANY 1**, City, LA   2001 – 2006
Programmer, **COMPANY 2**, City, LA   2000

MILITARY EXPERIENCE

Sgt., Laboratory Services, **Louisiana Army National Guard**, Lafayette, LA   1994 – 2000

EDUCATION

University of Louisiana, Lafayette, LA
BS in Computer Science (2005)

- Course work included: Data Structures, C++, Programming Languages, Compilers, Operating Systems, Mathematical Computation of Data Structures, Design Patterns, and Assembly

PROFESSIONAL DEVELOPMENT

Primary Leadership Development (Louisiana Army National Guard)

SECURITY CLEARANCE

Previously held Top Secret Security Clearance

TECHNICAL SKILLS

Windows, UNIX, C++, COBOL, Perl, scheme, smallTalk, Snobol, Glade, MS Office

ANIMAL CARE MANAGER
Address • City, FL 12345 • (555) 555-5555 ▪ name@email.com

PROFILE
Talented and accomplished Animal Care professional with extensive experience in supervising exotic and large animal programs in sanctuary and public display facilities. Proven ability to train and supervise personnel and volunteers, establish and direct husbandry operations, perform behavioral observation and enrichment, and coordinate health, safety, and public speaking programs. Adept at habitat design and construction, budget administration, special project management, and vendor relations management. Able to prepare and implement policies and procedures. Comprehensive background working with large felids as well as variety of other exotics.

PROFESSIONAL EXPERIENCE

ORGANIZATION 1, City, FL   2005 – Present
Director of Operations and Animal Care
- Oversee daily operation of preserve, including animal care, habitats, husbandry, acquisition and rescue of animals, safety, and landscaping.
- Train and supervise caretakers, handlers, and volunteers. Ensure compliance with all industry and organization health, safety, and welfare regulations. Implement operational policies and procedures.
- Assist with preparation and management of annual departmental budget. Additionally work with Executive Director and Board on Master Plan and Capital Campaign.
- Perform habitat design and supervise construction process. Obtain materials and equipment.
- Manage husbandry functions, including diet, veterinary care, observation, and enrichment program, for animal collection, including large and exotic felids.
- Lead weekly and monthly operational and enrichment meetings with keepers and volunteers.
- Assist with public speaking and enrichment programs, lead special projects as needed.
- Maintain compliance with USDA and Florida Fish and Wildlife Conservation regulations.

ORGANIZATION 2, City, NV   2004 – 2005
African Lion Handler / Caretaker
- Managed handling and care of approximately 10 African lions. Supervised and trained assistants.
- Coordinated transportation of animals from compound to MGM Hotel on daily basis.
- Carried out personal interaction with animals as part of educational programs for general public.
- Performed behavioral observation, led enrichment programs, cleaned and bathed animals, maintained habitats, assisted with veterinary care. Ensured all safety regulations complied with.

ORGANIZATION 3, City, FL   2000 – 2004
Animal Compound Manager
- Maintained compound and held responsibility for care of six large, exotic felids.
- Supervised and trained staff of three assistants and three volunteers.
- Accompanied USDA and Florida Fish and Wildlife Conservation officers on regular compound inspections. Ensured compliance with all safety and animal care regulations.
- Coordinated transportation of animals between habitats, maintained health records, carried out habitat design and maintenance. Assisted with rearing of young animals.
- Prepared individual diets and assisted with veterinary care. Administered medications.
- Delivered educational lectures to public, behavioral observations, and enrichment program direction.

ORGANIZATION 4, City, AZ

1997 – 2000

Animal Caretaker / Handler

- Directed physical care of large collection of felids, hyena, bear, wolves, and other exotics.
- Participated in non-rehearsed demonstrations, performed public education, and delivered public lectures. Coordinated movement of animals between habitats and display areas.
- Assisted with all daily husbandry functions and maintenance of habitats.
- Prepared individual diets, administered medications, and maintained animal records.

ANIMAL HOSPITAL, City, CA

1990 – 1993

Veterinary Technician

- Assisted with animal handling during routine medical examinations and surgeries.
- Performed care and feeding of animals, cleaned cages, and filled prescriptions.
- Maintained charts and records, operated x-ray machinery.

WILDLIFE REFUGE, State Park, CA

1990

Keeper

- Cared for wide range of exotic animals, including carnivores, primates, and great apes, at one of largest rescue facilities in United States. Promoted rapidly from volunteer to Keeper.
- Maintained and cleaned habitats, prepared and delivered meals, transferred animals.
- Observed and charted animal activities, facilitated rehabilitation of injured animals, assisted with conditioning of animals to perform natural behaviors to support release into wild.
- Worked closely with veterinarians, administering medications and examinations.

EDUCATION

Two years general education, University of Kentucky

TRAINING

Extensive training in exotic animal care

PROFESSIONAL MEMBERSHIPS

Member, American Association of Zookeepers

APPENDIX 2
SUGGESTED RESOURCES

I. Résumé Posting Sites

Here are a few of the sites I recommend to my clients as excellent places to post résumés online.

American Preferred	Hireforjobs	Monster.com
AmericasJobSource	HireNet	NationalJobBank
Bakos Group	Horizon Career	Net-Temps
Beyond.com	HotRésumés.com	PostJobFree
Career Exposure	Job Bank USA	Prohire.com
CareerBuilder	Job.com	QuintCareers.com
CareerJournal.com	JobAnimal.com	Résumés2Work
CareerMarketplace	JobCentral.com	SearchEase.com
ChiliJobs.com	JobClub	SmartHunt
CollegeGrad.com	JobGuru.com	Smuz
CollegeJobBoard	Jobing	TalentSpider
CollegeRecruiter.com	JobNugget.com	The Talent Bank
DealSplitStaffing.com	JobsExcite	Thingamajob.com
EmployerIndex.com	Jobstar.com	TigerJobs
FillThatJob	Jobvertise	USJobNetwork.com
GlobalPitch.com	JobWarehouse	Yahoo! HotJobs
HireAbility.com	Kakoon.com	ZillionRésumés
HireBreed	MegaJobSites.com	

II. Informational Sources.

These are sites where you can find resources to assist you with your job search, look up data on companies or the employment environment, and even read forums by professionals and have access to career counselors and recruiters.

Company of Friends

First Tuesday

ItsNotWhatYouKnow

QuintessentialCareers.com

Wetfeet.com

Vault.com

Hoovers.com

Learnwebskills.com

www.AmazingGraceCircus.org

www.jobstar.org/hidden

III. Professional Networking

Here are a few of the larger sites where you can post a résumé and at the same time network with other professionals - they're kind of the business version of Facebook or MySpace, and are growing increasingly more important in today's employment process.

The Ladders

LinkedIn.com

Ecademy.com

Networking for Professionals

Ryze

Delphi Forums

Ezboard

(Author's Note: At the time of writing, all the websites listed in this Appendix were current; due to the unpredictable nature of the economy and the internet, I cannot guarantee they'll all still be around by the time you buy the book!)

APPENDIX 3
PROOFREADING YOUR RÉSUMÉ

It may seem obvious that you should proofread your résumé and cover letter before sending them out, but in order to build a truly error-free document, you need to proofread like a professional editor, which is very different.

There are 6 steps to proper proofreading:

1. Spell and Grammar Check. After you've written the document, use your word processing software's built in spell check and grammar check to proof the document. Identify any potential mistakes and correct them. But beware of those pesky words that fool spell check - too/to/two; four/for, which/witch, etc. - and make sure you're using the correct spelling of the correct word for the sentence's meaning.

2. Print the document and read it yourself. Catch and correct any mistakes relating to spelling, spacing, punctuation, and content. Then print it again, and read it backwards. This proofreading technique usually turns up several punctuation and format errors. Correct those and print it again.

3. Give the résumé to two or three associates and have them read it. Not only will they probably find typos you missed, they might even have suggestions for including information you've forgotten.

4. Print another copy. Read the contact information and make sure it's all correct. Often a phone number or email address will have a typo.

5. Read the résumé and letter aloud. Is there something that doesn't sound right? A sentence that seems too long? If so, now is the time to correct it.

6. Print a final copy, and look at it from a purely format point of view. Is there too much white space? Not enough? Does it print correctly, or do you need to adjust the margins?

Remember, your résumé must be error-free when you send it out. This is your one chance to market yourself, and a simple mistake can ruin everything you've worked so hard to put together.

APPENDIX 4

PRINTING YOUR DOCUMENTS

Even if you're planning on emailing the résumé rather than sending out hard copies, it's important to print a copy before you send it out. The reason for this those margins that look perfect on the computer screen don't always print correctly. In fact, laser printers and ink jet printers don't always print the same as each other.

A general rule of thumb is to never set the top and bottom margins any smaller than 0.6," or an ink jet printer won't be able to keep everything on the proper pages. I see résumés all the time where the margins are set to 0.5" or even smaller, sometimes 0.15". When you try to print a résumé like this, the last few lines of each page end up on a separate page, and suddenly your two-page résumé is now three or four pages, and heading for the garbage can.

If you're planning on printing hard copies to mail or hand out, it's important to use a good printer and good paper, but nothing too fancy. The idea is to impress someone with your business professionalism, not appear as if you're sending a document to a king.

The Paper

Most people can get away with using a plain white laser printer paper, of thick stock (weight), so it doesn't wrinkle or tear easily. Rarely do you see anyone using résumé paper anymore. However, if you choose to use résumé paper, here is what I recommend:

Southworth Fine Linen, White. 24 lb, 25% cotton

You can purchase this paper at any good office supply store.

TIP: Never use any color except **white**. *HR Representatives do not like colored paper, or paper with patterns or designs on it.*

The Printer

I always tell my clients that printing on a laser printer is best, because the ink won't smudge or smear when you handle the document. However, if you have to use an ink jet printer, be sure to set the printer to print at the highest quality, and let the document dry well before handling it, so you don't get any smudge marks on it.

TIP: Never fold the documents if you're mailing them. Instead, place them in an envelope large enough to hold them flat.

APPENDIX 5
ACTION VERBS AND ADVERBS

On the following pages, you'll find a list of common action verbs frequently used in résumés, and a list of common adverbs. Neither of these lists is by any means complete; however, both should help you put together a résumé that really stands out from the crowd.

(Note: the action verbs are all listed in past tense, but you can also use them in present tense if describing your current job.)

1. Action Verbs

A

Accelerated

Accomplished

Achieved

Acted

Activated

Adapted

Addressed

Adjusted

Administered

Advanced

Advertised

Advised

Advocated

Aided

Allocated

Analyzed

Answered

Applied

Appraised

Approved

Arbitrated

Arranged

Ascertained

Assembled

Assessed

Assigned

Assisted

Attained

Augmented

Authorized

Awarded

B

Balanced

Began

Boosted

Briefed

Budgeted

Built

C

Calculated

Captured

Cataloged

Centralized

Chaired

Charted

Checked

Clarified

Classified

Coached

Collaborated

Collected

Combined

Communicated

Compared

Compiled

Completed

Composed

Computed

Conceived

Conceptualized

Condensed

Conducted

Conferred

Conserved

Consolidated

Constructed

Consulted

Contacted

Continued

Contributed

Controlled

Converted

Conveyed

Convinced

Coordinated

Corresponded

Counseled

Created

Critiqued

Cultivated

Customized

D

Debugged

Decided

Defined

Delegated

Delivered

Demonstrated

Designated

Designed

Detected

Determined

Developed

Devised

Diagnosed

Directed

Discovered

Dispensed

Displayed

Dissected

Distributed

Diverted

Documented

Drafted

E

Earned

Edited

Educated

Effected

Eliminated

Emphasized

Employed

Encouraged

Enforced

Engineered

Enhanced

Enlarged

Enlisted

Ensured

Entertained

Established

Estimated

Evaluated

Examined

Executed

Expanded

Expedited

Experimented

Explained

Explored

Expressed

Extended

Extracted

F

Fabricated

Facilitated

Fashioned

Finalized

Fixed

Focused

Forecasted

Formed

Formulated

Fostered

Found

Fulfilled

Furnished

G

Gained

Gathered

Generated

Governed

Grossed

Guided

H

Handled

Headed

Heightened

Helped

Hired

Honed

Hosted

Hypothesized

I

Identified

Illustrated

Imagined

Implemented

Improved

Improvised

Incorporated

Increased

Indexed

Influenced

Informed

Initiated

Innovated

Inspected

Installed

Instituted

Integrated

Interacted

Interpreted

Interviewed

Introduced

Invented

Inventoried

Investigated

Involved

Issued

J

Joined

Judged

K

Kept

L

Launched

Learned

Lectured

Led

Lifted

Listened

Located

Logged

M

Maintained

Managed

Manipulated

Marketed

Maximized

Measured

Mediated

Merged

Mobilized

Modified

Monitored

Motivated

N

Navigated

Negotiated

Netted

O

Observed

Obtained

Opened

Operated

Ordered

Orchestrated

Organized

Originated

Outlined

Overcame

Overhauled

Oversaw

P

Participated

Performed

Persuaded

Photographed

Pinpointed

Piloted

Pioneered

Placed

Planned

Played

Predicted

Prepared

Prescribed

Presented

Presided

Prevented

Printed

Prioritized

Processed

Produced

Programmed

Projected

Promoted

Proofread	Reported	Sponsored
Proposed	Represented	Staffed
Protected	Researched	Standardized
Proved	Reshaped	Started
Provided	Resolved	Streamlined
Publicized	Responded	Strengthened
Purchased	Restored	Structured
	Retrieved	Studied
	Reviewed	Suggested
Q	Revised	Summarized
Qualified	Revitalized	Supervised
Questioned	Routed	Supplied
		Supported
R		Surpassed
Raised	**S**	Surveyed
Ran	Saved	Sustained
Rated	Scheduled	Synthesized
Reached	Screened	Systematized
Realized	Searched	
Reasoned	Secured	
Received	Selected	**T**
Recommended	Separated	Targeted
Reconciled	Served	Taught
Recorded	Shaped	Terminated
Recruited	Shared	Tested
Reduced	Simplified	Totaled
Referred	Simulated	Tracked
Regulated	Sketched	Traded
Rehabilitated	Sold	Trained
Related	Solved	Transcribed
Remodeled	Sorted	Transformed
Rendered	Spearheaded	Transmitted
Reorganized	Specialized	Translated
Repaired	Specified	Traveled
Replaced	Spoke	Tutored

	Used	Volunteered
U	Utilized	
Uncovered		**W**
Undertook	**V**	Weighed
Unified	Validated	Widened
United	Verbalized	Won
Updated	Verified	Worked
Upgraded	Vitalized	Wrote

2. Adverbs

Accurately	Artistically	Imaginatively
Reliably	Effectively	Proficiently
Actively	Steadily	Successfully
Meticulously	Efficiently	Confidently
Resourcefully	Strongly	Independently
Creatively	Competently	Progressively
Responsibly	Energetically	Supportively
Analytically	Precisely	Consistently
Diligently	Substantially	Thoroughly
Significantly	Competitively	

SPECIAL BONUS DISCOUNT COUPONS

When all is said and done, you might decide you don't want to write your résumé by yourself. Or perhaps you know someone who needs a résumé written. Or maybe your company is paying you to get your résumé written professionally. Whatever your situation, you can use the coupon codes below (and share them with friends!) to get discounts on professional résumé writing services from **www.a-perfect-resume.com.**

Coupon Code 1: Perfect 001

Receive 15% off any Résumé Rebuild package at **www.a-perfect-resume.com**.

Coupon Code 2: Perfect 002

Receive a free asci, HTML, or ATS-formatted resume with the purchase of any resume package (value = $25).

(Offers cannot be combined with each other or any other discounts).

FREE DOWNLOAD!

For a free copy of my 25-page pamphlet "Interview Secrets," go to:

www.a-perfect-resume.com/Interview Secrets.doc

Not sure if your résumé needs help? I provide FREE résumé evaluations. Just email a copy of your current résumé to me at **sales@a-perfect-resume.com**, or post a copy to me from my website (**www.a-perfect-resume.com/quotes.htm**) and I'll be happy to review your résumé, let you know how I can improve it for you, and provide you with a free price quote for the new documents. My price quotes are always guaranteed for 12 months, and, unlike many other résumé companies, all my résumé packages include a résumé, cover letter, thank you letter, and free PDF version of the résumé for printing.

ABOUT THE AUTHOR

GREG FAHERTY, CPRW

A Certified Professional Résumé Writer and member in good standing of the Professional Association of Résumé Writers and Career Coaches since 1999, **Greg Faherty** brings more than 15 years of professional résumé writing experience to the table, with a better than 99% customer satisfaction rate.

Through his own company, **www.a-perfect-resume.com**, and his work as a senior writer for several of the largest internet résumé firms in the world, Greg's accomplishments include producing more than 10,000 résumés, serving as a subject matter expert for several newspapers and websites, and introducing cutting-edge business documents and résumé formats to the industry.

Greg's areas of expertise include, but aren't limited to, information technology, sales and marketing, executive management, education, human resources, pharmaceutical and medical industries, healthcare, and international business. In addition to résumés and cover letters, his services include international and academic CVs, federal résumés and KSAs, executive biographies, personal profiles, social media profiles, business card résumés, webfolios, and résumé distribution.

Follow him at Linkedin (www.linkedin.com/in/gregfaherty) and at Twitter (@gfahertycprw).

Made in the USA
Lexington, KY
23 January 2018